AMERIGO VESPUCCI

Pilot Major

PORTRAIT AND SIGNATURE OF VESPUCCI, 1508

AMERIGO VESPUCCI
Pilot Major

By FREDERICK J. POHL

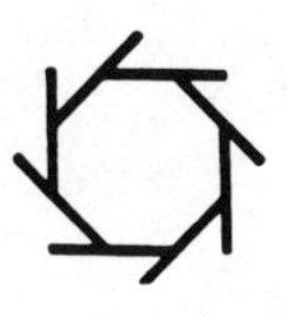

OCTAGON BOOKS

A DIVISION OF FARRAR, STRAUS AND GIROUX

New York 1979

Reprinted 1966
by special arrangement with Frederick Julius Pohl

Second Octagon printing 1979

OCTAGON BOOKS
A DIVISION OF FARRAR, STRAUS & GIROUX, INC.
19 Union Square West
New York, N.Y. 10003

LIBRARY OF CONGRESS CATALOG CARD NUMBER: 66-18056
ISBN: 0-374-96499-8

Manufactured by Braun-Brumfield, Inc.
Ann Arbor, Michigan
Printed in the United States of America

PREFACE

Columbus deserved immortal fame for his courage and indomitable will in pursuing his purpose. His principal accomplishment was his giving mariners "the keys to the ocean" – knowledge of the sailing routes where ships could be blown by prevailing winds across the Atlantic in both directions. As to places where he landed he was confused. To the day of his death he persisted in claiming they were parts of Asia.

That one could reach Asia in less than a month by a voyage westward was the most sensational "news" that had ever come to Europe. Almost everyone at first believed Columbus. Flushed with wild enthusiasm by the misinformation, eager adventurers went west to tap the wealth of India. All drew blanks. No one could find Asia where Columbus said it was. Something was wrong. Where were the rich cities of China which Marco Polo had visited? Where were the famous ports of India with which the Arabs traded so profitably and which the Portuguese under Vasco da Gama had reached by the long route around the Cape of Good Hope?

Merchants and business men as well as kings wanted to know what lands actually lay on the western side of the Atlantic.

Americo Vespucio, to use the Spanish form of the name Amerigo Vespucci, sailed to the West under the Spanish flag in 1499, with the theory that he might "turn a headland" into the Indian Ocean. In 1501 he sailed to acquire geographical information for the king of Portugal, who like the Spanish monarch, had been puzzled by the contradictory reports. On his two voyages, Americo discovered the Amazon and Pará Rivers, explored over 6,000 miles of continuous shoreline between Venezuela, which he named, and a harbor about 50° South on the coast of Argentina. In 1502 he presented proof of the existence of a hitherto unknown continent, "which we may rightly call a New World."

Americo demonstrated that this continent extended too far south to be India. His studies of longitude showed him that its east-west position was thousands of miles from the east coast of Asia, from which it must therefore be separated by another ocean broader than the Atlantic. Americo's proofs that there was a new continent which blocked direct westward passage to India, came as a great disappointment to Europeans. But it was verifiable fact.

To say that Columbus discovered America is a subsequent simplification of what actually happened in the drama of falsity and fact throughout which Cristoforo and Americo continued to be good friends.

With a realistic, scientific mind, Americo crossed the Atlantic and found out and reported what was really there. A geographer properly named the new continent "America" from "Americus," the Latin form of the name of the man who discovered it by exploring it. The name was euphonious, in harmony with the names of other continents. It was instantly and forever after on everyone's lips.

FREDERICK J. POHL

New York
January 20, 1966

FOREWORD

Two continents are named after Amerigo Vespucci. One-third of the land surface of the globe perpetuates his memory, so that no name in history has a more effective advertising than his, or a wider extension of fame, or a more permanent surety of preservation.

Vespucci has indeed been honored above other explorers, but he has also been vilified by many who have charged him with being an impostor, a charlatan of geography. While some have held that he, "by the discovery of America, rendered his own and his country's name illustrious," there are those who have rejected him, who have denounced him as a boaster, a fame grabber who never commanded a ship, a mountebank who preferred self-contradictions to truth. He has been accused of an unholy ambition to immortalize himself at the expense of Columbus, and he has been sneeringly referred to as "an obscure ship chandler." One of the climaxes of vilification was attained by the gentlemanly Ralph Waldo Emerson, who wrote in *English Traits,* in 1856: "Strange that broad America must wear the name of a thief! Amerigo Vespucci, the pickle-dealer at Seville, who went out in 1499, a subaltern with Hojeda, and whose highest naval rank was boatswain's mate, in an expedition that never sailed, managed in this lying world to supplant Columbus, and baptize half the earth with his own dishonest name!"

These extremes raise an important issue for inhabitants of the New World. Patriotic pride as well as good sportsmanship impels us to ask whether we have any reason to be ashamed of the origin of the name of our land. Did Amerigo Vespucci discover America, or is the name "America" an invention based upon false premises, and does it bestow an honor upon the wrong man? The question can be definitely answered, for an impartial study of Vespucci's life and voyages in the light of recent research clears away the cloud of misunderstanding and ignorance by which he has so long been obscured. The investigation will carry its reward, because it is always an exciting mental adventure to follow the mind of a man who perceived the most important fact of his generation before it was seen by anyone else.

The Vespuccian controversy has had a dramatic history. *Mundus Novus* and the *Four Voyages* (so-called Soderini Letter) were published in 1504, both purporting to have been written by Vespucci, and both of them were forgeries. The "first" of the four voyages, dated 1497, gave Vespucci priority of one year over Columbus on the coast of South America and also made him the first explorer of the coastline of Central America, Mexico, and the southeastern coast of the United States.

In 1507 Waldseemüller first used the name "America" for the continent of South America, and in 1538 Mercator applied that name to the northern continent. In the middle of the sixteenth century Las Casas attacked Vespucci on legalistic grounds that Columbus had priority, and in 1601 Herrera, accepting the forgeries as genuine, accused Vespucci of falsifying the dates of his voyages.

The three Vespucci letters from Seville, 1500, Cape Verde, 1501, and Lisbon, 1502, were first published as apocryphal, the Seville letter in 1745, the Lisbon letter in 1789, and the Cape Verde letter in 1827.

In 1846 Lester and Foster, in the first biography of Vespucci in English, accepted two of the genuine letters and at the same time uncritically retained the *Four Voyages.* M. F. Force, in 1879, was the first to suggest that the *Four Voyages* might be a forgery. In 1895 Harrisse wrote: "The four voyages of Americus Vespuccius across the Ocean remain the enigma of the early history of America."

In 1900 Gallois cleared Vespucci of having had anything to do with Waldseemüller's naming of America. The next year Uzielli thought the errors in the *Four Voyages* were largely due to the lack of an exact text of that narrative. Ober, in 1907, avoided taking sides in the controversy; he held the problem of the "first" voyage to be insoluble on the basis of the *Four Voyages;* he quoted extensively from it, however, as source material. He quoted also from the Seville and Lisbon letters, and he defended Vespucci's character against the logical consequences of the contradictions he had admitted.

Professor George Tyler Northup, a meticulous scholar, undertaking a textual study such as Uzielli had advocated, with the purpose of preparing reliable copies of Vespuccian documents for the use of university students being trained for research in American history, in 1916 published exhaustive studies of the texts, in which he raised grave doubts as to Vespucci's authorship of the *Four Voyages*. In 1926 the Italian scholar Alberto Magnaghi in his *Amerigo Vespucci, studio critico* repudiated *Mundus Novus* and the *Four Voyages*, advanced overwhelming historical and textual evidence that they were forgeries, and accepted as genuine the three letters from Seville, Cape Verde, and Lisbon. Magnaghi's conclusions have not been seriously challenged. The cumulative effect of the arguments of Professor Northup and of Magnaghi would seem to be conclusive, and such as no biographer can ignore.

Fortunately in the case of Vespucci, by claiming less one can prove more. This study is based upon a repudiation of *Mundus Novus* and the *Four Voyages* (Soderini Letter), and an acceptance of only the two voyages described in the genuine letters from Seville, Cape Verde, and Lisbon. These three genuine letters are herein newly translated. For assistance in doubtful points in translation I am indebted to Mr. Jordan B. La Guardia for the Italian, to Mr. Jacob Mann for the Latin, and to Mrs. Rosemary F. Rabus for the Spanish and the Portuguese. I have availed myself of the subject matter of seventy-three letters written to Vespucci, which were brought to light in 1903 by Ida Masetti-Bencini and Mary H. Smith and have been published only in Italian.

I wish to thank Princeton University Press for permission to quote from "Vespucci Reprints," The Soderini Letter, by George Tyler Northup. To Dr. Celestino Soares, specialist in Portuguese history and cartography, I owe more intimate acquaintance with the Portuguese claims of pre-Columbian discoveries beyond the Atlantic. I am grateful to Captain Victor Slocum, who lent ear to my nautical queries, and gave me the benefit of his experience in sailing along the South American coast. Other sources of technical knowledge are Mr. Ralph C. Urban, Mr. Samuel Mellor, and Mr. William Williamson, with their great interest in ships of sail. I am grateful to Professor Howard Wikel, of Purdue University, for assistance in the field of medieval history; to Mr. Adolph Zeltner for aid in mathematical calculations; to Dr. W. W. Francis, of the Osler Library at McGill University, for his kind co-operation in obtaining some astronomical data; to many helpful attendants at the New York Public Library, the Brooklyn Public Library, the Grolier Club Library, the Library of Congress, and the Huntington Library; and to Mr. Melvin V. Landon, formerly at the University of Maine, for his painstaking computations of the dates and times of conjunctions of the moon with Mars and with Jupiter during Vespucci's voyage in 1499. For many suggestions in matters of form and substance, I owe great thanks to Mr. Robert E. Farlow and Mr. Coley Taylor; and also to Miss Ida M. Lynn and Dr. William Bridgwater, of Columbia University Press. I owe more than thanks to Josephine, my wife, for invaluable assistance and unfailing encouragement throughout five years of research.

FREDERICK J. POHL

New York
July 10, 1944

CONTENTS

ILLUSTRATIONS

AMERIGO VESPUCCI

Pilot Major

Chapter One

PTOLEMY'S CHALLENGE

Primitive man's immediate sense perceptions told him that the earth was flat. Ancient philosophers upset the simplicity of this conception. Endeavoring to explain what upheld the flat earth, one wise man said that it floated on water, while another said it was supported by air and that at night the sun did not pass under it from the west to the east, but returned to the point of sunrise by going around the rim of it behind high mountains which kept the land in shadow. Giving heed to the insistence of mariners that the surface of the sea curved downward beyond the horizon, another ancient theorist asserted that the earth was not flat, but cylindrical in shape.

Cosmography became a science when Pythagoras pronounced the earth a sphere and when Aristotle convincingly explained this sensational theory. By the eighth century the Church had withdrawn opposition to the Pythagorean conception; and by the time the ancient authors were being widely studied, in the years of the Renaissance, the scholars throughout Europe had very generally adopted it. The Arabs in the twelfth and thirteenth centuries made maps of the world in the form of globes of silver and bronze; Sir John Mandeville, in the fourteenth century, upheld the sphericity of the earth; in 1457 Fra Mauro of Murano made a map of the world in the form of a globe; so did Paolo Toscanelli in 1474, and Martin Behaim in 1492. The sphericity of the earth was accepted by the learned in the fifteenth century, and no general deduction should be drawn from the much-publicized occasion when two appallingly ignorant Portuguese ecclesiastics, officially called upon to weigh the request of a Genoese adventurer for ships with which he proposed to reach the East by sailing west, declared his project to be nonsense, because they believed the earth was flat.[1]

In every generation there have been individuals unable to conceive of the earth as a sphere. Paul Kruger, President of the Boer

Republic, held to his flat-earth conviction, as did many of his followers. Ignorance was not confined to the Middle Ages. The history of science is concerned with those who accept truth and transmit it to others, not with those who reject truth. It is inconsequential in the history of geography that some unenlightened people in the fifteenth century still thought the earth was flat. Most of the scholars knew better. So did the mariners and traders and people who traveled.

Previous to the fifteenth century geography was not an independent science, but was included in the study of geometry and to some extent in the larger subject of cosmography, which included all branches of natural history. It was also interknit with astronomy and geology.

Students of geography retained the ancient division of the land surface of the globe into three continents: Europe, Africa, and Asia. At the nearest, or western, end of Asia was Jerusalem, and at the antipodes from Jerusalem, at the easternmost end of Asia was the Terrestrial Paradise, the Garden of Eden. "From the middle of the Garden," a bishop wrote, "a spring gushes forth to water the whole grove, and dividing up, it provides the sources of four rivers. Approach to this place was barred to man after his sin."

The scholars modestly admitted ignorance of much that lay nearer at hand than the mythical farthest point of creation. Such parts of Europe as Scandinavia and the Baltic were regions of mystery, and so was all of Africa beyond the Mediterranean fringe. Across Africa lay the torrid zone, where the sun was so hot it would burn a man black or curl him to a crisp. This was believed to be the condition, whether there was ocean or land at the equator. Many held that Africa did not extend to the equator, and others that both Africa and Asia extended far to the south and the east, so that the Atlantic and Indian oceans were enclosed and separate from each other. Land near the equator, if there were any, was thought to be uninhabitable. The south temperate zone, although it might well have a habitable temperature and might contain a separate antipodal continent or else extensions of Africa and Asia, was believed to be actually uninhabited; for were not all men descended from Adam, who had lived in the north temperate zone, and how could any of his descendants ever have passed through the killing heat of the tropics to establish a population in the southern hemisphere? The idea that there might be inhabited land in the southern hemisphere was held to be a perverse and heretical doctrine, contrary to Christian faith; for how could Christ have died for all men, as the Bible said, if some men lived in a part of the world to which it was impossible to carry His Gospel? Here was an unanswerable argument. If there were an "Austral," or southern, continent to balance against the northern continents, it must be uninhabited.

Asia and Africa and the remote parts of Europe were believed to be full of monsters. Many a region was infested with gryphes, a species of winged quadrupeds, which combined the more destructive anatomical details of lions and eagles. Gryphes were "positively" known to exist, especially by people who had never seen them. The largest and most powerful of all monsters was a kind of dragon who caused earthquakes; for, as the learned author of *De mundi constitutione* said, "The earth contains the animal leviathan, who holds his tail after a fashion of his own, so that it is sometimes scorched by the sun, and so the earth is shaken by the motion of his indignation." Let those on ships and along the shore beware of the wave stirred up when a flick of leviathan's tail hits the sea!

Far to the north dwelt the partly-human Hyperboreans, a sort of mythological reconstruction of Laplanders. In other distant regions were the Blemmyes, of alarming, though indefinite, characteristics. More completely described were the Anthropophagi or man-eaters; and the men whose heads grew beneath their shoulders; and the men who had one foot so large that they could hold it over their heads as a sunshade; and the men whose feet were advantageously hitched on backward, with the result that their enemies followed their tracks in the wrong direction. No one was adventurous enough to desire to meet any of these abnormal beings. Europeans were well satisfied to see pictures of them.

Certain other creatures whom every European male hoped particularly he might never encounter were the Amazons—fighting females, famed for their martial prowess, unnatural women who were not to be played with, dreadful women who were their own rulers and tolerated men, if at all, only at rare and capricious moments. No man who had ever attempted to pacify an infuriated woman could doubt the existence of tribes of feminine warriors.

Fortunately, the country of the Amazons was very far away, for everyone agreed that it was near the end of Asia, or on islands off the coast of Asia. The Amazons were always among the most potent of the terrors described by travelers, and if a man in his wanderings had come by chance to a village in a hunting or fishing season when only women and children were present, the tale he told of it might have persuaded his hearers that he actually had reached the land of the feminine battalions and that it was by a miracle that he had returned alive.

While imagination did its best to picture the inhabitants of distant portions of the three continents, there was a greater mystery as to what lay beyond them—if there were a beyond. No one was deeply concerned, save as a matter of speculation, for even the land distances were too great for travel; but when the question arose regarding what did lie beyond, men clung to a ready answer—the ocean. By this they meant the one and only ocean, encircling all land. Men had believed it to be there when they thought the earth was flat, as a peripheral stream, like a broad ring around the three continents. Now that they understood the earth to be a sphere, their conception of the ocean had evolved, for the three continents were wrapped around the globe and covered three-quarters—some said six-sevenths—of it, and the one ocean, filling its own center, occupied what was left. This view appeared to be supported by the statement in Genesis: "Let the waters that are under the heaven be gathered together into one place." A single ocean surrounding three continents had been analogous to Christian theology—the ultimate Oneness embracing the Trinity.

The idea of one ocean was not entirely theoretical. It was based upon some knowledge, though largely legendary, from tales of ancient voyages. Necho, the ruler of Egypt, was said to have sent Phoenicians on a voyage around Africa, for the pure purpose of geographical knowledge. These Phoenicians followed the coast, stopping to sow and reap grain for food, and two years after leaving the Red Sea they entered the Mediterranean by the Pillars of Hercules, and so returned to Egypt. They reported the remarkable fact, which, until men could explain it, cast doubt upon their story instead of corroborating it, that during a part of their circumnavigation of Africa, the sun from sunrise to sunset had been altogether on their right hand, or on the land side.

Hanno, the Carthaginian, was said to have sailed from Gades (Cadiz) around Africa to Arabia; and Caelius Antipater wrote that the Carthaginian navigator Himilco did what Hanno did. There was a statement by Posidonius, preserved by Strabo, that Eudoxus of Cyzicus sailed from Cadiz about 113 B.C. and voyaged around Africa as far as Ethiopia, and returned.

These tales, believed by some, denied by others, kept open and debatable the question whether Africa had an end, or whether the sea from Arabia to India was a closed sea, not at all connected with the ocean that lay to the west of Africa and Europe. The waters of India were possibly separated from the ocean on their eastern side by a southern extension of India, for men had no certain knowledge of the length of the Malay Peninsula—only vague reports.

Much debated, also, were questions as to how rivers are formed, or how they maintain a constant flow. Water was a mysterious element. There must be some way by which the salt water of the ocean returned upon the land to become the fresh water of rivers, else from the continuous flow of rivers into the ocean, the ocean level would rise and flood the continents. Yet how was this return accomplished? One theory was that ocean currents were caused by vast whirlpools, which sucked the water back down into the earth, to come out again as rivers.

Why did the Nile overflow at its maximum always in late summer instead of in the early spring like other rivers? Was its source the melting of mountain snows south of the equator, and did its waters come thence across the torrid zone through subterranean passages? Was the Red Sea really red? If so, was it made so by a fountain of red water? Was the sea made salt by the heat of the sun? Did the great amount of evaporation from equatorial waters cause the ocean in the torrid zone to become viscous and so make navigation there as impossible as amid the ice of the Arctic? Was Mt. Pelion two hundred and fifty miles from base to summit, and were the Alps fifty miles high? Was there a continent in the Southern Hemisphere? Was it true that in India men never slept in the daytime? Was there an island off the coast of India which was "never without leaves on its trees"? Was the Terrestrial Paradise at the eastern extremity of Asia, or in the south, as some said? Was it possible for men to visit it?

These and many other unanswered questions prevailed in the world for centuries, when legends were rife. In the Middle Ages Europe knew less about the earth than did some of the ancients, for the commercial decline of Rome brought with it a contraction of geographical knowledge.

The old trade routes to Asia overland across Asia Minor or Arabia to some port on the Persian Gulf or Indian Ocean for centuries brought to the Mediterranean world fragments of information concerning the Orient: myths and legends and romantic tales, along with bales of silks and fine cotton fabrics, precious jewels, drugs and perfumes, glass and metal and porcelain objects, and the highly prized spices—pepper, nutmegs, ginger, camphor, and cinnamon. They brought the legend of Prester John. In 1122 a Nestorian priest named Giovanni came from India to acquire information as to the proper investiture of patriarchs. He was invited to Rome and was received in the Lateran by Pope Calixtus II. He said he came from the capital city of the Indian Christians, of whom there had been a sizable community since the earliest centuries, and he so vividly impressed the people of Rome with his description of the wealth of India and the power of the Christians there that for three centuries following his visit men of the West believed in the legendary figure of a great ruler of a Christian kingdom near the eastern end of Asia. When Marco Polo returned in 1295 from his visit to the "Kingdom of Cathay," he truthfully reported that there was no Prester John in Cathay (China), so that this fact was available to scholars. Thereafter some said that Prester John resided in Ethiopia, in the mountains somewhere south of Egypt. Nevertheless, most of the people of Europe held to the legend of the Asiatic kingdom of Prester John. But wherever his kingdom was, men thought it would be a great support for all Christians if they could find Prester John and form an alliance with him against the Moslems.

The story of Marco Polo's visit to China upset also the identification of Cathay with the Terrestrial Paradise, but this was apparent only to the scholars. The book of Ser Marco Polo established in the minds of those who were interested in trade with the East the certainty that there was a water route between the coast of China and the coast of India, for Marco Polo had returned by water from the land of the Great Khan, sailing from the port of Zaiton in Cathay through a strait "between two islands," into the Indian Ocean. His voyage left no room for doubt that the Sea of China and the Sea of India were connected by a sea passage.

Following Marco Polo there were other travelers to the East: Friar Odoric, of Pordenone, Giovanni dei Marignolli, and Ibn Batuta—all in the fourteenth century. The early fifteenth-century travels of Nicolò de' Conti taught map-makers to divide "the Indies" into three regions: Persia, "India this side the Ganges," and "India beyond the Ganges." Some students of old maps believed that India was in the form of a peninsula, but this view was hard to accept, for it was contrary to the opinion of many.

And so it was that if an occasional merchant did journey all the way to India or to the Spice Isles the true story he had to tell, if he returned and was capable of telling the truth, was soon confused with many conflicting tales and with the fallacies conjured up by the imagination of stay-at-home folk. The distance to the ends of Asia was so great and the communication so slow that definite geographical knowledge did not gain wide acceptance. For the stories, as well as the spices, had to come by ship from the islands beyond India, and from India they had to be reshipped to Persia, Arabia, or Egypt. Thence they were brought overland by camel to Constantinople or Antioch or Cairo; thence by ship to various ports in the Mediterranean, principally to the trading cities of Italy, there to be distributed to other countries.

The cost of this transportation was excessive. Everywhere along the thousands of miles of travel, local potentates took toll and taxed the merchandise. The Sultan of Cairo charged one-third of the value of the goods passing through Egypt. When Constantinople fell to the Turks, in 1453, the unified Moslem power around the eastern Mediterranean got a grip on all the trade routes. The Mohammedan control soon forbade to Christendom any further direct contact with Asia and obscured knowledge of the East.

The challenge of the Moslem monopoly was sharply felt by Christian Europe, which made intensified efforts to break the stranglehold of the Turkish Empire. Italian trading cities built larger fleets and sought to establish firmer relations with their agents in Egypt and Syria. Chief among those cities were Venice, Genoa, Pisa, and Florence; and, strange to relate, it was Florence, an inland city, which became the most important trading center of all.

Why did Florence forge ahead of her seacoast rivals? The reasons were many. Genoa enjoyed an apparently unequaled site, with an excellent harbor; but Genoa, like Pisa, was on the wrong side of Italy, for the preponderance of lands and peoples and markets was toward the East. Genoa and Pisa were so near together that they hindered each other. Venice, on the other side of Italy, commanded the Adriatic and held her advantage over Genoa and Pisa in more direct contact with trading points in the eastern Mediterranean, but Venice could not compete with her rivals in trade with the West. Each of the seacoast cities had only half as much countryside to draw upon as inland cities. Florence, however, was surrounded on all sides by a large fertile region, and from her, roads went forth in every direction. Florence was on the principal north-south trade route through Italy and thus was much more accessible from Rome, Naples, and southern Italy than were the seaports which she in consequence outrivaled. She was in fact much better off for not being a seaport, because the large sums of money which entered the coffers of the papacy, brought to Rome by pilgrims from all parts of Christendom, were deposited in Florentine banks, since these funds were safer in Italy's largest inland city than in a coastal city that might be raided by pirates.

Every sort of guild or trade union existed in Florence. With more goods for sale than her own people could purchase, Florence adopted a policy of economic imperialism. Early in the fifteenth century she conquered Pisa, built up a large fleet, used Pisa, Livorno, and Piombino for her seaports, took away from Venice the lucrative grain trade of Naples, and then won over much of the commerce of the Mediterranean. Soon she had all the world for her customers.

Her large population made farm lands in her vicinity valuable, her landowners and money lenders flourished, and wealth and power came to her most successful families. She became the wealthiest city, the Wall Street of the fifteenth century. She had eighty banking houses and counting houses and controlled the credit system of Europe. Her coinage, the gold florin, because of the genuine metal in it, became standard throughout the continent. Her merchants went forth into all lands, and the activity of her agents in business everywhere gave rise to the saying that there were not four, but five elements: water, earth, air, fire, and Florentines.

Her merchant oligarchs formed a privileged class, which enjoyed individual freedom and developed the life of the mind, making Florence a republic of letters. No one understood so well as they that trade and learning were handmaidens. The torch of civilization was in their possession. They brought home precious manuscripts rescued from churches and monasteries threatened by the Moslem advance. Nicolò Niccoli, for example, collected eight hundred manuscripts. Cosimo de' Medici was the founder of the first public library in Europe. The appellation "Florentine" carried reflections of the stirring ferment in the city on the Arno, conferring a sort of distinction, for the Tuscan intellect compelled universal recognition by its outstanding vigor and alertness. Florence gave the world its leaders in art and in science. Leonardo the Florentine, Michelangelo the Florentine, Amerigo the Florentine, were names that became towering beacons on the widening horizon of mankind.

The story of the Renaissance is best revealed in the flowering of Florence. Out of her came a new spirit of inquiry, more valuable than the products of the East, more precious than pepper, cinnamon, nutmegs, cloves, and ginger; for the minds of Europeans, even more than their meals, needed spicing.

The new spirit of inquiry demanded definite knowledge concerning the habitable lands of this earth. Spurred on by the desire of merchants to extend their trade, men sought information everywhere—from the geographers of ancient times, from Arabian astronomers and cosmographers, from the authoritative writings of esteemed philosophers, from practical seamen's charts, and from more imaginative maps embodying chiefly their makers' guesses. Increasingly, however, men began to disregard authority and learned to rely on direct investigation. This had been the method of the ancients, and it was this method which dynamically influenced the fifteenth century.

The new spirit of inquiry received its chief impetus from the invention of printing, an invention whose importance outweighed even the greatest political event of the time. The capture of Constantinople was a loss of tremendous consequence to Europe. But the following year, 1454, the first book printed from movable type was published, and it was printing that gave birth to modern science.

Printing led to the overthrowing of authority, for it brought the minds of men into immediate contact with each other and into stimulating conflict. Before the days of printing, books were costly manuscripts, few in number, widely scattered, prized for their scarcity, and revered for their uniqueness. Except for the rare instances when they were assembled by men of culture and wealth, as in Florence, manuscripts were not available so that they could be easily compared. Printed books, however, were comparatively cheap and numerous; thus larger collections of works were possible, and books that contradicted each other lay side by side, inviting comparison and starting debate in their readers' minds. Which of the conflicting authorities was closer to the truth? Original investigation alone could tell. And so, in 1453 a door closed to the direct trade with the East; and in 1454 another door opened, the printed book, through which the thoughts of mankind would go forth to conquer the vast unknown in every direction.

While breaking free from authority in the field of geography, however, the new spirit of inquiry temporarily established as greater than ever the authority of one ancient author. Why it did so is important to relate. That author was Claudius Ptolemaeus, a native of Egypt, who recorded his findings as astronomer and geographer in Alexandria about 160 to 150 B.C. Ptolemy was at first famed for his astronomy, a work called *Megale syntax*, widely known as the *Almagest*, from the title, meaning "The Great," of a ninth-century Arabian translation of it. Although this work was based upon the erroneous theory of the ancients that the earth was the center of the universe, it gave considerable information as to the motions of the sun, the moon, and the planets.

Ptolemy may have been as well known for his geography as for his astronomy in his own day and for the first few centuries thereafter. But from the fifth century to the end of the fourteenth century his geography was not often mentioned. From 1406, however, when his geography was revived, or rediscovered and translated into Latin, Europe held him in reverence as a geographical authority, especially during the latter half of the fifteenth century.

His geography, called the *Cosmographia,* then had the highest reputation in spite of its inaccuracy, and even though several of his major conclusions had been challenged, it was recognized as authoritative by the scholars. Its reputation was established, not by his deserved reputation as an astronomer, but by his application to geography of an astronomical idea. Ptolemy had the basically important concept that "the fundamental principle of geography was the accurate fixing of position by latitude and longitude astronomically determined."

In imagination, we may draw upon the surface of the earth lines running parallel with the equator, or lines of latitude; and other lines of so-called longitude or meridian lines running from pole to pole and crossing the latitude lines. We may thus think of the earth's surface as marked off by crossing lines which can be identified by number; that is, by the degrees which the lines represent.

The new idea which Ptolemy seems to have contributed was that every point on the earth's surface could be or should be identified by determining through astronomical observations what are the degrees of latitude and longitude of the lines which cross at that point. This concept was exactly the kind of solidly-grounded proposition that the new spirit of inquiry demanded.

While Ptolemy did not carry out his own principle in preparing his geography, since he secured his information from a comparison of various authorities, from the itineraries of travelers in the ancient world, and from "Marinus" of Tyre, so that his geography was as full of guesses as anybody's, nevertheless his work assumed a scientific form. It consisted not only of maps but also of voluminous tables giving latitude and longitude for the cities of the earth, for the kingdoms, the seaports, the islands, and the river mouths. Knowing no more than did several other geographers, perhaps even less, he advocated what was a distinct scientific advance. His tables of latitude and longitude, though never accurate, were a step in the right direction and appealed to the mentally adventurous.

Ptolemy laid down the method by which he could be displaced. By the method he advocated, and by that method only, would the age-old questions be answered: What is the shape of the end of Asia? How far is it to the Indies? What is the true location of the Spice Isles? Does there exist a southern continent? Thus the popularization of Ptolemy's geography did not have the effect usual with the setting up of an authority. It did not fetter minds, but stimulated research to secure more accurate determinations of latitudinal and longitudinal positions.

Since it was a simple matter to find one's latitude by measuring one's angle distance from the Arctic Pole by means of the astrolabe or quadrant, the real difficulty in solving the Ptolemaic problem would be in finding a practical astronomical method of determining longitude, that could be used by explorers at unknown distances, in far regions of the earth, with the limitations of the hourglass as a time-measuring instrument. This, then, was the task for whose accomplishment the world had been waiting since Ptolemy's day, waiting for sixteen hundred years.

It was by no accident that Florence produced the man who first made a practical approach to meeting Ptolemy's challenge—Amerigo Vespucci. The cultural environment in that city of his birth, the incentive provided by the necessities of trade, the accessibility of manuscripts and printed books, the opportunities there offered for study, and the inspiration of great teachers, in combination with inherited qualities of mind and character, gave to the world the navigator and explorer who, devising a way to apply the Ptolemaic principle, dislodged ancient geographical errors and drew in large outline the first accurate picture of the geography of the globe.

Chapter Two

AMERIGO

A stranger coming into Florence in the middle of the fifteenth century would have found the town swarming with artisans of all trades: weavers and dyers, brocade and jewelry craftsmen, leather-workers, stonecutters, and intarsia-makers. In the narrow streets near Giotto's beautiful bell tower at the cathedral, he would have rubbed shoulders with silk buyers from Rome, wool buyers from Nürnberg, couriers from Spain, messengers and porters, *condottieri* of the merchant houses, peasants and priests and partisan soldiery. He would have seen much to admire in the imposing façades of the palaces of the Ruccellai, Altoviti, Pazzi, Spini, and Soderini families, and of the Medici, the richest of the merchant princes.

In the northwestern quarter of the city, bordering on the Arno, was the residence of the leading family of the district of S. Lucia di Ogni Santi, the stately and palatial mansion of the Vespucci. Early in the preceding century, when the Vespucci family first established themselves in Florence, they chose this district of Ognissanti, because it was most convenient to their country estates. It was in the section nearest the gate of the city known as the Porta della Cana (later called the Porta del Prato), and not far away, outside the walls, was their ancestral home in Peretola. They could readily escape to their countryseat whenever a political uprising in the city threatened their safety.

Their town house, with its frescoed walls and ceilings of beams, oaken furniture and plates of majolica and silver, presented a picture of comfort bordering on luxury, but not so luxurious as to dull the appetite or destroy initiative. Built upon an inner court, with a stone staircase leading to the second story, the mansion was large enough to be taken over by monks, in a later era, to be converted into a hospital for the poor—the Spedale di San Giovanni di Dio, at the corner of the Via Borgo Ognissanti and Via de' Porcellana.

Like many other houses which the Vespucci owned in the neighborhood, it proudly bore their coat of arms emblazoned upon its portals, a not very propitious escutcheon, consisting of a red field crossed by a blue band on which crawled a procession of golden wasps. "Vespa" meant wasp. Perhaps some revengeful deed, some ferocious action had caused the name to be assigned to the first of the Vespucci, but for many years there had been nothing waspish in the behavior of the clan. They were counted among the most cultured and widely respected of the aristocratic families of Florence. On an average of two years out of every three during the last hundred years some member of the family had occupied a prominent public office. And now there was Amerigo, the grandfather, who would spend thirty-six years all told in the high position of chancellor of the *signoria,* or secretary of the senate, the governing body of the oligarchic republic. His son, Ser Nastagio Vespucci, would likewise be prominent in the political life of the city. He, too, in 1455 and 1459, would be chancellor of the *signoria,* and from time to time chancellor of various guilds.[1]

To this distinguished family was born Amerigo, Nastagio's third son, named for his grandfather. Let us be exact enough to note that this birth was not in 1451, a date which the capacity of many writers for repeating errors has caused to be widely accepted. The baptismal record is evidence that in our calendar the date was in March of 1454.[2] And in this fact was an ironic fate, for this child born in the first year of the new age of the printed book was to be the first notable victim of unscrupulous printers.

Most of the questions one would like to ask about his youth remain unanswered. We do not know what special friendships, as he grew from boyhood into manhood, what intimates, what love interest, what relations with the Church, what financial vicissitudes, what travels were his. But to compensate for the meager factual record of his formative years we have a clear picture of his physical appearance when he was eighteen, for a portrait of him at that age was painted by one of the great Renaissance artists, Ghirlandajo. (See the illustration on the facing page.) In 1472 Ser Nastagio commissioned Ghirlandajo to paint a family group for the wall of the chapel built by Simone di' Pero Vespucci in 1383, which ultimately became part of the church of S. Salvadore d' Ognissanti. In the por-

MADONNA WITH VESPUCCI FAMILY, BY GHIRLANDAJO

trait of Amerigo, placed immediately at the left of the central figure of the Virgin, the brush of the artist recorded dark brown eyes, aquiline nose, and strong lips and chin, framed in an oval countenance under thick, dark, loosely waving hair. From Amerigo's own words we know that he was not above medium height. Ghirlandajo showed him to be a hearty, lusty youth, upon whom both nature and culture had laid a quality of gentleness. His body was built for endurance, for facing odds in a conflict, while the fineness of his features indicated sensitivity. His face carried an air of completeness: it was lively, full of adventure; it glowed with a winsome kindliness. In this group, dominated by the Madonna, in which all the persons were intended to show religious fervor, young Amerigo had the poise of one who was going to think things through for himself. His eyes particularly caught the artist's attention: eyes underlined with humor, beneath powerful lids and high-arched eyebrows; eyes which his somewhat slanting forehead seemed to set most naturally at a slightly upturned angle; clear, widely-spaced eyes, made for seeing far.

It was indeed a splendid fresco, the Vespucci family group, with each face strongly individualized. Ghirlandajo was only twenty-three years of age, at the beginning of his career, yet his painting showed all the qualities for which he was later to become famous: balanced composition, distinctive portraiture, clear and powerful draughtsmanship.[3]

The priest in the Vespucci family picture was Amerigo's uncle Giorgio Antonio. He was in all the family counsels, was mentioned frequently in family correspondence, and was an all-important influence upon Amerigo. Giorgio Antonio will bear much looking at, for we know that Amerigo went to school to his uncle, and in this single fact is contained the longest and the least-known chapter in his story.

Giorgio Antonio Vespucci was renowned throughout his native city for his learning and for his character. Always dressed in such spotless clothes that he was popularly called "the mirror of Florentine piety and probity," he was a canon and became dean of the cathedral. He was a scholar, a collector of manuscripts, and the owner of a splendid library, which he finally divided and gave to the library of the Monastery of San Marco, to the library of the

Medici, and to the cathedral. He was in touch with the leading thinkers of Florence, with the humanists and the Hellenists and, above all, with the Platonist Marsilio Ficino, who taught the doctrine that the divinity of man could be attained through self-development and admitted three guides for humanity: reason, experience, and authority, of which he held experience to be supreme. In the face of Christianity's claim of uniqueness, Ficino declared that variety in religions was an admirable ornament of the universe. Acquainted with such men as these, Giorgio Antonio had his hand, as it were, on the pulse of the Renaissance.

He saw that medieval scholasticism, or learning limited by the narrowest orthodoxy, was unsatisfactory food for an active intellect. He was one of the men who turned to the classics of the old pagan world, fervently embracing their broadening ideas with little fear of heresy and without disturbing at first the complacency of the Church. There was more freedom of thought in the early Renaissance than after the Protestant Reformation began, for it was the Reformation which alarmed the Church and in effect rang a tocsin for persecution.

This brilliant uncle of Amerigo's put his erudition to good use as master of a school for the sons of noblemen. Under his tutelage Amerigo acquired a love for Vergil, Dante, and Petrarch and became skilled in mathematics and in Latin. Testimony to Giorgio Antonio's discipline and excellence as a teacher is to be found in the proficiency with which Amerigo wrote his Latin. When the plague made its terrifying periodic visits to dwellings devoid of sanitation, in which it was as threatening a menace to the well-to-do as to the impoverished, members of the Vespucci family removed from the city and temporarily resided in their villa at Trivio Mugelli. On one such occasion, when Amerigo was twenty-two, he wrote the following letter in the language of scholars:

With respectful greetings to his father, the notable and distinguished man, Anastasio de' Vespucci, at Florence—
Honored Father,

Do not be astonished at my not having written you during the past few days. I certainly supposed my uncle, when he arrived, would have satisfied you on my behalf. In his absence I scarcely dare to employ Latin in my letters to you, since I blush at some of my errors in my native tongue. I have been busy recently in copying out Latin rules and idioms that I may thus use, so that upon my return I shall be fortified to show you my notebook in that section in which thoughts you have expressed have been collected. Whatever else I am undertaking and how I am behaving, you have learned, I think, from my uncle, whose return I ardently desire, so that with your help and with his I may the more dexterously apply myself both to my studies and to your precepts. Giorgio Antonio, three or four days ago, gave several letters to you to a learned and zealous priest, Ser Nerotto, to which he wishes you to reply. Beyond that there is no news, except that every one desires to pack up and move and come to the city. For all that, the day of our return is not yet, though they think it will not be long delayed, unless the plague should strike with greater terror, which may God avert!

He [Giorgio Antonio] commends to your care the case of a poor unfortunate neighbor of his whose sole expectation and resources depend upon our house, which he has discussed with you at length. He beseeches you, accordingly, that you would take upon yourself all his affairs and set them in motion so carefully and diligently that with you present he will suffer as little loss as possible in his absence. With him or after him, I shall hasten to you forthwith. May you all prosper happily for a long time. Give the whole family my greetings, and remember me to mother and then to my other elders.

In Trivio Mugelli, October 19, 1476.

Your son
Amerigo Vespucci.

Ser Nastagio was obviously a lover of good Latin, and in composing this letter his son took pains to please him. The notebook he referred to was undoubtedly the little paper notebook still extant in the Riccardi library. On the last page, amid ink stains and fantastic disfigurements, is inscribed, "Amerigo, son of Sir Nastagio Vespucci, wrote this little book." The contents, consisting of quotations from the Italian which he had chosen for translation into Latin, expressed his determination to spend less time in sleep and idle amusements and to "tire himself out a little" in earnest endeavor. This notebook was further credit to the influence of the character of Giorgio Antonio.[4]

But there was another field in which Giorgio Antonio's effect upon Amerigo was more consequential, the field of the physical sciences. He instructed Amerigo in the teachings of Aristotle and Ptolemy, firing his nephew with the particular ambition of adding to the sum of human knowledge, especially in astronomy, cosmography, and geography. This ambition shaped Amerigo's career.

This major effect of Giorgio Antonio's teaching was in opposition to the will of Amerigo's father; for Ser Nastagio had decided upon a mercantile career for the lad, in accordance with the custom of selecting a younger son to enter commercial life. Qualities of aptitude, intelligence, energy, versatility, and judgment in Amerigo caused his father to choose him as the one who should devote himself to business and advance the family fortunes; indeed, Amerigo's character was indicated by this choice. Certainly his whole future was conditioned by his father's decision not to send him to the University of Pisa with his three brothers, but to keep him in Florence for more practical training.

He was fortunate, considering the limitations of formal scholasticism in education, in that he was not sent to Pisa. Conventionally-trained, fifteenth-century intellectuals were more disposed to respect the learning of the past than to pursue independent researches. If Amerigo had become a product of Pisa, he might have accomplished nothing greater than his brothers did. As it was, he was in the good company of irregularly educated men of the Renaissance, such as Leonardo da Vinci and Shakespeare.

During Amerigo's early manhood his eldest brother became a notary and married.[5] His second brother, Girolamo, went to the Near East, where he established residence in Rhodes as the family's representative and joined the Knights Hospitalers of St. John of Jerusalem, a religious order which formed the eastern outpost of Christendom in its struggle against the Turks and later transferred from Rhodes to Malta and became known as the Knights of Malta. Amerigo's younger brother, Bernardo, entered the woolen business and upon one occasion went on a commercial trip to Hungary. Neither Girolamo nor Bernardo seems to have been very successful.

In one respect Amerigo's interest in cosmography and geography linked up with his father's choice of him for a business career. Cosmography and geography, in the fifteenth century, became separate sciences, and a distinction was made between them which was unknown to the ancients. Cosmography was theoretical; it included physics and the problems of astronomy, or of the heavens in relation to the earth. Geography was the practical science, the study of things useful to a merchant—"pratiche di mercatura," or commer-

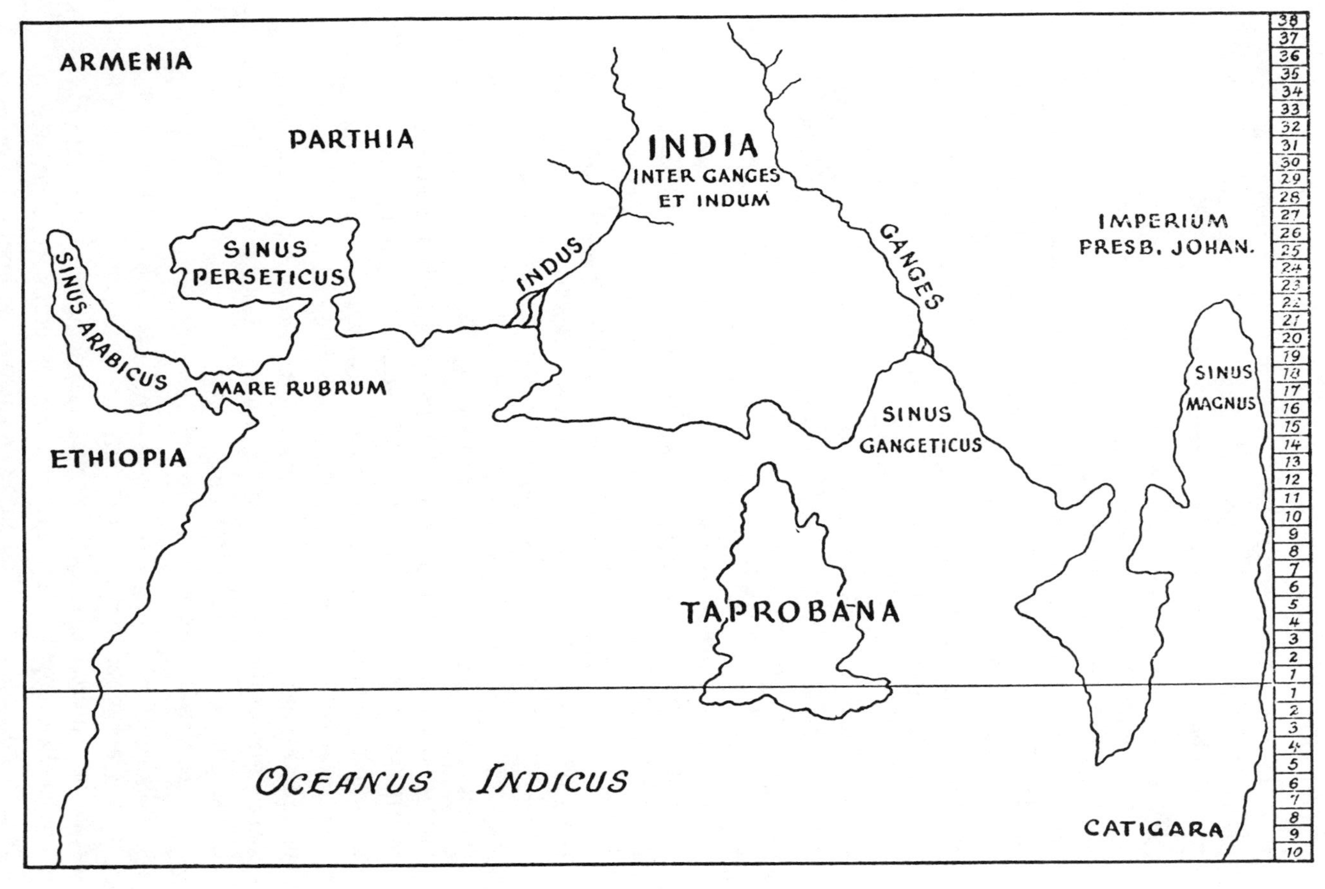

MAP OF THE EAST—PTOLEMY

cial science, consisting of knowledge of the countries of the world, their location, their trade, their resources, their people—all the available information. It was knowledge of distant countries especially, because goods obtained from distant countries commanded higher prices and afforded greater opportunities for profit.

Some of the maps which Amerigo studied for this purpose were large rolled parchments which could be spread out on a table, having the corners weighted down with cubes of marble to make them lie flat. They were beautifully decorated with water colors, the seas green, the mountains ultramarine, the land partly yellow and partly carmine, and the legends gilded. Other maps were in an atlas and pictured the Ptolemaic conception of the world east of Egypt, drawn by hand on vellum. Here was all the East, toward which Europe had been looking for centuries. A Ptolemaic map showed the Nile and the Red Sea, Arabia Felix, Arabia Deserta, the Persian Sinus, the Indus River, the land of India, the Ganges and the Great Sinus, the island of Taprobana, the kingdom of Prester John, and the farther regions of India down to the Cape of Catigara at the farthest corner of the map. In that far region beyond the Ganges and the Great Sinus, close to Catigara, in its strategic corner, was said to be found the strait described by Marco Polo, a sea route from Java and the Spice Islands and Cathay, a narrow opening between two islands, like the slender neck of a wine bottle, through which the most valuable products of the earth, spices and silks and jewels stowed away in the ships of the Arabs and the Great Khan, flowed in a concentrated stream. What geographical fact could be of greater interest to a lad whose lifework, it appeared, was to be trading in merchandise from the East? No wonder Ptolemy's geographical picture burned into Amerigo's imagination. No wonder he literally memorized that exciting portion of the map and never afterward forgot the Ptolemaic latitude of Catigara—eight and a half degrees south of the equator.[6]

There was a scholar in Florence who was further advanced in cosmography and geography than any other man of his time, and he was a fountainhead of inspiration for anyone who was, like Amerigo, interested in these sciences. His name was Paolo dal Pozzo Toscanelli (1397–1482). He was an executor testamentary of Nicolò Niccoli, who died in 1437 and whose books, assigned to the Monastery of San Marco, constituted in Florence the first public library in Europe.[7]

Toscanelli was the grand old man of Florence. He had studied astronomy under Prosdocimo de' Beldomandi, and had returned to Florence about 1424. Thereafter, he had taken no journeys, but had traveled in mind to better purpose than any man of his generation. He assembled many priceless manuscripts and the earliest examples of printing.[8] He was the head of the large wholesale and banking house of Pozzo and had close business relations with the Medici, his family specializing in skins and spices. A doctor of medicine of great learning and skill, he accepted no remuneration from the poor among his patients. He was an ascetic and a vegetarian and drank no wine, but he liked company and sought out travelers who had been to the East and from them collected tales of adventure, always seeking to winnow out the truth from the chaff of superstition and exaggeration. He had the sincerity and humility of a scientist.[9]

Messer Paolo advanced calculations of the precession of the equinoxes and ascertained variations of the ecliptic. He did what the Greeks had done, and the Arabs. He observed reality in its physical appearance, gaining knowledge by research and inquiry, not by faith in tradition or by mere deductions. He was not content with theories or with reading the works of commentators upon ancient writers. Of all his activities, that which was most likely to excite a youth of Amerigo's propensities was his study of comets. He wrote a treatise on comets containing a record of observations remarkable for exactness of time and position. He had observed five comets in thirty-five years: one in 1433, another in 1449 and 1450; then a very prominent one in 1456, another the following year, and finally the comet of 1472. He did not hold with the popular superstition that comets appear on special occasions to give notice or warning of important events on earth—for he believed that all objects in the heavens follow their own motions and that they do not make prophecies. He wittily said in his old age that once in his youth he read a prophecy from the skies: "I ascertained that the stars decreed my early death! That prognostication has been disastrously discredited!" In 1468 he established the gnomon in the cathedral of Florence. This gnomon was a meridian line which was used for determining

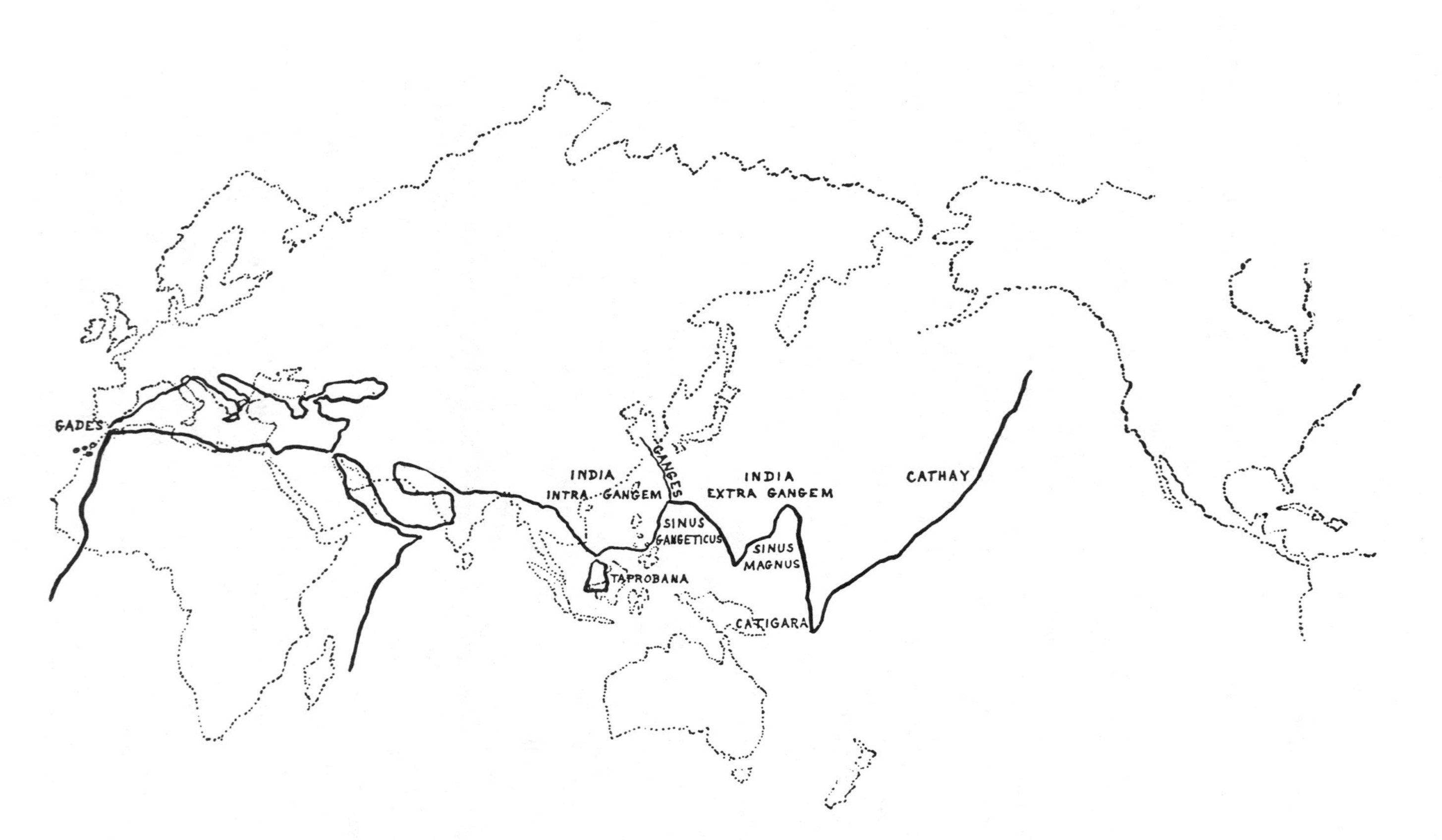

PTOLEMY'S MAP SUPERIMPOSED ON MODERN MAP

the dates of movable feasts and was extraordinarily accurate for the age in which it was constructed.

He was an enthusiastic map collector and map-maker, and unquestionably the greatest cosmographer of his day. His computation of the length of a degree of longitude at the equator, and hence of the circumference of the earth, was more nearly accurate than any one before him had ever made, though means of proving it so was still lacking. The over-extension of Asia to the east, as misrepresented by all previous cosmographers, was another matter entirely, and neither Toscanelli nor anyone else during his lifetime had any opportunity of ascertaining that error.

He gave to some Portuguese ambassadors and through them to Prince Henry the Navigator the idea of sending ships to attempt the circumnavigation of Africa in search of a route to India, since the direct routes were blocked by the Mohammedans. Years later, in 1474, he propounded to a Portuguese friend, Fernando Martinez, the more sensational idea of reaching India by sailing westward. Soon afterward he received several letters of inquiry from a young Italian in Portugal named Cristoforo Colombo. Toscanelli replied to Colombo by sending him a copy of the original letter to Martinez and also a "navigator's chart" of the Atlantic. The letter to Martinez declared that "there is a very short route from here to the Indies . . . by way of the ocean, a route which I estimate to be shorter than that which you seek to find by way of Guinea. . . . While the route has never been followed, it is not very far across the sea." Cristoforo Colombo was completely won over, and he wrote again to Toscanelli most enthusiastically, and Toscanelli again replied, encouraging Colombo in his new purpose and saying: "I note your noble and ardent desire to go to the countries of the Orient by way of the western ocean, which is indicated upon the map I sent you." [10] These letters to Colombo were always thereafter treasured by this ambitious youth and were left among his papers after his death. From Toscanelli this Colombo either first got the idea that became the ruling passion of his life, which he attempted to carry out in his voyages, or else, having originally come by the idea, he valued the support which Toscanelli's expression of the idea lent to his adventurous plan.

Another youth who sat at the feet of "Paul the Physicist" was

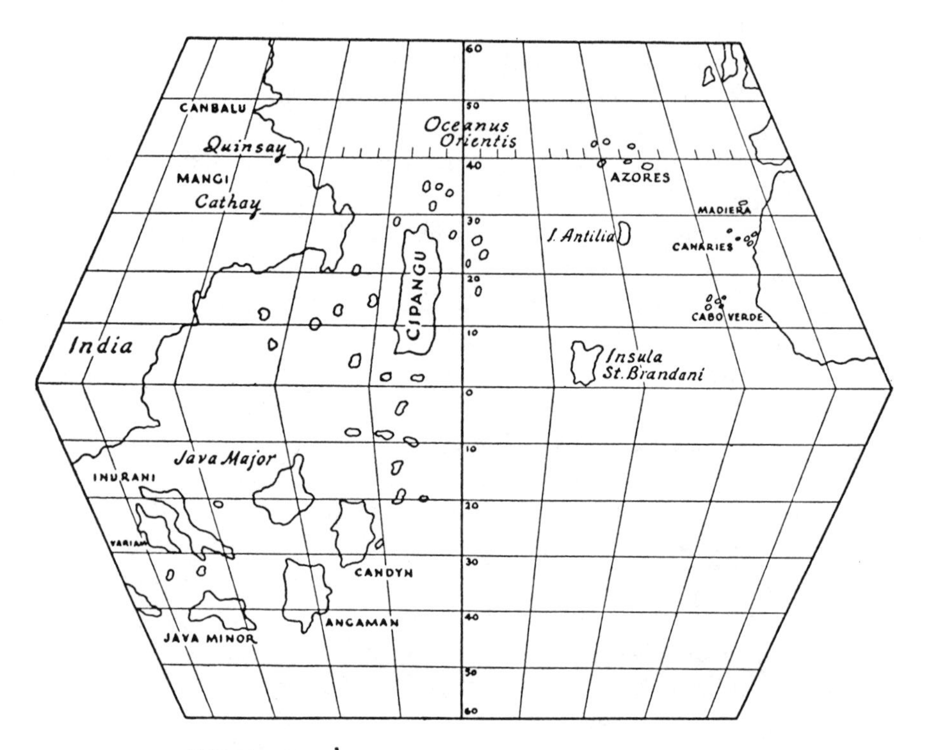

TOSCANELLI'S MAP, 1474, RECONSTRUCTED

that student of nature with an inquiring mind, Leonardo da Vinci, Amerigo's elder by two years. Leonardo, who borrowed a quadrant from Carlo Marmocchi and picked up knowledge in most extraordinary ways, came to Toscanelli seeking help in problems of mathematics and learned more than he came for. Toscanelli initiated Leonardo into his observant attitude toward reality, starting him on his lifelong quest for the truth behind all the manifestations of beauty and physical appearance. The influence of Toscanelli upon Leonardo da Vinci is authoritatively stated by Antonina Vallentin, who says in her biography of that great Florentine, "The man who exerted the decisive influence over Leonardo was Paolo dal Pozzo Toscanelli." [11]

Although no proof of their having met has been found, Italian writers repeatedly assert that Amerigo Vespucci and Toscanelli were personally acquainted. Indeed, it would seem that they must have been. Consider all the circumstances: the close connection between Amerigo's uncle, a scholarly monk of the Monastery of San Marco, and Paolo Toscanelli, a director of the library of that monastery; also, Amerigo's special interest in geography, cosmography, and astronomy, which would have led him to the famous savant; and the fact that in order to meet Toscanelli, Amerigo had only to ask his uncle for an introduction, if one were needed. Toscanelli lived near the public well in the Santo Spirito quarter, just across the Arno from the neighborhood of the Vespucci residence. Even if by some miracle Amerigo and Toscanelli never met, the younger man was undoubtedly informed by his teacher uncle of all that Toscanelli had to contribute to the education of a future geographer, especially of his sensational idea of reaching Asia by sailing westward.

In the year 1478 occurred one of the most dramatic events in Florentine history. Giuliano de' Medici was assassinated during a service in the cathedral by members of the Pazzi conspiracy. Giuliano's brother Lorenzo fled from the uplifted weapons of the conspirators into the sacristy and escaped with his life. The populace at once rose against the conspirators, and "Lorenzo the Magnificent" was thereafter undisputed ruler of Florence. Piero Vespucci, one of Amerigo's distant relatives, aided the escape of a friend who was one of the conspirators, and for this Piero was arrested by

Lorenzo and was sentenced for life to the city prison, the *Stinche,* which was probably as noisome as it sounds. He was released two years later through the intercession of his friend King Ferdinand of Aragon. The incident has been mentioned to show that the Vespucci family had important contacts with Spain. Indeed, the family had a long tradition of friendship with Spanish royalty. Half a century earlier, Alfonso of Aragon, who was also king of Sicily, had given to one of the Vespucci, Giovanni di' Simone, the privilege of placing a vase containing a rose on the family coat of arms.

In 1479, the year following the conspiracy, Florence suffered a defeat in war and was compelled to submit to a hard peace. Severe taxes were levied to meet the financial terms of the peace settlement. Life was then no bower of blossoms in the banking houses of Florence, and the Vespucci family fortune was reduced.

One of the principal influences in the life of Amerigo was Guidantonio Vespucci, a distant cousin (Amerigo's great-great-grandfather was a brother of the great-grandfather of Guidantonio), who was a prominent lawyer (Doctor of Laws) and diplomat and a man of letters. In the year of the Pazzi conspiracy, when this illustrious jurist was sent as Florentine ambassador to France, he took the twenty-four-year-old Amerigo with him to the court of Louis XI as his attaché and private secretary.[12] Amerigo spent two years in Paris and at the French court, and during that time he wrote out his cousin's official reports. When Guidantonio returned to Italy in 1480, he went as ambassador to the pope to claim absolution for the Pazzi conspirators. He was again ambassador to the pope in 1482 and in 1484. A decade later he was the Florentine ambassador to Charles VIII at Milan. He was the most distinguished member of the Vespucci family, was several times *priore,* and twice *gonfaloniere di giustizia,* the chief executive of Florence, in 1487 and in 1498.

From Guidantonio, Amerigo gained much practical wisdom in dealing with men, acquired insight into the devious ways of kings and courts, and learned how effective in diplomacy simple integrity of character can be. Family correspondence shows that Guidantonio and Amerigo had high regard for each other and that there was close contact between them throughout the years.

At the time Amerigo returned to Florence from France his

father was chancellor of the exchange. Under his father's direction he gained further experience in business. He also continued to study physics and the sciences and acquired "other knowledge of the most useful kind."

The death of Ser Nastagio Vespucci, in April of 1482, the same year in which Toscanelli died, compelled Amerigo to become the chief money-earner of his family, as the only one of the four sons directly trained for business. In fifteenth-century Florence leaders in business often became leaders of the state, since the career of business attracted men of highest intelligence and broadest culture. Amerigo was soon given an opportunity to show how well he had been prepared to take a distinguished place in trade and imaginative enterprise, for he almost immediately qualified as an executive. In 1483 he was chosen to be *maestra di casa,* or manager of the firm, of the cadet branch of the Medici.

Pier Francesco de' Medici, a first cousin of the father of Lorenzo the Magnificent, had bequeathed great wealth to his two sons. Under Cosimo, the Medici fortune had become the greatest in Europe, and in 1451 "a liberal half" had been assigned to Pier Francesco. When Amerigo took charge, the elder son, Lorenzo di Pier Francesco de' Medici, to give him his full name, was barely twenty, and the younger son, Giovanni, was seventeen. Amerigo's duties were to handle all financial affairs for his young patrons and to conduct their business in a manner profitable to them. The choice of Amerigo to manage this house of the Medici was a compliment to his judgment and character. His was a position of great trust and responsibility.

Giovanni was the most handsome and attractive of all the Medici. When he was nineteen, he was engaged to Maria, daughter of Lorenzo the Magnificent, but she died before they could wed. Some years later, though a commoner, he won the heart of a duchess; and she, Catherine Sforza, married her irresistible lover against the wishes of her proud Milanese relatives. This was the most ambitious marriage any Medici up to that time had achieved.

The brothers Lorenzo and Giovanni di Pier Francesco did not share in the financial opportunities open to Lorenzo the Magnificent through his political control of the city, and they were consequently jealous of the elder branch of the family and connived with others to secure its downfall. They appealed to the populace by calling themselves "Popolano," and two years after the death, in 1492, of Lorenzo the Magnificent, they accomplished the banishment of the elder branch.

Before Amerigo began to serve the "Popolano" Medici, Savonarola, friend of Amerigo's uncle Giorgio Antonio, had already arrived in Florence. Savonarola surpassed all his fellow monks of the Order of San Marco in his fanatic zeal for reform. He was the determined enemy of Lorenzo the Magnificent, taunting Lorenzo on his deathbed, setting all Florence by the ears, and becoming temporary master of the city.

In the midst of these fierce conflicts Amerigo struggled with the problems of trade, buying and selling, securing credit and acquiring information in foreign ports, handling agents, and procuring the safe transportation of goods. Of little importance, but of interest to us nevertheless, were the kinds of goods he handled. He dealt in fish, wine, cherries, buttermilk curds, mustard, cloth, shirts, handkerchiefs, sheets, towels, bed curtains, mulberry seed, tapestry, carpets, tablecloths, napkins, silver forks, spoons, saltcellars, knives, satchels, poultry, pigeons, goblets, "200 casks of vermilion at 21 soldi per cask," and so forth.

He was expected to produce profits and was to blame if anything went wrong. For at least sixteen years, nine of them in Florence, he labored for Lorenzo di Pier Francesco de' Medici and his good-looking brother, remaining in his native city much of the time, but facing the discomforts and dangers of travel when duty required. He journeyed to Piombino, Leghorn, and Pisa. Several times, perhaps, but certainly once or twice, he went on business trips to Spain, before he settled there permanently. Against the competition of rival houses he strove to advance the prosperity of his patrons. Fully appreciative, they kept him in their employment, for he was uniformly successful. And his efforts in their behalf were duly rewarded through his personal income.

Flush, with money to spare, Amerigo indulged his hobby of collecting maps and books relating to cosmography and astronomy. His enthusiasm for geography impelled him to buy a map of sea and land made at Mallorca in 1439 by Gabriel de Velasca ("Valsqua" on the map). This map was a portolano, with vertical and horizontal lines also, drawn on a whole skin. It represented the known world from the western ocean to Arabia, showing part of the Red Sea and the Persian Gulf. It was profusely adorned with miniatures, with pictures of kings in Africa and Asia, and with flags in Europe and North Africa. It was colored in red, blue, green, and gold. The map had a very interesting subsequent history and was later described as "the most artistically illustrated cosmographic sea chart, the very finest, most exact and completest of its kind in its epoch." Amerigo paid a hundred and thirty ducats for it, as he recorded in his own handwriting upon the margin. This sum was the equivalent of more than four hundred dollars.[13]

How Amerigo spent his time during his last nine years in Florence may be deduced from the seventy-three surviving letters written to him by members of his family, by comparative strangers, by one of his employers, and by various merchants and agents with whom he had dealings. Quotations from these letters show that he had many friendships, that many people looked to him, the rising young business man, for aid, relying on his willingness as well as his ability to help them, and that he cheerfully carried the burden of relatives and dependents. They show the changing fortunes of his family, give several hints as to his personal life, reveal in some detail the nature of his business, and indicate why he finally left Italy for Spain.

They show that he lived in the Medici house as a friend, almost as a member of the family. His employers, being younger than he, made him their confidant. Semiramide, Lorenzo's wife, requested him to procure a cap of gray silvered velvet, with a plait in the middle, for her infant son, Pier Francesco. She asked him to ascertain Pier Francesco's head size and to send stockings for two of her other children and an ivory comb for her little daughter. When Amerigo's uncle Giorgio Antonio was taken ill with a flux at six o'clock on November 15, 1489, he was cared for with great solicitude by Lorenzo and Giovanni de' Medici in their house until he was pronounced cured five days later.

Amerigo's employers were men of culture, who read books and patronized artists. In a postscript to a letter to Amerigo, Lorenzo wrote, "If Friar Piero Rosso or other monks of S. Maria Novella ask you for that book of theirs which they loaned me, have it given to you by my Gianmaria and return it to them; and without waiting for a request, send the other book to S. Marco." Amerigo himself was lending books. A relative named Piero, captain of the Florentine military force of occupation at Pisa, wrote that he wished to borrow Amerigo's copy of some sonnets.

Among the most revealing of the letters to Amerigo, were those from his brother Girolamo, in 1488 and 1489. Girolamo wrote of having been robbed of all his clothing save one suit, and he declared himself completely dependent upon Amerigo. He complained that their mother had given everything to their brother Antonio. Amerigo had borne the burden of the family after his father's death, though Antonio, to whom their mother was so partial, was the ostensible head of the family business and was able to afford marriage and a large family. Significantly, it was to Amerigo that the indigent Girolamo turned in his distress.

His younger brother Bernardo wrote him from Hungary that the king there had set Carlo Macinghi, a Florentine, in a tower, and Bernardo begged his brother to collect money, "which it is believed has more power than the king," to procure the prisoner's release. A letter from a member of Amerigo's entourage showed that he was a person of recognized influence, whose good offices were valuable.

In a letter from Spain there was a hint as to Amerigo's personal life. Juane de Tosiñana from Burgos, on August 18 of one of the years from 1488 to 1491, inquired as follows, addressing Amerigo as "Brother":

> I have concern to know how your daughter is and the mother, and the one called Francisca. Remember me to them. Let me know if Lesandra is well, not that I wish her well, but to know if she is dead or alive, since she has had little regard for me, and I have less for her . . .

The salutation suggests a brother-in-law relationship, which argues a marriage; but no such marriage was recorded in Florence. It may be that Amerigo's daughter was illegitimate. But in view of the fact that there is proof of a formal marriage in Spain, though no record of the date of it, it is interesting that the inquiry came from that country. The Vespucci family tended to observe the convention of depending upon the eldest son to marry and carry on the family, and in accordance with this tradition Antonio was, as far as we know, the only one of the Vespucci brothers married in Italy.

The blasting moral force of Savonarola, castigator of sinners, rocked Florence to the depths. No man in Florence could escape feeling something of his influence. Certain phrases in Amerigo's letters, however, imply a complete lack of sympathy with religious fanaticism, and in any case, Savonarola's interference with the old ways of life in the city did not continue to affect Amerigo, whose business called him away at the very time when the preaching monk rose to power. Far off in Spain, he had no share in the machinations of his two young patrons, the "Popolano" brothers, who, under cover, later led in the uprising against the Prior of San Marco, and thus, more than any other two men were responsible for the shame brought to Florence by the burning of Savonarola.

While on a business trip to Spain, Amerigo, according to Pier Rambaldi, wrote to a friend who had requested him to purchase a ring, "You see my reply is delayed so many days because I am writing in Spain, and cannot leave, but this very hour I will go shopping for you in the market here." The voyage between Leghorn and Barcelona, with fair winds, took perhaps ten days. Amerigo had already been to Spain (Castile) at least once when his patron Lorenzo wrote to him on the eve of another trip to Spain:

> Because of the fact that within three days you must start for Spain to meet the young man of Tommaso, I do not know what to reply, because through their communications, in my opinion, they have written lies enough, and they mismanage our affairs. It would seem that our affairs should be taken out of their hands rather than be turned over to them once again. Donato tells me he has left in the establishment a certain Giannetto Berardi. Inform yourself there of his character, whether he is a good man in whose hands our firm would be secure. It seems to me better to withdraw from Tommaso and give the business to him. And in this matter it will be necessary to make some better bargain. I will be there [at the home office, presumably] up to Sunday, for a short while. As for the reports of that imprudent one, I tell you that if I had believed them, I would not call for such an accounting, but because I think them lies, I do not estimate much value. As to the affair of Alonso, just as with Sandro, see if you can arrange it before my return; and if not, when I am there, we shall provide.
>
> Make Geri hurry to settle that account which gives me enough annoyance remaining as it does, for my rent is dependent upon it. Speed-

ily conclude dealing with Tommaso, for there is no need of that business. That is how I understand it, since I am here, and since you have been to Castile. And if there is no need for that business, bring the affair to a termination, doing it in such fashion that we shall not be compromised. Donato knows very well that I told him I did not wish him to withdraw before this business had been accomplished. That is all.

Lorenzo

At Cafaggiuolo, September 24, 1489.[14]

Two years later, toward the end of 1491, Lorenzo's commitments in Spain required Amerigo's presence there again. Spain was then the land of greatest business opportunity, and foreign merchants, particularly Italians, were welcome there for various reasons growing out of political conditions. It was not one country, but several countries in process of being welded together. Chief among these political entities were Aragon and Castile, which had been united by the marriage of King Ferdinand and Queen Isabella. Ferdinand really should not be mentioned first, for as long as Isabella lived he was the less important. He was tall and handsome, with a bright and roving eye and a persuasive tongue, which influenced, but could not deceive, his wife, least of all with regard to his concubines and illegitimate children.

Isabella of the golden hair and blue eyes was of Lancastrian ancestry and, like an English lady, possessed of great dignity. She was "Queen of Castile, Leon, Aragon, Sicily, Granada, Toledo . . . Seville, Sardinia, Cordova, Corsica . . . Gibraltar, the Canary Islands, Countess of Barcelona, Sovereign Lady of Biscay," and so forth, with many emergency titles to spare, so that without false impersonation she could travel incognito. When she came to the throne, the country was in an unhappy state: the coinage was debased, and robbers and cutthroats abounded. With firm resolution Isabella took hold of chaos and brought swift order. She established the Royal Constabulary, which consisted of troops of horsemen who galloped here and there, appearing unexpectedly and executing lawbreakers with a brace of arrows. Isabella herself was an accomplished horsewoman, and often by her presence lent persuasion to the power of her police.

She supported the Holy Office (official name for the Inquisition).

There seemed to her to be satisfactory reasons for the persecution of heretics, for Spain was overrun with Moors, and if she and her consort were to succeed in driving out the followers of the Prophet, they must secure unity among the Christians by every possible means, including a crusade against all unbelievers. In addition to this tactical advantage, she believed that a confession of faith was spiritually bolstered by blood sacrifices and burnt offerings. As for the inquisitors themselves, there was no doubt of their enthusiasm, since they came into possession of one-third of the goods of each condemned heretic.

The Holy Office hopefully opened for business in 1481, and it received immediate popular patronage in the form of accusations against Jewish tax collectors. The Queen's confessor, Tomas de Torquemada, became Inquisitor-General in 1484, and before his unlamented demise, fourteen years later, he was responsible for the public burning of ten thousand persons and the slaughter of unrecorded thousands in the torture chambers. This peculiarly Spanish conception of religion flourished, of course, because of lack of intellectual culture such as existed in Florence, where the burning of Savonarola, diabolic as it was, had motives less piously pretentious.

The common people in Spain insisted upon making a discrimination considered reprehensible by the inquisitors, for while the people approved of the extermination of Jewish tax collectors, they sought to preserve Jewish physicians, almost the only physicians they had. Thus, while inquisitors hunted heretics, the populace in many places hunted inquisitors, who had to be saved by the Queen's officers. In 1490 Pope Innocent VIII sent a legate to inquire into the proceedings of the Holy Office, but resourceful royalty bribed the legate to make a vain inquiry, and the too-innocent pope was deceived.

Since Jews were prohibited by the Holy Office from acting as merchants, there were many openings for foreign traders. During the ten years in which King Ferdinand and Queen Isabella were fighting to expel the Moors, while the fortunes of war fluctuated, and one out of every twelve inhabitants was in the army, opportunities for war profiteering attracted merchants of all nationalities. Spain, out of touch with the principal trade routes, was comparatively poor, though famous for her Arabian horses, Segovian armor, and Toledo blades. On the other hand, since Italy was the land of greatest prosperity and refinement in all Europe, Italian merchants were especially welcome in Spain.

Because of fear of French domination of the world, most of Europe desired the strengthening of Spain as a rival of France and hence approved of Spain's attainment of unity and her rise to power. Italy in particular was fearful of France and looked to Spain for salvation. King Ferdinand ultimately led in the formation of a league to expel the French from Italy, seeking to effect the realization of Italian hopes by seizing from the French as much of Italy as he could for himself. In preparation for this rescue, he continued his family's policy of befriending all Italians, especially of courting the favor of the influential citizens of the leading Italian cities.

To such a Spain, Amerigo went,[15] welcome as a merchant, doubly welcome as an Italian and a Florentine. And after he established contacts there, Spanish affairs increasingly demanded his attention, until the Spanish end of his business became the center of it.

Chapter Three

FROM MERCHANT TO EXPLORER

The turn of the year 1492 found Amerigo in Barcelona. A few days after the triumphal entry of Ferdinand and Isabella into Granada, he and Donato Nicollini wrote to Lorenzo:

> As it is necessary for one of us, either Amerigo or Donato, to proceed in a short time to Florence, we shall be able to give you better information on all points by word of mouth than can possibly be done by letter. As yet it has been impossible to move the freight of salt, for want of a vessel, since for some time, we are sorry to say, no ship has arrived here which was not chartered. Be assured that if one arrives we shall be active in your interests.
>
> You will have learned from the elder Donato the good fortune which has befallen His Highness the king. Assuredly the most high God has given him His aid; but I cannot relate it in full. God preserve him many years, and us with him.
>
> There is nothing new to report. Christ preserve you.
>
> Donato Nicollini
> Amerigo Vespucci
>
> We date this January 30, 1492.

In March, 1492, Amerigo was in Cadiz, and at the end of the year in Seville, where he established his residence. Pietro Logoluso says that a letter has been unearthed by Davari, the custodian of the archives at Mantua, which was written by Vespucci at Seville on December 30, 1492, addressed to Corradolo Stanga, and carrying the signature: "Ser Amerigho Vespucci, merchante fiorentino for Sybilia."

Seville was a proud city that boasted that she had been built by Hercules, enwalled by Julius Caesar, and refortified by Ferdinand III, who expelled the Moors. At the time Amerigo arrived, one of the principal buildings was the famous Court of Oranges. This was part of an ancient mosque and was used as a patio of the great cathedral which had been built by the ambitious Sevillians "to be equaled by none," the largest cathedral in the world. Close to the cathedral rose the gigantic minaret of the ancient mosque, the marvelous Giralda tower. Near the cathedral converted Moorish architects were being employed in the work of restoration of the Alcázar, the old fortress of the Moors.

Across the Guadalquivir River was the district of Triana, named after the Roman emperor Trajan. There, in the neighborhood of the old Gothic church of Santa Ana, were the dockyards, and lodging houses for sailors and the homes of men who followed the sea.

For Amerigo life in Seville was very different from that in Florence. He was no longer burdened with the immediate concerns of his relatives, no longer under the daily beck and call of his employer, but was free to exercise more initiative in dealing with merchants, and he very soon began to play a part in connection with maritime enterprises. First as agent for the Medici, and then also as successor to Berardi, the leading outfitter of ships, he rose to prominence. He lived among mariners, in an atmosphere where his special knowledge of cosmography and geography, his love of maps and skill in making them, were most fully appreciated.

At the river landing in the Triana district he saw something of the process by which lads from the country were transformed into sailors. There, whenever a young boy popped up with ambition to become a sea captain, he was asked whether he knew how to steal a cat. The law required a ship's master to have cats aboard to keep down rats, and if he could not buy cats, he must "get them on board in any manner." A youth of likely age to become a sailor was informed of the one way he could avoid taking a whipping from the ship's master—by passing the chain. If the captain hit him, the loafers in Triana told him, he could run into the bows and stand beside the anchor chain. Then if the master came at him with a belaying pin, he should slip to the far side of the chain. There the captain was not permitted to touch him. But if he did, the sailor might call his messmates to witness that the master had broken the rules by passing the chain, and then he could legally hit back.[1]

Half-starved apprentices were tempted to skip out and run away to sea by a description of sailor's fare, which was meat and wine for dinner three days a week and porridge the other days, and for supper, cheese or onions or sardines. If this menu did not entice, a hungry lad was told that most ships were also supplied with oil and vinegar, rice, stockfish, lentils, plums, almonds, garlic, mustard, salt, and honey.

In Spain, any man could become a sailor. In Portugal, it was said, a man must first have proper instruction and must learn to be a carpenter or a rope-maker, or a caulker, or a blacksmith, or a plank-maker, so that he could be really useful on a voyage.

At the beginning of the year 1493 Amerigo heard the mariners talking of the most famous voyage that had ever taken place, the voyage of the Portuguese Bartolomeu Dias to the Cape of Good Hope, from which he had returned five years earlier.

In Triana, Amerigo occasionally heard it mentioned that a Spanish expedition had departed the preceding summer from Palos, under an Italian fellow, Cristoforo Colombo, whose name in Spanish was Cristóbal Colón, who had got himself appointed admiral and sailed away westward into the ocean to find India, with three ships. His crew, it was said, were the lowest scrapings from the waterfront: Castilians, Biscayans, Aragonese, Andalusians, an Irishman, an Englishman, one or two converts, and some fellows from France or Flanders and from Italy. Half of them were jailbirds. This Admiral Colón had boasted that all the world would hear of him, but the Portuguese had been clever enough to refuse him aid. It was a pity the Spanish king and queen had let themselves be persuaded to sacrifice three caravels to such a dreamer; for Colón was gone forever—lost at sea, they said. Everybody had prophesied it in August, when he sailed, and there had been the worst storms in fifty years during that winter. Admiral Colón was undoubtedly in the Port of Missing Ships and would never be seen again, even though he had with him, more's the pity, the best pilot of Spain, Juan de la Cosa of Biscay. Everybody who knew the ocean said Colón had been engulfed by waves, God rest his soul!

No one could guess how far west Colón had ventured before he was overwhelmed, but a student of cosmography like Amerigo would have been keenly interested to hear that Colón had asserted that he did not expect to have to sail anywhere near as far as Bartolomeu Dias had already sailed in the western ocean on his voyage to the Cape.

Three months after Amerigo's arrival in Seville the sailors of

Triana were shouting that Colón had found a Spanish route to India, straight westward. He had beaten the Portuguese at their own game. Why seek India around the far end of Africa, when the great and glorious Colón had found for Spain a direct route to the Indies?

It was the middle of March, 1493. Spain was exultant. Colón had humbled the egotism and pride of the Portuguese, who had never done boasting of having rounded the Cape of Good Hope. Imagine the envy of Bartolomeu Dias, who in Lisbon witnessed the return of Colón and was the first gentleman there to greet him! In Cadiz, in Seville, in Barcelona—in all Spain—merchants and mariners, courtiers and commoners, were delirious at the prospects of the riches open to them now that such immediate contact with eastern Asia had been so spectacularly established. Everywhere men were saying: "Such a short distance! Little more than a month's voyage! To think that all the time the Indies were so near! The Admiral reached them in just a few weeks! They are only twice as far beyond the Azores as the Azores are from Cadiz!" [2] The success claimed by Colón made the world seem smaller than most people had dreamed.

At first almost everyone was satisfied that the Admiral had proof of what he said he had done. Behold the six Indians he took to Barcelona to Their Majesties and the four he left in Seville! They surely came from near the Ganges. They were not Africans, for they were not black like Senegals and Ethiops, but were a sort of copper brown, as it was said men are in Asia. It was true that they were unlike any inhabitants of the East that had been described, and when men tried to talk with them and mentioned the names of kingdoms and cities in Asia, they showed no recognition. From what country were they? But even if no one knew what to think of them, the Admiral had earned all the honors Their Majesties bestowed upon him.

The facts that interested seamen were that he had lost one of his three ships, that it had been announced that he was almost immediately to sail again to India, and that this time he would have an immense fleet and thousands of men, who would be sure to bring home great riches. Those who failed to secure permission to sail with him would be the unlucky ones.

Amerigo was tempted, like everyone else, to run away from business and take passage to India. But his patron Lorenzo was relying upon him to discharge certain duties, and he could not desert his post under the plea of romantic ambition or thirst for adventure.

The voyage of Columbus made geography a political issue, for it caused the rivalry of Portugal and Spain instantly to flare anew. The Treaty of Toledo in 1480 had given to Portugal the Canaries and islands opposite Guinea, and beyond. Under that treaty Portugal claimed all land south of the Canaries. A papal bull in 1481 gave Portugal the isles south to the Indies, "beyond, behind, and across the Ganges." Now, in 1493, the reported findings of Columbus had thrown everything into confusion. In less than seven weeks after his return Spain and Portugal were threatening each other with war. The pope was called upon to settle the dispute between them. On May 4 he issued a bull dividing the unknown regions of the world in half, reserving to Portugal everything east of a meridian line one hundred leagues west of the Azores or Cape Verde Islands, and giving to Spain everything west of that line.

Portugal protested. The Portuguese were not satisfied with one hundred leagues, because of the adverse currents and unfavorable winds near parts of the African west coast, which they believed could be avoided only by sailing far out to the west on their way to the Cape of Good Hope, through waters which the papal bull would deny to them. They were determined to have the division line shifted farther west. Again at risk of precipitating war, they put pressure upon Spain, so that on June 7, 1494, by the Treaty of Tordesillas, the Line of Demarcation between the possessions of Spain and Portugal was moved from one hundred leagues to three hundred and seventy leagues west of the Cape Verde Islands.

During the summer of 1493 Columbus and Vespucci were both in Seville. The Admiral of the Indies, now in his season of greatest glory, was preparing a large fleet of three transports and fourteen caravels, on which fifteen hundred men eager to take passage to India would soon set sail with him. It is likely that along with other merchants Amerigo invested money in the second voyage of Columbus, and it is also probable that his business brought him into personal contact at this time with his fellow countryman. Another Italian then in Seville who may have met Columbus was the stout-hearted Giovanni Caboto, who was ambitious to reach China across the western ocean.

Columbus, whom men in Spain called the "Very Magnificent Lord Don Cristóbal Colón," was a stately figure—a little past forty, possessed of great natural dignity, with light grey eyes, a long nose, a high forehead, and hair that had turned white ten years earlier. His distinguished personality had made it easy for him all his life to impress other men with his importance, even if he had not readily won their support. This commanding physical presence, which gave him the advantage in meeting opposition, was both his strength and his weakness, for while it enabled him to initiate a world-stirring project, it habituated him to a fatuous reliance upon his own judgment, often ill-informed. He had the aplomb of a great leader and also the disregard of facts which is fatal to success. He could foretell the signs of an approaching hurricane, but he could not adjust himself to a disconcerting reality which did not jibe with his romantic preconceptions. He had proved himself one of the world's greatest in imagination and initiative, but he had already doomed himself to disappointment by an obstinate insistence upon interpreting facts to please his mystical fancy.

At this period he was in high fettle, a man who had made the world wag his way. Nevertheless, he showed annoyance at many of the questions he was being asked, as though he were incurably suspicious of an interrogator's motives. If anyone in his hearing ventured the comment that he had not publicly mentioned having put into port at any of the famous cities of India, his answer was ready and sharp—that he had been near the great cities of India; that the inhabitants he had met along the coast were only fishermen; and that the wealthy region lay just beyond. He firmly declared, "I discovered what Ptolemy calls 'the islands beyond the Ganges,' and I also reached the mainland of Asia!"

As to his estimate of the circumference of the earth, he said flatly:

> Experience has shown it, I have discussed it with quotations from the Holy Scriptures, and computed it with the situation of the terrestrial paradise which Holy Church has approved. I see that the world is not so large as the common crowd say it is, and that one degree on the equator is fifty-six and two-thirds miles [Roman miles]. This is a fact

one can touch with one's fingers. I am not one of those carried astray by the new calculations. The length of a degree is fifty-six and two-thirds miles. This is a fact, and whatever any one says to the contrary is only words.

This assertion, if it came to Amerigo's ears, must have sounded astonishing, for Amerigo's estimate of a degree was sixty-six and two-thirds miles. Columbus was so firmly self-taught that he could not be re-educated.

He set sail on his second voyage in September, 1493. He was in a hurry to forestall any expedition from Portugal and to carry aid to the thirty-nine men on Española [island of Haiti], left there to build a fort, because the *Santa Maria* was there wrecked, a catastrophe which he had described in his first official report with the words, "I left them also one caravel." In the large fleet that now departed with him, there were hundreds of stowaways. As for the legitimate crews and passengers, no care was taken to provide suitable persons to exploit and colonize the Indies, but the bad fellows whom nobody wanted were crowded into the ships for good riddance. In the war against the Moors (1482–1492) thirty thousand professional destroyers, called "taladores" or "gastadores," had been trained to cut down trees, corn, vines, and gardens and to demolish houses belonging to the infidels. Many of them were among the men who now sailed with Columbus, confidently expecting him to transport them speedily to India, where they could prey upon the fabulous wealth of the valley of the Ganges. A few weeks later, when they found themselves in the midst of a population of wretched Caribbean savages, their rage against him was extreme. They began to ask embarrassing questions. Where was India? Where were the gilded palaces and treasure houses of jewels? Where was Calicut? Where was the kingdom of the Great Khan? Having insisted upon his title, Admiral of the Indies, Columbus seemed partly an impostor and partly ridiculous, and he was in an unenviable position as a royal governor attempting to control the brutal and embittered white men under him, who were good for nothing but ruthlessness and treachery.

In desperation he identified the land he had named "Isabella" as the mainland of Asia, in order to silence critics and satisfy the disgruntled. Isabella was called by the natives "Cuba," which he interpreted as a form of "Kubla." He said it was the kingdom of Kubla Khan (China), and he required the notary Fernán Pérez de Luna to go to each caravel and compel all to sign that this was mainland.

> If they had any doubt or knowledge of it, that he besought them to declare it, in order that at once he might remove the doubt and make them see that this is certainly mainland. And if any should contradict him at any time, there should be imposed upon him in behalf of the Admiral a fine of one thousand maravedis for each occasion, and that his tongue should be slit; and if he were the ship's boy or a person of such degree, he should be prepared for this penalty by receiving a hundred lashes.

Columbus thus made his own geography. The natives, of course, of both Española and Isabella maintained that Isabella was an island. On June 12, 1494, Columbus signed a declaration "that he had never heard of or seen an island having an extent of three hundred and thirty-five leagues of coast from east to west, without having got yet to the end of it, and that he now perceived that the mainland turned toward the SW and SSW; that he had no doubts about its being a mainland, but, on the contrary, believed and would maintain that it was a mainland and not an island, and that before one had gone many leagues, sailing along the said coast he would find land inhabited by civilized people instructed, and with a knowledge of the ways of the world. . . ." He seems to have persuaded himself to the day of his death that Puerto Rico was Cipangu (Japan) and that Cuba was the mainland of Asia on the coast of China between Zaiton (Changchow in Fukien) and Quinsay (Nanking).

The Declaration of Columbus that he had identified the mainland of Asia came to Spain, but so also did persistent reports that no civilization even remotely resembling that of Cathay (China) or of India had yet been discovered. An Irish Friar, Bernardo Boyle, who had returned from the West, felt it his duty in the name of God's truth to expose the humbug. Boyle accused Columbus of having made a false claim of discovery at the outset, for he quoted the natives of Española as saying that Columbus and his crew in 1492 were not the first white and bearded men they had seen, but that others had arrived at their island a few years earlier.

When Columbus returned from his second voyage in 1496, there were no grand public receptions for him. His sincerity was called into question. He said he had found Asia, but nobody else could find it. It was undeniable that he had found new islands, but he could not escape responsibility for the collapse of great expectations, and the loss of money to those who had invested so enthusiastically in his second expedition.

His uncompromising demands contributed to the coolness with which he was received at court. He was a hard bargainer, a stickler for his shares and percentages of all the wealth obtained from all the islands and continental land (if any) across the western ocean—one-third of all gained by trade therewith, a tenth of all found therein, and an eighth part ownership of all lands and everything else, plus a salary befitting his rank as Admiral, Viceroy, and Governor. Such was the contract he had insisted upon early in 1492 before he would agree to sail on behalf of Spain on his voyage of discovery. But now King Ferdinand and Queen Isabella realized that if he were allowed to pocket his full legal share of the wealth of all newly discovered lands there would be scant pickings and insufficient incentive for others. Their Majesties had begun to repent of their bargain, which promised to make the Genoese adventurer a more powerful and richer potentate than themselves, and they were disposed to favor those whose terms were cheaper. Against the wishes of Columbus, navigation to the Indies was thrown open to all, while he himself had to wait two years for ships for a third voyage.

The letter written to Amerigo by Lorenzo di Pier Francesco in 1489 had expressed suspicion of the probity of the managers of Lorenzo's business in Spain, had requested Amerigo to investigate, and had suggested his transferring the business into the hands of Berardi. Amerigo found Berardi trustworthy, and in turn won Berardi's esteem. The two men became collaborators, if not actual partners.

Berardi was engaged by the Spanish government to furnish supplies for twelve ships being prepared for trade and further exploration in the West. Four of these were ready in August, 1495, and set forth under Juan Aguado, who was sent to investigate Friar Boyle's accusations against Columbus. Before the remaining eight were ready, Berardi lay dying, and shortly before his death, in December, he left this statement in his will:

> I declare and avow as God's truth and upon the salvation of my soul, that the Señor Admiral Don Cristóbal Colón owes me and is obligated to give and pay for his current bill one hundred and eighty thousand maravedis, a little more or less. . . . I declare in your presence that I request and ask as a favor of the said Señor Admiral that he please pay to Jeronimo Rufaldi and to Amerigo Vespucci, my executors, the said sum which he owes me.

Berardi called Amerigo his "agent and especial friend."

Amerigo was commissioned, January, 1496, to complete the financial part of the contract with the Crown left unfulfilled by the death of Berardi. On January 12 the royal treasurer, Pinelo, paid him ten million maravedis.[3] The maravedi was worth about as much as an English penny, so that this sum represented something in the order of several thousand dollars. Another four ships were very soon ready, and they set sail in January, but met with a tempest and returned for repairs. On June 17, three set sail under Peralonso Niño; they returned to Spain on October 29. By the next January, Amerigo had two of the eight ships ready for P. Fernández Coronel. Though we have no record of Amerigo's whereabouts, he was at this time probably in Andalusia, in Seville, or in San Lucar from mid-April, 1497, to the end of May, 1498, while the six ships were being prepared for Columbus.

If during this period Columbus and Amerigo engaged in conversation on problems of geography, the question which Amerigo most probably would have wanted to ask is whether on his third voyage Columbus expected to sail into the Great Sinus (Bay of Bengal) around the Cape of Catigara, which Ptolemy placed at eight and a half degrees south of the equator. If Columbus were thus called upon to answer this question, he must have told Amerigo what he told others, "that he intended this time to sail more to the southward, to find out whether King John of Portugal was mistaken, who affirmed that there was land to the south."

A few months later word came to Spain from Columbus in Española that after having dispatched the other ships to Española by the direct course, two from Spain and three from the Canaries, he had himself sailed to Cape Verde and thence somewhat south of west and had made a landfall at ten degrees north, and there had found an island which he named in honor of the Three Persons in the Godhead—Trinidad. Between Trinidad and what he called the

"Land of Parias," he had sailed with a current of fresh water into what he called the "Gulf of Parias." He had given the name "Coast of Pearls" to the land west of the north exit from the Gulf of Parias, and from the Coast of Pearls he had turned toward Española.

For one who believed, as Amerigo did, that the water route to India was south of the equator, it was exasperating to hear that Columbus had not turned south from the island of Trinidad to search for that route. What a pity, when he might have found the passage by which Marco Polo, homeward bound, had sailed from Cathay into the Indian Ocean on his way to Persia! How could he have been content to steer north and away from it? Did he love his Española so much? It was as though his heart were where his vested property interests lay. Like a householder choked with many possessions, he seemed chained to his islands, of which he was governor by virtue of discovery and by contract with the Crown. Had he deliberately dropped his ambition to visit the famous cities of India?

Indeed, for him to have turned south from Trinidad would have appeared like a confession that he had not found a route to India after all. There was also a very understandable motive for his being more interested in his island of Española than in India, for his contract with Their Hispanic Majesties made him a man of wealth and importance in newly-found lands like Española and Isabella, which were inhabited by primitive people, but he could not expect to rule over the civilized peoples of India and Cathay, who were the obedient subjects of great potentates. Furthermore, since other men were receiving commissions to explore beyond the western ocean in violation of his exclusive contract, he was on the defensive to hold what he had already discovered, and so he naturally preferred to make a sure thing of Española, lest by seeking to possess more he lose all. This, at any rate, is implicit in what he stated as his first reason for failing to explore the Land of Parias. His piling up of arguments to justify his decision to turn northward to Española makes it clear that he was conscious that this was the step in his career for which he might be held most subject to criticism.

Whatever his motives, and they were assuredly complex, he seemed incapable of perceiving with realistic mind the lands which he had sighted. He interpreted their appearance with a mirage of fables of literary origin: the place where "all women are communal," the island of women, the island of matriarchy, the land where the Amazons live, the Terrestrial Paradise at the antipodes from Jerusalem, and the kingdom of the imaginary Prester John. His passion for romance was uncurbed. Illusion was stronger than experience, for to him, discovery signified not only the finding of something new, but the recognition in reality of the creations of imagination and traditional faith.

Thus, the northwestward-flowing current of fresh water through the Gulf of Parias seemed to him too large to have come from a river, and he was unwilling to explain it in any other way than that it was of supernatural origin flowing directly from the Terrestrial Paradise, which was therefore somewhere southeast of the island of Trinidad. The Land of Parias he declared to be an eastward extension of Asia which led to the easternmost point of creation, which one could never reach, because in order to do so, one would have to sail uphill. In all seriousness he wrote:

I have seen so much irregularity in the elevation of the polar star in latitudes where it seems near the horizon, that I have come to a new conclusion respecting the earth; namely, that it is not round, as they describe, but of the form of a pear, which is very round except where the stalk grows, at which part it is most prominent; or like a round ball, upon one part of which is a prominence like a woman's nipple, this protrusion being the highest and nearest the sky, situated under the equinoctial line, and at the eastern extremity of this sea, where the land and islands end.

This bump on the earth, or protrusion, Columbus said was "the most elevated point of the globe." He wrote home to Spain:

I have never found any account by the Romans or Greeks which fixes in a positive manner the site of the Terrestrial Paradise, neither have I seen it given in any authentic map of the world. I have no doubt that if I could pass below the equator, after reaching the highest point of which I have spoken, I should find a variation in the stars and in the waters; not that I suppose that elevated point to be navigable, or even that there is water there; indeed I believe it is impossible to ascend thither, because I am convinced it is the spot of the Earthly Paradise, whither no one can go without God's permission.

All this was nonsense to a realistic student of cosmography like Amerigo. The third voyage of Columbus brought to Amerigo's mind the need for another type of explorer. His own ambition had been fired by what Columbus had attempted—and failed—to do; and he now decided to do some exploring himself.

Columbus had not found a passage to India, and there were already hundreds of witnesses to his failure. Every report from Española added to the certainty that he had not found the strait known to the mariners of Cathay, through which Marco Polo and other travelers had passed. Vasco da Gama, meanwhile, had sailed from Lisbon for India by a route definitely opened to the Portuguese by the work of Bartolomeu Dias in rounding the Cape of Good Hope. Da Gama had not yet been heard from, but it seemed very possible that he would be successful. Spain's only chance lay westward. Any man who could reach India by sailing in that direction would be both the Dias and the Da Gama for Spain. Amerigo determined to find the western sea route to India and, going through it, to be the first to reach India directly from Europe. What fame would be his after he had sailed past the Cape of Catigara into the Great Sinus and had shown the way from Spain to the cities of India and the rich market places, of which he had heard tales ever since he was a child!

It was quite in the Vespucci family tradition for him to take to the sea. When he was ten, had not his cousin Bernardo been captain of a Florentine galley and later Captain of Livorno? Had not a relative named Giuliano been an executive in charge of maritime affairs for Florence, as well as Commissioner of War, and had not another cousin, named Piero, commanded the Florentine fleet against the corsairs before he went as ambassador to the King of Naples? Furthermore, was it not in the tradition of the Vespucci to assume positions of leadership? Had not Piero Vespucci been chief magistrate of Milan, and had not Giuliano Vespucci, after having been ambassador to Genoa, become governor of Pistoia? Had not numerous members of his family been the chief administrators of law and justice in Florence? Had not his own brother Antonio already twice followed in the footsteps of his grandfather and of his father in being chancellor of the *signoria?*

Having made up his mind to become an explorer, it was a comparatively simple problem for him to shape circumstances to his will. In addition to his family connections and family tradition, he had all the qualifications for a ship's commanding officer: his age, forty-five, his robust constitution, his proved ability as an executive and manager in the complex business of equipping ships and engaging in international trade, his practical knowledge of the materials and supplies needed on a protracted sea voyage, his skill in cosmography, cartography, mathematics, and astronomy, his intelligent and inquiring mind, his acquaintance with all the aids to navigation at that time known, and his progressive ideas regarding the application of his knowledge of astronomy to the business of determining one's location on the surface of the earth.

He was acquainted with great merchants whose financial interests were potent in the policies of royal treasuries, trade commissions, and officials in control of commerce and maritime appointments. Among his compatriots, some of them his friends, in Spain were Del Nero, of Valladolid, Antonio del Giocondo, Fr. Corbinelli, and Clemente Sernigi, a very wealthy merchant; and among the Spaniards, Juan de Piero Sances and G. Rana, of Valencia, and Diego, of Salamanca. Agents of the Medici firm in Seville and Lisbon were Giovanni da Empoli, Piero Rondinelli, Simone dal Verde, and Andrea Corsali. He had only to let his friends and compatriots know his purpose in order to find men willing to aid him with their political influence and their resources. Through his business connections he obtained the permission which he sought.

When it was settled that he was to go exploring, the question may have arisen as to whether his nephew Giovanni should be taken on the voyage. Probably the answer was "No," since the boy was scarcely old enough to go to sea. Ferdinand Columbus was fifteen before he sailed with his father on a voyage. Whether or not the twelve-year-old Giovanni Vespucci accompanied his uncle and received instruction on board ship, he was later described by Peter Martyr as having learned from his uncle "the art of navigation, and skill in calculating degrees."

Part of what Amerigo explained now or later to Giovanni was that the ancient method of sailing in the Mediterranean according to compass directions would not do on the western ocean, where directions as well as distances were any man's guess. Latitude could be easily determined by observing with the astrolabe or quadrant the altitude of the pole star, but longitudinal distance was "a more difficult thing." For their longitude, up to that time, navigators had to rely on dead reckoning or their opinion as to the extent of each day's run.

They could not determine longitude definitely, because they had no means of knowing time with accuracy; that is, the time in the port whence they had sailed. On board ship no clock would work, since the rolling would upset the clock mechanisms which then existed. The hourglass was not accurate, for the extreme motion of a ship tended to delay the flow of the sand even to as much as four minutes an hour. Even when the hourglass was suspended to keep it nearly vertical, after days and weeks at sea it could not be relied upon to give the correct time of the port from which the ship had sailed; for there was always the inaccuracy of several seconds in turning the glass when all the sand had dropped, and there was danger of irretrievable loss of time through the inattention of a ship's boy assigned to watch and turn the glasses. Nevertheless, as Amerigo pondered the problem he began to think he saw a way of determining longitude with some approximation to accuracy, and to that end he provided himself with tables of the ephemerides of the moon and the planets.

It was arranged that he was to sail in an expedition under the nominal leadership of Alonso de Hojeda (or Ojeda). Hojeda was a young aristocrat who had amused Queen Isabella by dancing a jig on a plank extended from an upper window of the Alcázar in Seville, and he was a favorite of Bishop Rodrigo Fonseca, who was in active charge of affairs relating to the Indies. Hojeda was a man of proved courage and ambition, for he had served as lieutenant in the second expedition of Columbus. Juan de la Cosa, who had been owner and master of the shipwrecked *Santa Maria*, and captain of the *Niña* on the second voyage of Columbus, was to go as one of the pilots of the expedition.

Amerigo went in twofold capacity—as astronomer, or as "one who knew cosmography and matters pertaining to the sea," quoting the words of Herrera, an early sixteenth-century historian, and also, Herrera said, "as a merchant." "Por mercader" meant as representative of the moneyed interests and thus as director of the policy and the purpose of those ships which his merchant backers had supplied. It would be his duty afterward to inform his backers of the commercial opportunities uncovered by the voyage. The details of the voyage show that he was not compelled to take orders from Hojeda, but was in an independent position, having two ships and freedom to steer them where he wished, within the limits which their captains deemed safe. Indeed, since the expedition was a commercial venture and was expected to pay for itself (as we know from Amerigo's subsequent statement that the two ships he was with succeeded in making a slight profit "above the cost of the ships"), Amerigo's backers must have insisted that the route to be followed by the sailing masters conform to the promising plan expressed by Amerigo: "It was my intention to see whether I could turn a headland that Ptolemy calls the Cape of Catigara, which connects with the Sinus Magnus."

Chapter Four

THE VOYAGE FOR SPAIN

The expedition set sail from Cadiz on May 18, 1499. Practically speaking, it was under divided leadership, for Amerigo, as was proved in the event, was under no compulsion to keep his ships in consort with those of Hojeda. However, strength of numbers in a combined fleet gave them greater safety until they were out of reach of interference from the Portuguese. The logical procedure for the total of four, some say six, ships thus united for mutual protection was for them to continue in consort across the many leagues of ocean at least until near their landfall, but thereafter to separate and explore the new coast in opposite directions.

That this plan was followed, there is convincing evidence. Hojeda and La Cosa made their landfall at about five degrees south of the landfall of Columbus on his third voyage, or somewhere on the coast of French or Dutch Guiana. Fevered with the prospects of enriching himself on the "Coast of Pearls," so enticingly named by Columbus, Hojeda was eager to turn northward from his landfall, and did so, following the coast, as he later testified under oath: "I came upon the mainland in the south, and followed the coast thereof ("corrió par ella") about two hundred leagues until I reached Paria, going out by the 'Dragon's Mouth' [leaving the Gulf by the north exit]." The statement is made by Antonio Cánovas del Castillo that Hojeda and La Cosa, after twenty-seven days of ocean navigation sighted the Land of Parias, "where they did not disembark." Vespucci's letter to Lorenzo tells us that he crossed the ocean in twenty-four days and that his company, after more than a month of exploration along the coast, did disembark in the Land of Parias: "We put into a gulf which is called the Gulf of Parias. . . . We went ashore in the boats." Hojeda was on a pearl-hunting expedition. Amerigo's ships refused to tarry in the Gulf of Parias, even when the natives offered to procure many pearls for them. From Española, Columbus wrote: "Hojeda came in five days." Amerigo wrote that it took his ships seven days to sail from the continent to Española. From evidence that will later be submitted we know that Amerigo's two ships were more than two hundred leagues south of Trinidad on August 4. The thirty-two days from that date to September 5, when Hojeda and La Cosa arrived in Española, were not enough to have made possible Amerigo's arrival in Española with the others, what with his spending twenty days in one place, taking seven days to sail from the continent to Española, and exploring more than two thousand miles of coastline, to say nothing of the many hours he was ashore in at least four or five different places. He did not arrive in Española until after the 23d of September. Amerigo's experiences, so convincingly related in his letter from Seville to Lorenzo, were written without foreknowledge of the argument we now deduce from them and must be accepted as truthful unless disproved. All the facts we know show that Amerigo's two ships were not in consort with the two ships of Hojeda and La Cosa from their landfall in June to their arrival in Española. They were certainly not in consort on their return to Spain, where they arrived two months after Hojeda and La Cosa had arrived. The conclusion seems inescapable that Hojeda and La Cosa did not accompany Amerigo on the last leagues of his first ocean crossing to his landfall or at any time thereafter.[1]

On this first voyage of Amerigo's his ships were driven by a steady fair wind. They sailed about thirty-seven hundred miles in twenty-four days. On or about the twenty-seventh of June at a latitude a little south of four degrees north, the lookouts on the mastheads of Amerigo's ships sighted land ahead. This was the first view any Europeans had ever had of the coast of Brazil. It was south of Cape Cassipore, near the northern end of Brazil. Amerigo's landfall in Brazil preceded that of Vicente Yañez Pinzón by seven months, that of Diego de Lepe by eight months, and that of Pedro Alvares Cabral by ten months.[2]

When they came close upon the land, they saw a low line of green, a level stretch of forest rising in the sea with the freshness of creation. In the boats, half-a-dozen men in each, they rowed toward shore. How sweet the smell of verdure, of woodland! How powerfully the air was scented! A compounding of many odors—

of forest undergrowth, of flowers and gums and resins, of wet wood and rotting leaves, of redolent barks and luscious fruits, of stagnant pools and delicate perfumes! There was more to smell than to see.

Amerigo's men were so much impressed by the fragrance that the name they gave this country was a sort of pun, a play upon a word that meant a richly perfumed unguent, or fabled food of the gods, "ambrosia." They called Brazil the "Land of Saint Ambrose" (tierra de S. Anbrosio), without reference to the date of that saint's name in the Church calendar. This and other place names given by the Vespucci expedition of 1499 were recorded on Juan de la Cosa's map the following year.[3]

Mud flats and shallow reaches made it impossible in most places for the boats to get near the line of trees, but where it was possible, they found there was no shore. Trees grew out of the water, their interlaced branches, hung with moss and lianas, forming an impenetrable wall. This solid green barrier faced them everywhere. The edge of the forest was the edge of the sea.

The ocean here was fresh, not salt. Otherwise, there could not have been this touching of forest and sea. They found the water fresh and filled their casks and drank of it, so that they were not incommoded by their inability to land.

They applied various terms to this region: "flats," "mudbanks," "flatlands," "overflowed coast" (llanos, motes, las planosas, costa anegada). If, as seems possible, the Ptolemy map (Ruysch, 1508) has some place names based upon Amerigo's account of his voyage, the men on Amerigo's ships probably named a river here, the "River of Fragrance" (Rio de Flagrãza).

Amerigo either ordered or persuaded the captains to turn the ships southward, for at this point, certainly, his will dominated. "We pointed our prows to the southward, since it was my intention to see . . ." he says in his letter to Lorenzo. Following along the coast, they found that the forest wall continued for many leagues, and they were unable to discover any place where they could go ashore.

On the second of July they turned into a great gulf a hundred and fifty miles wide. They called this broad waterway the "Gulf of Santa Maria" (G. de St Ma—the Visitation of Our Lady, July 2), thus carrying out the custom of mariners of naming after the saint on whose calendar date they first saw it, a noteworthy feature of a coast, such as a cape, bay, river, harbor, high land, or island. In the Gulf of St. Mary, which was the estuary of the Amazon, they found flat land (tierralana) and "sea higher than the land" (mas alta lamar quela tierra), and many islands. In that humid wilderness they encountered thunderstorms that blackened the dark shadows in the forest wall. Lightning played about the ships, and blue flames appeared on the mastheads and yardarms. "St. Elmo's fire," sailors called it, and so they named the delta of the Amazon the "Islands of St. Elmo" (Yllas de St. Elmo).

The water was fresh and flowing out to sea, and so they knew that here was no passage into the Great Sinus, but the mouth of a river, of a size incredible. They now understood why they had found the ocean fresh along all that coast. They sailed through the estuary and into the broad delta, until they were at least one hundred miles from the ocean, and even there the river was astonishingly wide, mighty beyond any theretofore imagined. Where they could at one time see both sides of the river, they measured it, and judged its width to be four leagues, or sixteen miles. And Amerigo recorded that the flow was from west to east.

Because they had not yet found any place where they could go ashore, by reason of the tangle of forest rooted in the swamps, they determined to go even further up the river to see if there might be found a break in the wall of trees. They dropped anchor, and unshipped the boats, and put in them provisions for four days. Amerigo went with twenty men well armed, and they rowed by turns continuously for two days, having the light of a waning moon on the river for the latter half of each night. They ascended seventy-two miles further up-stream, looking for an opening in the forest, or some human habitation. Many times they attempted landings, but always they were prevented by the density of the stems and branches of the trees. They saw no dwelling or house of any kind, or any native of the region; but they "saw positive signs that the hinterland was inhabited," for here and there behind the impenetrable wall of green rose columns of smoke. And so they called the mightiest river of the world the "River of Concealed Fire" (Rio de Foco Cecho). This was at any rate the first name given to the Amazon (Ptolemy map—Ruysch, 1508).

The same map indicates that they gave it, or a branch of it in the delta, a second name—"River of Birds" (Rio des Aves), because of the multitude of waterfowl and the parrots of beautiful plumage and because of the entrancing melodies that poured from the throats of invisible songsters nesting in the thick foliage.

From the Amazon the ship sailed southward and entered another immense river estuary (the Pará), which they named the "Rio Grande." This they penetrated for nearly a hundred miles, until they measured a width of three leagues, or twelve miles. Amerigo recorded the fact that here the flow of the stream was from south to north.

In the delta of the Amazon Amerigo observed that the North Star had dropped to the horizon and that he was at the equator. At noon he drew the members of the crew to him and explained the significance of sunshine which throws a shadow to the south; but at night, when he studied the sky of the Southern Hemisphere, he had no companion. No one else was willing to stay awake to make drawings of the relative positions of the stars in order to identify the south celestial pole; no one else appreciated the importance of the task; no one else was willing to sacrifice comfort and sleep for the benefit of future navigators. Night after night he made an astronomical observatory of the deck of his tiny ship, and faced the discouragement of poor visibility in the tropic atmosphere, and struggled with inadequate instruments.

All this brought about a transformation in him. The pursuit of wealth, the dream of acquiring jewels and cargoes of spices, which he had shared with other men, was no longer his chief incentive. As a result of having thrown himself into this adventure, through an intensification of responses to fresh experience, he felt himself a new person—as though for the first time he was really beginning to live. His most compelling motive now was to add to man's understanding of the earth which he inhabited. He had an itch for learning, perhaps the more intense for his having been denied the university education which his brothers had received. He had been a business man with a scholar buried in him; now that he was free to follow his hobby, the scholar subordinated the man of business. Acquisitiveness surrendered to inquisitiveness, as he proceeded with his nightly study of the stars.

His lifelong interest in astronomy and geography became an all-absorbing passion. It was now his ambition to be the first to identify the polar star of the southern firmament. But being so near the equator, he could not determine which of the stars close to the horizon was nearest to the South Pole. Then, one night, he observed that there were four stars which must be near the pole, because they appeared to have very little motion in revolving about the pole. When he saw them, his heart was uplifted and he felt the thrill of a great revelation, and there came to his mind some lines of Dante pertaining to stars in the Southern Hemisphere.

After about twelve days of exploration in the Amazon and Pará, Amerigo sailed southeastward for seven hundred to eight hundred miles. He went as rapidly as possible for a good third of this distance, because the size of the two rivers indicated an immense land area in their vicinity; and it neither seemed reasonable to expect to find close to such rivers the sea passage which he sought, nor had he yet attained the southern latitude at which he believed that sea passage to be. From the fourteenth to the twenty-fourth of July he followed the shore, naming the first two hundred miles the "Quiet Coast" (Costa Plaida). The huge Bay de S. Marcos was named the "Beautiful Gulf" (Golfo Fremoso).

His pilots recorded the outstanding features of the coastline, such as "level" (plano), "sandy coast" (costa de arena), "River of Trees" (Rio de arboledos), "Point Beautiful" (P. fermoso), "similar coast" (costa pareja, meaning "more of the same"), "Black Mountain" and "Gloomy River" (M. Negro and Rio Negro), and "Gulf of Reefs" (G. de arecifes).

They had set up crosses here and there in the act of taking possession of the country, but now they were out of wood, because they had not been able to land to cut more wood since they had departed from Gomera in the Canaries. They expressed this deficiency in the naming of the "River of the Lack of a Cross" (Rio dele fallo una cruz).

Beyond a promontory which they called "Sandbank Point" (Punta del medano), they came to another point, which they named, "Cape Santa Maria" (St. Mary Magdalen, July 22). They then passed "sandbanks" (motas arenosas), and on the 22d or 23d, entered a "River of Empty Casks" ("Rio de bazia bariles") to take on water, because the sea off shore was not fresh, as had been the case at the equator and north of it.

On July 24 they continued along the coast past a "zone of sand" (plaia de arena) and a "Point Beautiful." Beyond each point which they rounded, their progress became increasingly difficult, because, as the line of the coast turned more sharply to the southeast, they were more and more exposed to the coastal current. This current was caused by the pressure of the equatorial current where the direction of the coast forced the equatorial current to veer sharply to the northwest. The rapid flow thus set up was adverse to their sailing.

While the south equatorial current moves across the ocean at a speed of only sixteen miles a day before it is divided by the Brazilian elbow, the current which it creates off the northeastern coast of Brazil advances to speeds of forty, sixty, and even eighty or more miles a day. Where Amerigo a few days later received maximum assistance from it, it sometimes runs with a speed of three and one-half knots. This current pours into the Caribbean and eventually helps to form the Gulf Stream.

Amerigo's ships attempted to evade the coastal flow by sailing directly out to sea. They sailed thus "on a leg of forty leagues," Amerigo's measure of the league on this voyage being four miles. Nevertheless, they did not escape the "ocean current which ran from southeast to northwest, and was so great and ran so furiously" that the ships could make no headway against it, even with a "brisk fair wind."

Very likely the "fair wind" was more abeam than astern, and they may have run into rough water from some previous stiff blow or into some between-current rip. In any case, the caravels of Spain did not steer well because they had no fin keels or anything in the construction of their hulls to prevent a sidewise motion. They had no jib or any effective rig to hold the head up into the wind. On that first day out they sailed only twenty leagues. The next day they did no better, and before the day was over the signal perforce was given to alter course and sail with the current to the northwest.

This defeat was a bitter disappointment to Amerigo. He thought he had been getting near the entrance to the Great Sinus, but now his hopes were shattered. As his ships swung around to their new course, he wondered how the ships of the Great Khan had ever succeeded in making the sea passage to India. Marco Polo had spent two years in sailing from Cathay to Persia, but had not reported any such difficulty as was presented by this current.

He believed that the Cape of Catigara lay at about eight and a half degrees south and was therefore only a short distance farther down the coast; for he reckoned his own latitude when he left that coast as somewhere between six and six and a half degrees south. Actually, he was at about three to four degrees south, between Punta de Jericoaquára and Punta de Mucuripe. So large an error was made possible by the fact that the North Pole was below the horizon, and he had not been able to determine definitely the true South Pole. Refraction made faulty the observation of the familiar stars near the horizon.[4]

The northwest course of the two ships was set to make a landfall at or near the point of their first landfall a month before, so that from that point they could explore the coast to the north. The total voyage from the beginning of the new course to their sighting of land at what they called "Cape Saint Dominic," at four degrees north, was between thirteen hundred and fourteen hundred miles. Amerigo estimated it very closely as three hundred and sixty-one leagues.

Each day's run of each ship was recorded in its proper place on the world chart which Juan de la Cosa made the following year, on which he showed all the Spanish and English discoveries beyond the Atlantic. The saints' names are evidence that the numbers denoting the track of two ships on this map are a record of navigation during July and August, corroborating Vespucci's narrative and precluding the possibility that the navigation was made by Pinzón or De Lepe, both of whom did their exploring in the following winter. To date no one has offered any explanation of these numbers or has even called questioning attention to them, and any explanation other than the one here given would be rendered untenable by the dates involved. Subsequent injury to La Cosa's map unfortunately destroyed the record of the first two or three days of sailing of one of the ships, which for clarity may be designated as A. The full record of ship B was preserved. According to Amerigo's account of the "floundering around," the ships were within signaling distance of each other at the end of "the leg of forty leagues"; and since ship B completed the forty leagues sometime during the second day, ship A did so also.[5]

A daily run was computed from midnight to midnight. Speed and distance could only roughly be estimated, though a captain who was familiar with his ship, after years of experience with her, could sometimes guess rather closely what she was doing under any particular spread of sail, with the assistance of a log line. When companion ships were no longer in sight of each other, they were not necessarily lost to each other if the captains of both knew which was in the lead. The one in the lead might take advantage of good winds and increase her lead, knowing that later she could shorten sail and let her consort catch up with her. Since ships could sight each other from their topmost rigging at a distance of between twenty and twenty-five miles, they could find each other as long as they kept within ten or twelve miles of the track they had mutually agreed upon.

In the case of Amerigo's navigation, ship B, which was apparently the faster of the two and was perhaps farther to the east when the decision was made to change course, took the lead on July 25, the second day, and held it until she was forereached by ship A on July 28. Ship A increased her lead of three leagues to twenty-two leagues on July 29, but on July 30 ship B gained nine leagues, sailing thirty leagues to the twenty-one sailed by A. On the last day of July ship B gained another eight leagues, sailing twenty-eight as against twenty, and on the first of August gained another five, sailing fifteen as against ten, and caught up with ship A. That night a strong wind rose, and the two ships thereafter kept close to each other. While the sailing capacities of two ships might vary considerably in normal or very light winds, they would drive before the wind at much the same speed. Thus on the second of August, with a strong following wind and the assistance of the current that rose in speed to three and one-half knots, both ships made a run of eighty-one leagues; they made sixty leagues the next day, with the wind abating.[6]

They now judged that they had proceeded far enough on the northwest course, and having begun to find the water of the ocean a trifle less salt, they knew they were approaching land, and made a right-angle turn to the southwest (marked on Juan de la Cosa's map

"8L," meaning eight points of the compass, right angle turn), and sailed thirty leagues to land. On this day they sighted a cape (Cape Orange) at a little above four degrees north, and named it "Cape Saint Dominic" (C. de S. Do), for Saint Dominic, August 4. This establishment of the date August 4 makes it manifestly impossible that Juan de la Cosa, who arrived with Hojeda in Española on September 5, could have been on either of the ships that ran the courses recorded on his map. On the portion of his map shown on the facing page the northern edge is the one with the large compass dial. The northwest direction line followed by Vespucci's ships is the one that passes through the island of Trinidad. The river nearest to Trinidad is the Orinoco. The broad line representing the equator is drawn through the estuary of the Amazon, to the south of which another estuary is identifiable beyond question as that of the Pará.

The Juan de la Cosa World Chart, 1500, is the first map, now known, made after 1492, which pictures discoveries on the western side of the Atlantic. It will be seen that place names are not indicated as far east as the Brazilian elbow, but only as far as Vespucci's two Spanish ships were able to sail in that direction. The map contains no place names contributed by Vicente Yañez Pinzón, who in January, 1500, explored the coast from ten degrees south, northward to the Brazilian elbow; but to the east of the Brazilian elbow there is an inscription attesting to the fact of Pinzón's exploration, erroneously dated as of the year in which Pinzón set sail from Spain: "This cape was discovered in the year 1499 for Castile, Vicente Yañez being the discoverer thereof."

Amerigo's landfall on August 4 was a little to the north of his landfall in June, and a little to the south of where Hojeda and La Cosa had made their landfall. Their landfall was probably at "Rio de holganca," the name signifying repose, tranquility of mind, or recreation, such as men would have welcomed after an ocean crossing. Hojeda and La Cosa gave the name "climate of nudity," or "country of nudity" (Plaia de cordoba) to the region where they first saw naked savages.

Now, one month later than Hojeda and La Cosa, Amerigo followed the coast northwestward, observing "overflowed land" (plaia

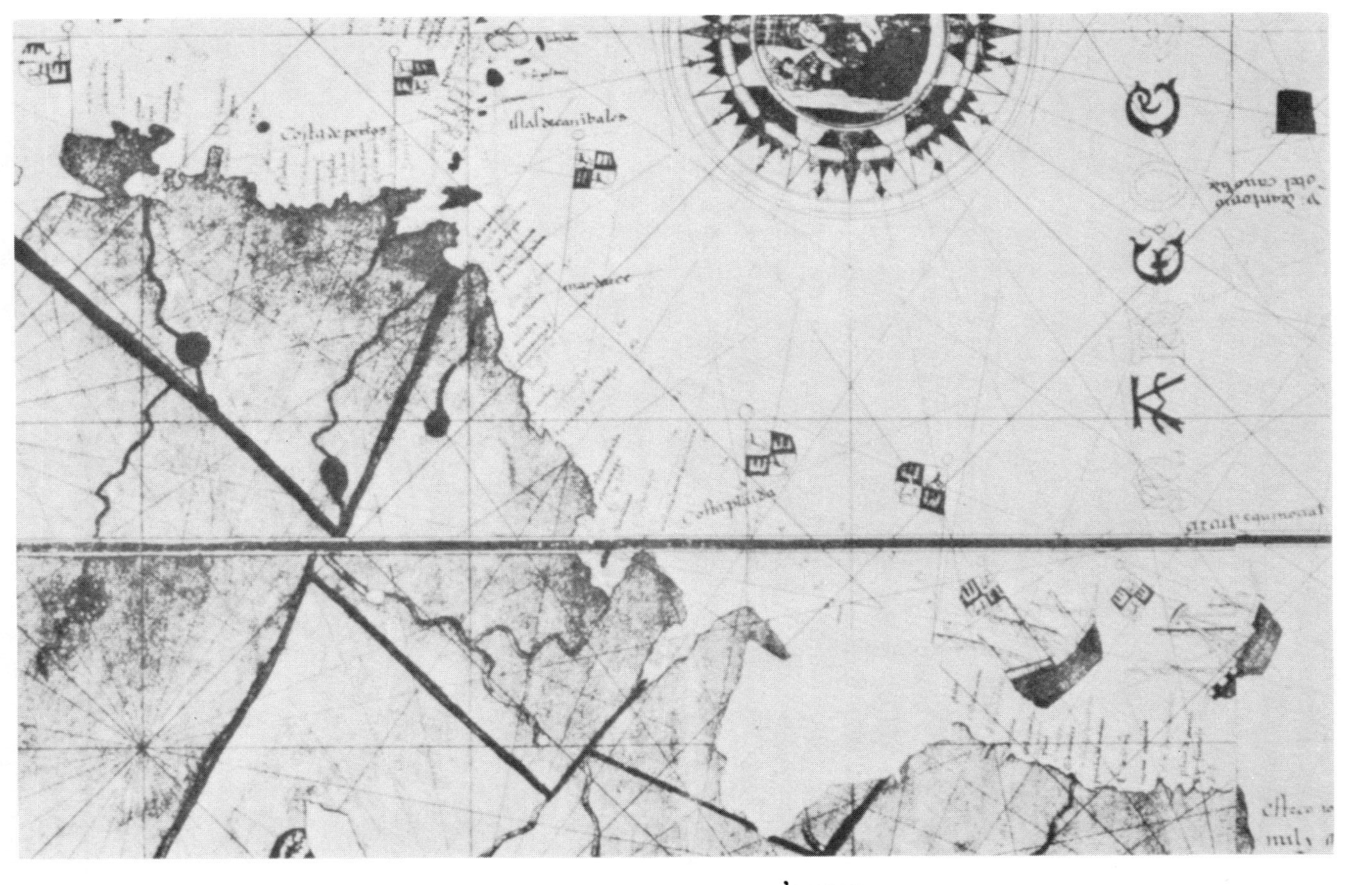

PORTION OF JUAN DE LA COSA'S MAP, 1500

anegada) and "flat land" (tierallana). With the aid of the coastal current he rapidly explored between six hundred and nine hundred miles of coast in about one week, not seeing any inhabitants until they reached the island of Trinidad. There his observation as to the color of the skin of the natives was keen: "grayish and brownish yellow." His reaction to the cannibals was likewise that of a realist, for he immediately began to investigate their dietary habits.

For a time his Spaniards behaved like gentlemen and did not rob the kind people ("Las Gaias"?) who gave them breakfast. They were treated to two breakfasts and one banquet, with wine, on Trinidad and in the Gulf of Paria, from about August 11 to 13. They were tempted with pearls to linger in the gulf, but they would not hold back. Amerigo had other purposes. M. F. de Navarrete, who disapproved of Vespucci, later wrote in intended condemnation what was really a high compliment: "Amerigo Vespucci did not bring home many pearls, for imitating badly the acts of the Admiral [Columbus], the desire to push on for discovery was greater than for the acquisition of riches." Though there were free breakfasts and pearls, there was no passage to India in the gulf that had been visited and named by Columbus.

Amerigo had begun to persuade himself that he might find the route from Cathay to Catigara farther to the west. But that hope soon died. As he expressed it: "After we had sailed about four hundred leagues continually along one coast, we concluded that this was mainland; that the said mainland is at the extreme limits of Asia to the eastward, and at its beginning to the westward."

Some three hundred miles west of the Gulf of Paria, beyond the Coast of Pearls, there was a change in the character of the natives. The Indians along the "Coast of Brave People" (Costa de Gente Brava) resisted the landing of the Spaniards. A severe fight occurred on or about the sixteenth of August, in which many of Amerigo's men were wounded with arrows. The site of the battle was later called "Port of Arrows" (Porto Flechado) and "Burned Village" (Aldea Quemada), because after the victory over the natives the Spaniards "massacred one hundred and fifty of them and burned one hundred and eighty of their houses." This was probably in the region of La Guaira. Immediately afterward, "since we were grievously wounded and weary, we returned to the ships and went into a harbor to recover, where we stayed twenty days, solely that the physician might take care of us."

During these twenty days, from about the seventeenth of August to the fifth of September, Amerigo evolved a valid astronomical method of determining longitude.

Previous to this voyage of his, mariners had only the most inaccurate method of knowing their longitude, for they had guessed at their east-west distances by dead reckoning. They guessed at the speed of their ships by throwing a chip of wood overboard from the bow and estimating the time it took for the stern of the ship to come abreast of the floating chip or by counting the number of knots in a log line that ran out while the sand was falling in a small, one-minute glass. Columbus acquired superior skill as a dead reckoner when he discovered that by counting his heartbeats he could measure more accurately than other dead reckoners the time his ship took to sail its own length.

Amerigo Vespucci brought a fresh mind to the problem of the determination of longitude, and was the first man to place it upon a scientific basis. Of course no means of determining longitude that could be used on board ship while at sea as a continuous guide in navigation was possible until a great deal of spade work had been done in preparing really accurate tables of the positions and motions of celestial bodies and until precise measuring instruments could be produced, especially one that could keep accurate time on a moving ship. The more immediate necessity was to put into practical execution the project outlined by Ptolemy:

> The correct course would be for any person attempting to draw a map of the world, to lay down as the basis of it those points that were determined by the most correct observations, and to fit into it those derived from other sources, so that their positions may suit as well as possible with the principal points thus laid down in the first instance.

The task was to be accomplished from various stations on land and was to fix the meridians of the principal capes, ports, islands, and so forth throughout the world and thus lay the foundation for accurate geographical knowledge. This work Amerigo commenced on the night of the twenty-third of August, 1499.

He hit upon the method of measuring lunar distance in relation to the time of a conjunction, a conjunction being the passing of a planet by the more swiftly-moving moon. What commended his method to his own mind was the relatively great speed of the moon through the zodiac. That speed is thirty-three minutes of arc per hour. The motions of the other planets were too slight to furnish satisfactory data for a computation of longitude, given the limitations of astrolabe,[7] quadrant, and hourglass as measuring instruments. The possibilities of the method he devised were vastly superior to those of the method Ptolemy mentioned and the Arabs had occasionally used, that of timing eclipses, or noting the time of an eclipse in relation to noon, in two different places.[8] The frequency of the moon's conjunctions with major planets, several each month, offered many more opportunities for making observations than did eclipses. Furthermore, one could make an observation for lunar distance from a planet at any time within eight or ten hours of a conjunction, either before or after it; and the chances were easily twenty-one out of twenty-four that the moon (together with the planet near it) would within eight or ten hours of the conjunction occupy a position in the night sky. Except when moonrise occurred during the three hours between 5 A.M. and 8 A.M., the moon and the planet would be in the night sky either during the night previous to a conjunction or on the night following or on both nights.

Amerigo had expended much thought on this problem and had made various attempts to solve it.[9] All met with failure until those twenty days of enforced leisure gave him an opportunity to observe from the land a conjunction of the moon with Mars. Now, while wounds were healing, he had six days and nights in which to establish his local midnight, in anticipation of the conjunction.[10]

It was impossible to catch the moment of noon by measuring the shadow of the sun; for he was only a little more than ten degrees from the equator, and at that latitude at that time of the year, the sun being almost exactly overhead on the sixteenth and seventeenth of August, there was a very short shadow cast within an hour of noon. During the first few days of enforced leisure he observed that the sun cast shadows in each of the four principal directions of the compass in the course of a day, and at noon, no shadow at all.

Now that the shadows of the sun were of no use to him, since they were too small for his measuring, he had to have recourse to something else to find the moment of noon or of midnight. Obviously, if he ascertained either one, noon or midnight, he could get the other by measuring with hourglasses the twelve hours from one to the other. The best he could do was to observe the sunset and the sunrise and halve the time between them by careful check with his hour glasses and minute glasses. To catch the moment of sunset and the moment of sunrise, he had to find a place on a neck of land extending northward from the coast, from which he could see the sun at a water horizon both evening and morning. After two or three consecutive nights of measuring the length of time between sunset and sunrise, he could ascertain the progressive increase or decrease in that length of time and thus compute its length for the night following, on which night he could the more accurately halve the time and establish the apparent solar midnight within something like five minutes. For this purpose he stayed up night after night, studying the heavens, while his men slumbered. The illustration of the scene pictures, an armillary sphere in one hand and a pair of dividers in the other, a somewhat stocky figure, with aquiline features in profile, eyes searching the stars, a mouth firm and refined, a face of rapt intelligence.

Of the night, the twenty-third of August, he wrote:

> There was a conjunction of the moon with Mars, which according to the almanac was to occur at midnight or a half hour before. I found that when the moon rose an hour and a half after sunset, the planet had passed that position in the east. That is to say that the moon was about one degree and some minutes farther east than Mars, and at midnight her position was five and a half [copyist's error for "three and a half"] degrees to the east, a little more or less.

The statement that at midnight the moon was "five and a half degrees to the east" must be a copyist's error for three and a half degrees, for nothing else will fit with his observation of lunar distance when the moon rose. At the time of moonrise (about 7:40 P.M.) he correctly observed a lunar distance of "one degree and some minutes" of arc, for at that time the lunar distance was actually one degree and about seventeen minutes of arc. By midnight two degrees and twenty-three minutes were added to this. Whatever errors were made on that night of August 23, he could not

VESPUCCI STUDYING THE STARS, BY STRADANUS

have made the mistake of measuring three degrees and forty minutes of arc as five and a half degrees. At his local midnight the moon and Mars were high in the heavens, within twenty-five degrees of zenith, and an error of two degrees in observation was impossible. The lunar distance at midnight could not have been five and a half degrees, for that would have represented ten hours in longitudinal time and would have been possible only from some meridian west of the Isthmus of Panama, in the Pacific Ocean. The observation of lunar distance at the time of moonrise was not essential to Amerigo's computation, but it served as a check against his observation at his local midnight. It is fortunate that he included it, for it confirms the evidence which shows that the lunar distance could not have been at midnight "five and a half degrees," and that the "five and a half" must be a textual error for "three and a half." The copyist was probably confused by the "five and a half hours" mentioned in the next sentence of his letter, which might have led an unthinking scribe to write the same number of degrees as hours.

On the night of August 23, Amerigo was at about 10° 35′ N. and probably at about seventy-nine degrees west of Ferrara, or at about sixty-one degrees west of Cadiz, as is deduced from a study of his voyage. Ferrara is at 44° 51′ N. and 11° 38′ E. Cadiz is at 36° 32′ N. and 6° 16′ W. The longitudinal distance between the two cities is seventeen degrees and fifty-four minutes, or approximately eighteen degrees. While Regiomontano's almanac omitted Cadiz, it gave the longitudinal distance from Ferrara to Toledo as one hour and twenty-four minutes; to Cordoba as one hour and twenty-seven minutes; and to Lisbon as one hour and forty minutes. Thus it practically compelled the deduction that the longitudinal distance from Ferrara to Cadiz was about one hour and thirty minutes, or twenty-two and a half degrees. Regiomontano was much nearer to the correct eighteen degrees than Ptolemy's *Geography*, which gave the distance as twenty-nine degrees.

If we believe that Amerigo observed three and a half degrees of arc of lunar distance at midnight, we find that he erred by ten minutes of arc. Ten minutes of arc of lunar distance represented a little more than eighteen minutes of time, and a little more than four and a half degrees of longitude.

The following data are the results of a modern computation [11] for

August 23, 1499, Old Style, and are introduced for comparison with Amerigo's observations.

Sunset at Amerigo's position	6:10 P.M. (approximately)
Moonrise at Amerigo's position	7:40 P.M. (approximately)
Time of conjunction at Ferrara	10:59 P.M.
Time of conjunction at Amerigo's position	5:20 P.M.
Time elapsed since conjunction at Amerigo's local midnight	6 hours 40 minutes
Lunar distance at Amerigo's local midnight (6 hours 40 minutes at 33 minutes of arc per hour)	3 degrees 40 minutes of arc.

Amerigo's letter continued:

> By such means was made the proportion: if twenty-four hours equal three hundred and sixty degrees, what do five and a half hours equal? I found that I had come eighty-two and a half degrees. So much I computed to be the longitude from the meridian of the city of Cadiz. . . . Up to this point I have told how far I sailed toward . . . the west.

Clearly the "eighty-two and a half degrees" was his computation of his farthest west longitude on the shore of the great land he explored and did not refer to his longitude on the night of August 23. The words, "Up to this point I have told how far I sailed toward . . . the west," take on rational meaning only when they are interpreted as referring to the "eighty-two and a half degrees." But a study of his voyage shows that he was nowhere near his farthest west on the shore of the land on August 23. He was at his farthest west about the middle of September. The passage beginning "By such means was made the proportion" thus is to be dissociated from what precedes it, since it refers, not to the observations of August 23, but to unstated observations on a night in September. The fact that the text of the original Italian is infrequently divided into sentences helps support this interpretation. To make the point clear, one should begin a new paragraph with the words "By such means." Amerigo gave the observed data of August 23 in his letter to his patron, because that was the first time he used the method of lunar distance, and those details were memorable. But his longitude on that night would be of no direct interest to his patron, while his longitude at his farthest west on the shore of the newly-explored land was a geographical fact of interest and importance to all merchants and future explorers and cartographers.

Let us examine Amerigo's conclusion as to his longitudinal distance from Cadiz at his farthest west, on or about September 15, when he was about sixty-six and a half degrees west of Cadiz (seventy-two and a half degrees west of Greenwich, eighty-four and a half degrees west of Ferrara). In giving it as "five and a half hours" or "eighty-two and a half degrees" he was making an error of sixteen degrees, or one hour and four minutes of time. This error could have been caused by Regiomontano's *Ephemerides astronomicae;* for Regiomontano, whose sidereal day began with noon and who gave "Hour 1" as the time at Ferrara of the conjunction with Jupiter on September 15, made Amerigo think the conjunction would occur at Ferrara soon after midday, whereas the actual time of its occurrence at Ferrara was nearer to 11 A.M.

Even if Amerigo made observations for his farthest west at Cape de la Vela as late as September 19, when there was a conjunction of the moon with Mars, the cause of his error was the same, for Regiomontano's almanac seems to have been consistently at fault in timing the moon late by an hour or so, in 1499.

With the aid of preparations which were well within the capacity of the scientists of the day, Amerigo's method of determining longitude could have yielded very satisfactory results. Efficient use of it required the careful timing of conjunctions at a port from which ships sailed into distant regions, so as to correct any error in the almanac, and also the provision of navigators with tables giving the hour and minute of sunset for each day of the year at various latitudes.

It should be understood, of course, that reliable observations could be made only from land or from the deck of a ship in still waters. Knowing the date and the latitude, one need have a clear sunset, at which minute he would start his hourglasses—the same procedure being carried out at the home port for later comparison of records. With quarter-hour and minute glasses one could determine his local midnight very closely, within the limits of an error of perhaps five minutes; and with the astrolabe or quadrant one could observe the lunar distance to within perhaps a tenth of a degree of arc, equivalent to twelve minutes of time, or three degrees of longitude. The amount of time to be allowed for parallax could be estimated to within a minute or two.[12] If an average of repeated observations were taken, the errors would tend to cancel out. Thus, by Amerigo's method, with means no better than were available at the end of the fifteenth century, it is reasonable to say that the distances in longitude between a given port in Europe and various stations in the lands to the west of the Atlantic could be determined reliably within approximately two degrees.

After the development of precise measuring instruments and subsequent careful charting of the heavens and more exact computations of the motions of the moon, the use of lunar distances from the sun and fixed stars became more and more practicable. This extension of Amerigo's method then became the accepted one and continued so for more than three hundred years. The possibility of determining longitude at sea by the use of a portable timekeeper of great accuracy was first mentioned in a publication by the Flemish astronomer Gemma Frisius, in 1530. Vain attempts to construct a successful chronometer were made by a Dutchman in the seventeenth century, and it was not until 1765 that John Harrison won a prize for inventing and constructing a chronometer "good enough to determine longitude within thirty miles after six weeks at sea." This means that it was within three seconds a day of correct, which was better than clocks ashore at that date. Chronometers were made available to seamen and were used extensively after 1775.

For many years after the chronometer came into general use the fundamental principle of Amerigo's method continued to be employed. In the account of the voyages in the eighteenth century of Captain James Cook we read: [13] "Lunar observations, in their turn, are absolutely necessary, in order to reap the greatest possible advantage from the timekeeper; since, by ascertaining the true longitude of places, they discover the error of its rate." Captain Cook is quoted by Von Zach as follows: "The method of lunar distance from the sun or stars is the most priceless discovery which the navigator ever could have made, and must render the memory of the first discoverer of this method immortal." [14] Amerigo, therefore, took an immense step forward in 1499 in attacking the problem of longitude, and his initial achievement must be ranked as one of the great accomplishments of human genius. The very simplicity of the expedient to which he resorted emphasizes the credit which belongs to him for doing what no one before him had ever done.[15]

After the men who had been wounded by Indian arrows were healed of their hurts—save one, who died—the ships resumed their navigation westward. They named the gulf where the coast turned northward the "Gulf of Torment" (Golfo Delinferno), which men later called the Gulf of Triste. The heat and hardships of the voyage were making their impression. After the ships came out of that gulf and were sailing well off shore, they saw an island to the north, and sailed to it. Amerigo said it was "fifteen leagues distance from the mainland." This island might have been Bonaire, more than fifty miles off the coast, but it was more probably Curaçao, forty-six miles from the mainland. Hills on the latter island are several hundred feet higher than those on Bonaire, so that Curaçao was more likely the one sighted while the ships were still within sight of the mainland. More than half the trees of the island were of dyewood, for which reason Amerigo called it "Brazilwood Island" (Y. de brasil). "Brasilia" had for centuries been the name of an imaginary island in the Atlantic, and was also the name for the red dyewoods used in the Middle Ages.

He also called it "Island of Giants" (gigan.), in memory of his ludicrous adventure there in the house with the seven giantesses and the timely entrance of the thirty-six giants with paddles. He was a good humorist, capable of laughter at his own expense.

From the Island of Giants he went to another island (Aruba) ten leagues distant, where he discovered a population "which dwelt in houses whose foundations had been built in the water like Venice." He named Venezuela (Veneçuela—Little Venice) on or about the ninth of September.

It is the present writer's opinion, if "Vericida" (from the Ruysch map, 1508) was named by Amerigo's expedition, that as he turned south from Aruba into the Gulf of Maracaibo, his preconceived certainty that the passage into the Great Sinus could be found only in a southern latitude, must have been in question for the moment. It seems probable that he thought this gulf would lead to a passage into the Great Sinus, since at the southwestern corner of the gulf he saw a break in the shore line, and with expectation temporarily renewed and growing excitement as he came nearer, he found islands that flanked the entrance to a passage toward the south. He would have jubilantly recalled that Marco Polo had said that the fleet of the Mangi had sailed between two islands when it entered the strait that led from the Sea of Cathay to the region of India! With elation based upon the momentary conviction that he had at last found the way to the goal of his voyaging, he would have eagerly sailed into Maracaibo Strait. His enthusiasm would have mounted as he noted that this passage was five to nine miles wide and the water of it salt. His theory as to the western route to India was to be gloriously substantiated! Here, indeed, was the promise of a great triumph in discovery!

If this was his assumption, it proved ill-founded. Enthusiasm was crushed when he found the strait only ten leagues in length, and south of it only a great lake. Disappointment was commingled with disgust. He felt he had been cheated by appearances. He had aroused the expectations of the crew, and now he was deeply mortified. And so he expressed his chagrin by naming the gulf which had humiliated him "Golfo de Vericida" (Deceitful Gulf, the Slayer of Truth). The Italian word "vericida" was the equivalent of "menzognero," which meant "lying." The above interpretation is tenable unless "Vericida" was a copyist's error for "Veneçuela."

He sailed northward out of the Deceitful Gulf, rounded the Cape of Expectation (C. de Espera), and followed the coast to the north and west. With scholarly interest he noted the many different languages among the natives. The people of the newly discovered regions interested Europeans as much as did the lands themselves, for natives transported to Europe were visible evidences of what had been found, and through ignorance concerning the appearance of the inhabitants of India, they were considered proof that Columbus had reached India, as he believed. The reasonable expectation had been entertained that the people found in the West would be those mentioned in the traditional geographies as living in the East. By hasty assumption as to their country of origin, the Caribbean islanders brought home by Columbus were called "Indians." Columbus described these naked savages as poor fishermen on outlying islands and along the shores of Asia. He believed that the races named by early travelers to the East would be found dwelling inland. Ethnological error was piled on geographical error to make the world seem smaller and the East and the West closer together than had been imagined. Amerigo, however, observing the natives, began to refute this shrinkage. He took issue with the accepted view of all the scholars, who said that the total number of languages on earth was seventy-seven. He made the challenging statement that there were more than a thousand. The existence of so many separate language groups made him suspect that the earth, instead of being smaller, as Columbus said, was somewhat larger and more populous than had been supposed.

But now his studies were for a time curtailed, for of necessity his voyage had soon to be concluded, since the ships were becoming unseaworthy. They "leaked endlessly." Teredo worms were eating the hulls, and Amerigo recorded the fact with the Italian word "bacoia," which meant "maggots." He also gave to the locality the Spanish word "aguada," which meant "water on board." The ships had been continuously at sea for nearly four months, and even with "two pumps going constantly" the crew could not reduce the water in the hold. "The men were worn down with fatigue and hardship, and the provisions were growing short." The men began to curse so loudly that Amerigo named the region "Sato de Verbos" (Field of Cursing).

In spite of the condition of the ships and the temper of the men, he was loath to discontinue the exploration. He rounded the northern end of the Goajira Peninsula and followed the line of the coast beyond it, which he found dropping away to the south and southwest. But it had become imperative to repair and reprovision the ships and to rest the men. And so, upon the advice of the pilots it was decided that the ships should turn back and sail away to the island of Española, which was now "inhabited by Christians" and, the pilots declared, lay due north from their position.

They remained, however, on the shore of the mainland during the night of September 15, Amerigo's insistence upon delay being a further cause for curses. On the night of the fifteenth, at the "Cape de la Vela" (Cape of the Vigil or Attendance without Sleep—"vela" meaning time devoted at night to work of any kind), he made observations concerning the conjunction of the moon with Jupiter and computed his farthest west longitude. The cape was properly named "Attendence without Sleep," for he had to be up all night, since moonrise occurred after 3 A.M. at his position and his observations had to be made between then and dawn, previous to the approaching conjunction.

The theory that at his farthest west he observed the conjunction of the moon with Jupiter on September 15 is supported by the proximity of Cape de la Vela to "M. de S. Eufemia" on Juan de la Cosa's map, the calendar date for Saint Eufemia being September 16. Hojeda and La Cosa had arrived on the island of Española on September 5, and so could not have named "M. de S. Eufemia." I do not follow the suggestion of Alberto Magnaghi that Amerigo waited at Cape de la Vela, after having named the Sea of Saint Eufemia, until the nineteenth of September to observe the conjunction of the moon with Mars. He was too desperately in a hurry because of the condition of his ships. In his letter he says that he observed conjunctions with the "other planets," not exclusively with Mars.

The whole voyage along the coast from his farthest south to his farthest west he estimated as "seven hundred leagues or more." He had in fact seen about three thousand miles of shoreline. But now, on the sixteenth of September, the pilots took charge and steered the ships out into the "Sea of Saint Eufemia," sailing by the wind in seven days a distance of four hundred miles north to Española.

Whether Amerigo's two ships temporarily joined those of Hojeda at Yaquimo or put into some other port on Española, we do not know. We do know that he had to get his ships repaired during a time of bloody squabbling between Hojeda and a man named Roldán who was nominally serving Columbus. It is unlikely that Amerigo or the men with him had any part in the dispute. Whereas several men of Hojeda's crew were killed in the fighting on Española, not one among the men of Amerigo's ships was thus slain. Not that his fighting with natives on "the Coast of Brave People" had been any more virtuous than Hojeda's fighting with his fellow Christians, but it appears that Amerigo either did not participate in the quarrel or was fortuitously in another part of the island. The murder and treachery in the hearts of some of the Spanish adventurers were foreign to his temperament. His way was to do everything through co-operation and in conference with others—a lesson he had learned in business. "We agreed" was his frequent phrase.

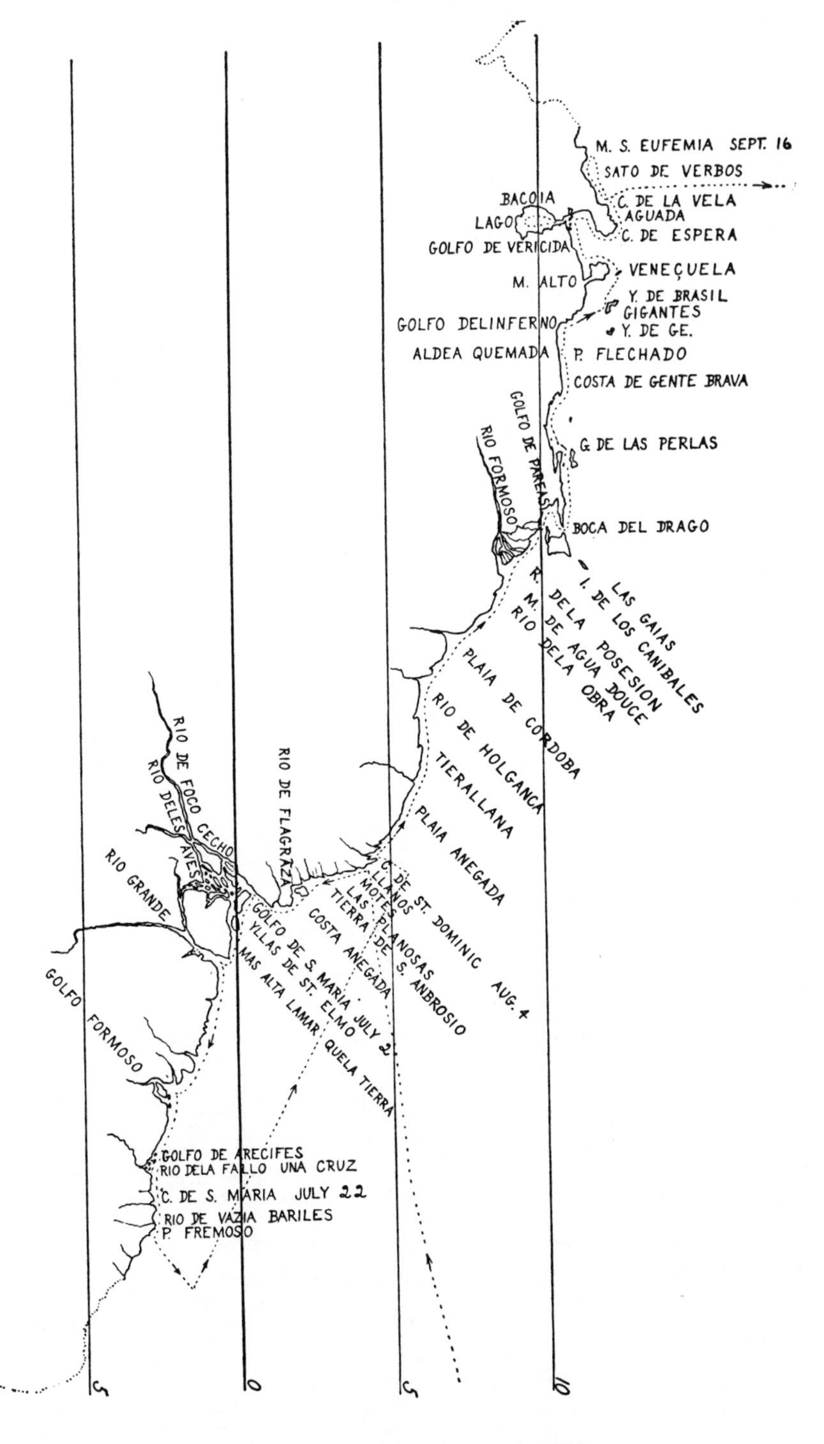

SPANISH VOYAGE OF VESPUCCI

Furthermore, his credit through his connections with the Medici and other Florentine bankers and merchants, must have helped make acceptable in Española his promises to pay for the materials with which he repaired his ships.

He sailed from Española about the end of November, while Hojeda and La Cosa, it seems, remained there until spring. Amerigo spent the winter months battling storms among the Bahama Islands, in constant peril of reefs and shoals. Once before, he had pursued his explorations to the limit of the crew's endurance; and now again he courted danger with terrible hardships, until after four months, because of sheer weariness and shortage of food and water, the crew began loudly to complain.

There had been no opportunity for his men to acquire riches. Now, "after nearly a year at sea," the ships' company pressed for an end to the voyage. A conference was held and an agreement was reached to adopt the only means at their disposal by which they could clear the costs of the voyage with a profit to themselves—to take home slaves. And so they went to certain islands and seized over two hundred natives.[16]

Amerigo's attitude toward slavery was like that of other white men, and indeed it could not openly have been any different in a day when it was possible for a man who had been moved to tears by the plight of slaves in a market to pray to God to be forgiven for his heretical emotion. It was widely argued that the fear of slavery kept believers from heresy.

Those Indians who were carried off as slaves to Spain were fortunate compared with their fellows who were left in the West Indies. Under the cruel hands of fiendish and bloody-minded Spaniards, thousands of Indians among the islands had already suffered extermination, by direct slaughter and by the conditions of living forced upon them. The native population of San Juan Bautista (Puerto Rico) was on its way to practically total extermination. Nine-tenths of the natives in Española perished within ten years. Even Queen Isabella, who heartily approved of the horrors of the Inquisition in Spain, was becoming convinced that the Indians "should be converted with more gentleness."

In Española, Amerigo had seen the beginnings of the brutal regime of the Conquistadores, against which Las Casas, "the Apostle to the

Indians," and a few of the friars later raised voices in vain protest. In succeeding years, from Spanish Puerto Rico to Spanish California, even many of the Indian missions were slave-owning plantations, built by forced labor, against which the Indians recurrently revolted. Columbus himself had founded the West Indian slave trade when he sent five shiploads of natives to Spain in June, 1495.[17]

The islands from which Amerigo took the slaves may have included some of those off the southern tip of Florida, though this is unlikely. By his own reckoning he went further west by a degree and a half among the islands north of Española than he did along the coast of the great land to the south of it.

His voyage home with the slaves was at first more to the north than to the east, to take advantage of the winds and currents, until he caught the prevailing winds from the west for the crossing to the Azores. This navigation in March, April, and May took sixty-seven days. He arrived at one of the southernmost and easternmost of the Azores and spent several days there laying in water and provisions. This the Portuguese allowed, whereas they had attempted to imprison Columbus seven years before; for now they recognized the rights of Spain beyond their own claims to the West. From the island of the Azores, because the wind was contrary and the ships could not make headway by beating to windward, Amerigo went roundabout by way of the Canaries and the island of Madeira. This additional navigation took close to another month, so that it was about the middle of June when he arrived in Cadiz.

~~

Chapter Five

VESPUCCI'S LETTER FROM SEVILLE, 1500

[To Lorenzo di Pier Francesco de' Medici]

Most Excellent and Dear Lord:

It is a long time since I wrote to your Excellency, solely for the reason that nothing had occurred worth remembering. My present writing will give you the news of my return from the Indies a month ago by way of the ocean. ["Indies" meant the islands off the coast of Asia, even though Ptolemy's geography taught that they were many degrees distant from India.] By the grace of God I was brought safely to this city of Seville. I believe your Excellency will be pleased to hear of the success of the voyage and of the most wonderful things which it was my lot to observe. If I am somewhat long-winded, let my letter take the place of fruit as a last course at table when you are in a mood for belching.

Your Excellency will please to note how with the permission of his Highness the King of Spain, I set out with two caravels, on the eighteenth of May, 1499, on a voyage of discovery across the western ocean, and followed down the coast of Africa until I reached the Fortunate Isles, which are now called the Canaries.[1] After I had laid in all necessary provisions, having made our orisons and supplications, we raised sail at an island called Gomera, and pointed our prows to the southwest and sailed twenty-four days with a stout breeze, without sighting land. At the end of twenty-four days we raised land [at about four degrees north, on the coast of Brazil] and found that we had sailed for about thirteen hundred leagues to that land from the city of Cadiz, by means of a southwest wind. [This meant distance sailed over the course he had covered, via the Canary Islands, not distance in a straight southwest direction.] Seeing the land, we gave thanks to God, and put out our boats with about six men each, and pulled toward the shore. We found the land heavily covered with trees which were most amazing not only in height but in their greenness, since they are never denuded of all their leaves. They had a fragrant smell, being all aromatic, and gave forth such tonic odors that we were greatly invigorated.

We followed the edge of the land in the small boats to see whether we could discover a place to jump ashore. What a world of shallows it was! We rowed hard all day until nightfall, but were prevented from penetrating inland not only by the shallowness but by the density of the forest through which we could never find so much as a chimney opening. We decided, therefore, to return to the ships, and attempt a landing in some other region. We observed one remarkable fact in this part of the ocean. Always when we approached within twenty-five leagues of the coast [Magnaghi suggests that "25" may be a copyist's error, and thinks Amerigo may have more accurately written "15"], we found the water fresh like that of a river and drank of it and filled all our empty casks. Having rejoined the ships, we raised anchor and set sail. We pointed our prows southward, since it was my intention to see whether I could turn a headland that Ptolemy calls the Cape of Catigara, which connects with the Sinus Magnus. In my opinion we were not a great distance from it, according to computed longitude and latitude, as hereinafter stated.[2]

Sailing southward, we saw two most tremendous rivers [the Amazon and the Pará] issuing from the land, one coming from the west and flowing to the east, and having a width of four leagues, which is sixteen miles. The other flowed from south to north, and was three leagues, or twelve miles, wide.[3]

I believe these two rivers, by reason of their enormous size, create the fresh-water area in the ocean. Having observed shallows all the way down the coast, we decided to enter one of these rivers with the boats and to work along close to the bank to find either a place to jump ashore or an inhabited region. We put the boats into commission, and placed in them provisions for four days, and with twenty men well armed started upstream, and with two days of rowing worked in eighteen leagues. We attempted landing in many places, but found a thick swamp everywhere and the branches of the trees so thickly interlaced that a bird could scarcely fly through them. Thus following up the river, we saw positive signs that the hinterland was inhabited, but since the ships were in a dangerous position in case a storm had sprung up, we decided at the end of two days to return to the ships and take the will for the deed.[4]

What we saw that was indeed a sight was an endless number of birds of ungainly shapes. [The word is *bruttissima*—"ugly," "grotesque." Vespucci thus gave us the first European reaction to the appearance of toucans.[5]] Some were a brilliant scarlet; others green spotted with lemon; others all green; still others black and flesh-colored. And the singing of other birds lodged among the trees was so soft and melodious that we often paused, wonderstruck at its sweetness. The trees were so beautiful and so fragrant that we thought we were in a terrestrial paradise.[6] Not one of those trees or its fruit was like those in our part of the globe. In the river we saw a great profusion of fish of many species.

When we had regained the ships, we weighed anchor and set sail and continued to sail southward. In following this course, we stood out to sea on a leg of forty leagues. We encountered an ocean current which ran from southeast to northwest, and was so great and ran so furiously that we were terribly frightened and hastened away out of this great danger. The current was such that the waters of the Strait of Gibraltar and around the lighthouse of Messina were those of a pool by comparison. It was such that when it struck our bows we could not make any headway, even though we had a brisk fair wind. Perceiving the hazards in this floundering around, we decided to point our prows to the northwest and sail to northern parts.

As I know, if I remember correctly, that your Excellency understands something of cosmography, I have in mind to note how much we had to learn in order to navigate by means of longitude and latitude.

I certify that we sailed so far south that we entered the Torrid Zone and passed the Tropic of Cancer. You may have it as a positive fact that for several days while sailing in the Torrid Zone we saw four shadows of the sun, as the sun stood at zenith at midday. [These were the days when he was west of the Gulf of Paria, after mid-August, for then only during the whole voyage and at that latitude was the sun directly overhead at noon.] I explain it that the sun, being in our meridian, did not have any shadow, all of which I had occasion many times to demonstrate to the rest of the company, and I took as witness each one of the burly boys who do not know how the solar sphere moves through the circle of the zodiac. One time I saw the shadow to the south; at another time to the north; at another to the west; and at another to the east; and sometimes for one or two hours of the day we had no shadow at all. We sailed so far south in the Torrid Zone that we found ourselves standing under the equinoctial line [at the equator] and had both poles at the edge of our horizon. Having gone six degrees beyond the equator, we lost the north star altogether. The stars of Ursa Minor, or better to say, the Guards, which revolve about the pole were scarcely visible.[7]

Very desirous of being the author who should identify the polar star of the other hemisphere, I lost many a night's sleep in contemplation of the motion of the stars around the South Pole, in order to record which of them had the least motion and which was nearest to the pole. I was unable to succeed because of the many bad nights I had and with such instruments as I used, namely, the quadrant and the astrolabe, and other means of measuring the swing of the stars. I did not observe any star which had less than ten degrees of motion around the pole. While I was at this work, I recalled a passage of the poet Dante which occurs in the first chapter of the "Purgatorio," in which he invents a fiction of a flight into the heavens in our celestial hemisphere and his finding himself in the other hemisphere. Endeavoring to describe the Antarctic Pole, he says:

> "I turned to the right hand, and gave heed
> To the other pole, and saw four stars
> Never seen save by our first parents.
> The heavens appeared to rejoice in their rays.
> O widowed northern region,
> Since thou art deprived of beholding these!"

It seems to me that the poet in these verses wishes to describe by the "four stars" the pole of the other firmament, and I have no reason to doubt that what he says may be true; because I observed four stars in the figure of a cithern, which had little motion. If God grants me life and health, I hope to return at once to that hemisphere and not come back without identifying the pole. In conclusion I state that our voyage extended so far south that our distance in latitude from the city of Cadiz was sixty and one-half degrees [obviously a copyist's error], because at the city of Cadiz the pole is elevated thirty-five and one-half degrees, and we found ourselves six degrees beyond the equator. [Actually less than three degrees. The error was caused by refraction, which affects the apparent altitude of stars seen near the horizon, and by Amerigo's inability to determine the true South Polé from a position so near the equator.]

This will suffice as to latitude. You will observe that this navigation was during the months of July and August and September, when the sun is more continuously above the horizon in our hemisphere, and describes the greater arc by day and the lesser by night. While we were at the equator or within four or six degrees of it, in July and August, the difference in length between day and night was not perceptible. Day and night were about equal, or differed very slightly, if at all.

As to longitude, I declare that I found so much difficulty in determining it that I was put to great pains to ascertain the east-west distance I had covered. The final result of my labors was that I found nothing better to do than to watch for and take observations at night of the conjunction of one planet with another, and especially of the conjunction of the moon with the other planets, because the moon is swifter in her course than any other planet. I compared my observations with the almanac of Giovanni da Montereggio, which was composed for the meridian of the city of Ferrara, correcting with calculations from the tables of King Alfonso.[8]

After I had made experiments many nights, one night, the twenty-third of August, 1499, there was a conjunction of the moon with Mars, which according to the almanac was to occur at midnight or a half hour before. I found that when the moon rose an hour and a half after sunset, the planet had passed that position in the east. That is to say that the moon was about one degree and some minutes farther east than Mars, and at midnight her position was five and a half degrees [copyist's error for three and a half, as explained in Chapter Four] to the east, a little more or less.

By such means was made the proportion: if twenty-four hours

equal three hundred and sixty degrees, what do five and a half hours equal? I found that I had come eighty-two and a half degrees. So much I computed to be the longitude from the meridian of the city of Cadiz. Giving to each degree sixteen and two-thirds leagues, I found my longitudinal distance from the city of Cadiz to be thirteen hundred and sixty-six and two-thirds leagues, which are fifty-four hundred and sixty-six and two-thirds miles. [He should have said thirteen hundred and seventy-five leagues; he omitted the half degree.] The reason why I give sixteen and two-thirds leagues to each degree is that according to Ptolemy and Alfragano the circumference of the earth is twenty-four thousand miles, or six thousand leagues, which being divided by three hundred and sixty comes to sixteen and two-thirds leagues for each degree. This reasoning I confirmed many times by checking with pilots their locations on charts, and I found it true and valid.[9]

It appears to me, most excellent Lorenzo, that by this voyage of mine the opinion of the majority of the philosophers is confuted, who assert that no one can live in the Torrid Zone because of the great heat, for in this voyage I found it to be the contrary.[10] The air is fresher and more temperate in this region, and so many people are living in it that their numbers are greater than those who live outside of it. Rationally, let it be said in a whisper, experience is certainly worth more than theory.[11]

Up to this point I have told how far I sailed toward the south and toward the west. Now it remains for me to inform you of the character of the land and the nature of the inhabitants, of their customs, of the animals we saw, and of many other things most worthy of remembrance which fell under my observation. Let me say that after we turned our course toward the north, the first land that we found to be inhabited was an island [Trinidad] ten degrees from the equator. When we came up with it we saw a great multitude along the shore who stood staring at the wonderful sight. We rode at anchor about a mile from the land and manned the boats and went ashore with twenty-two men well armed. When the people saw us leaping ashore and discerned that we were of a different nature—because they have no beard or clothing, the men, like the women, appearing just as they issued from the wombs of their mothers, without covering any shame, and because of the difference of color, they being grayish and brownish yellow and we white—they had fear of us and betook themselves to the woods. With great difficulty, by means of signs, we reassured them and negotiated with them. We discovered that they were of the breed called cannibals and that the majority of them lived on human flesh. Your Excellency may hold this for certain, that they do not eat one another among themselves, but they sail in certain vessels which they call "canoes," and with these canoes they drag their prey from the islands or mainland, from tribes which are their enemies or are not allied with them. They do not eat any women, except those they possess as slaves. And these things we verified in many places where we found such people, because we often saw the bones and skulls of some that they had devoured, and they did not deny it; the more they boasted of it, the more their enemies stood in fear of them. They are people of affable comprehension and of beautiful physique. They go entirely naked. The weapons they carry are bows and arrows and small shields. They are religious people of great courage, and very excellent bowmen. In conclusion, we had dealings with them, and they conducted us to one of their villages that lay two leagues inland. They gave us breakfast and everything we asked of them, but they gave more through fear than affection. And after we had stopped with them all one day, we returned to the ships, remaining friendly with them.

We sailed along the coast of this island and saw the inhabitants of other large villages along the seashore. We landed in a skiff and found them waiting for us, all loaded with provisions, and they gave us the wherewithal for a very good breakfast of their native dishes. Seeing they were such kind people, who treated us so well, we did not resort to seizure of anything of theirs.

We made sail and put into a gulf which is called the Gulf of Parias. [The Gulf of Paria was first entered and named in 1498, by Columbus. This is worth noting in view of the many assertions later made by others, never by Vespucci, that he had preceded or that he said he had preceded Columbus by a year in reaching the shore of South America.[12]] We rode at anchor at the mouth of a very large river, which causes the water of this gulf to be fresh. We saw a large village close to the sea, where there were so many people that we were astonished. All were unarmed. In token of peace, we went ashore in the boats, and they received us with great display of affection. They conducted us to their houses, where they had very good preparations for a collation. There they gave us three rations of wine to drink, made not of grapes but of fruit, like old-fashioned beer, and it was extremely good. There we ate many fresh prunelike fruits, a very peculiar sort of fruit. They gave us many other fruits all different from ours and very good to taste, and all having aromatic flavor and odor. They gave us some small pearls and eleven large ones, and they told us by signs that if we would wait several days they would go fishing and bring us many of them. Not caring to delay, we departed with many parrots of various colors and with good friendly feeling. From these people we understood that those of the island above-mentioned were cannibals and ate human flesh.

We emerged from this gulf and followed along the coast. We saw continually great numbers of people, and when they were so inclined we bargained with them, and they gave us what they had and everything we demanded of them. They all go naked as they were born, without having any shame. If all were to be related of how little modesty they have, it would be entering upon obscenity. It is better to keep silence.

After we had sailed about four hundred leagues continually along one coast, we concluded that this was mainland; that the said mainland is at the extreme limits of Asia to the eastward and at its beginning to the westward. For it often happened that we saw various animals, such as lions, red deer, wild boars, rabbits, and other land animals which are not found in islands, but only on the mainland. Going inland one day with twenty men, we saw a serpent [an anaconda]. In truth, that serpent's length was eight extended arm lengths, and its thickness as large as I am in the waist. We were very much frightened by it, and the sight of it caused us to return to the sea. Many times we happened to see most ferocious animals and huge serpents. Sailing along the coast, we discovered each day an endless number of people with various languages.

When we had sailed four hundred leagues along the coast, we commenced to find people who did not desire our friendship, but stood waiting for us with their weapons, which they held in readiness, and when we approached the shore in the boats, they resisted our landing, so that we were forced to combat with them. ["Costa de Gente Brava."] At the end of the fight they broke from us with loss. Since they were naked, we made a great slaughter of them. It often happened that sixteen of us fought with two thousand of them, and at the end we routed them and massacred many of them and pillaged their houses.

One day we saw a great number of men standing in battle array to prohibit our landing. We put armor on twenty-six men carrying sharpened weapons and covered the boats because of the arrows which they shot at us and which always wounded some of us before we jumped ashore. [At "Puerto Flechado," Port of Arrows. Navarrete thought Puerto Flechado was Chichirivichi, which is near Punta Tucacas; but it seems more likely that it was not so far west.] After they had defended the land as far as they could, we finally leaped ashore and fought against them with extreme hardship. The reason they held out against us with more courage and greater force was that they did not know what a weapon the sword is or how it cuts. Thus we battled with them, but so great was the multitude of men who charged upon us and so many were their arrows that we could not remedy it. As if we had abandoned hope of conquering, we turned our backs in order to jump into the boats, and while thus retreating and being put to flight, one of our sailors, a man of fifty-five years of age who had remained as boatguard, seeing the danger we were in, leaped from boat to shore, and with a loud voice called out: "My lads! Face your enemies! God will give you the victory!" Throwing himself upon his knees, he prayed aloud, and then making a great resistance, struck at the Indians, and all of us jointly with him, wounded as we were, so that they turned their backs and began to flee. Finally we routed them and massacred one hundred and fifty of them and burned one hundred and eighty of their houses. ["Aldea quemada."]

Since we were grievously wounded and weary, we returned to the ships and went into a harbor to recover, where we stayed twenty days, solely that the physician might take care of us. All were saved except one who was wounded in the left breast.

Thereafter we resumed our navigation. On this same coast it happened that we often fought with an endless number of men and always defeated them. Thus sailing along, we came upon an island which was situated fifteen leagues from the mainland. ["Gigan—Y. de brasil," which is Curaçao, forty-six miles from the mainland. "Y. de ge," which is Bonaire, fifty miles from the mainland, is not referred to in the text of the letter, nor is any hint given as to the meaning of the name. The island with the double name is the one on which Vespucci had the comical experience with giants, and also saw much dyewood (Brazilwood). On the mainland between "gigan—Y. de Brasil" and "Veneçuela," the La Cosa map gives "M. Alto," which was undoubtedly the Paraguana Peninsula.] At our arrival, since we saw no people and the island looked favorable to us, we decided to explore it, and eleven of us landed. We discovered a trail and set ourselves to walk on it two leagues and a half inland; we met with a village of twelve houses in which we did not find anyone except seven women. They were of such great stature that there was not one of them who was not taller than every one of us by a span and a half. When they saw us they were very much afraid of us. The chief one of them, who was certainly a discreet woman, by signs hauled us up to a house and made them give us refreshments. When we saw such noble women, we determined to carry off two of them, who were young women fifteen years of age, and make a present of them to the king. They were creatures whose stature was certainly above that of average men. While we were thus plotting, thirty-six men arrived, who entered the house where we were drinking, and they were of such lofty stature that each of them was taller when upon his knees than I was when standing erect. In fine, they were of the stature of giants in their great size and in the proportion of their bodies, which corresponded with their height. Each of the women appeared a Penthesilea, and each man an Antaeus. When the men entered, some of our fellows were so frightened that at the moment they thought they were done for. The warriors had bows and arrows and tremendous oar blades, finished off like swords. When they saw our small stature, they began to converse with us to learn who we were and whence we came. We gave them soft words for the sake of amity and replied to them in sign language that we were men of peace and that we were out to see the world. In fact, we judged it wise to part from them without controversy, and so we went by the same trail by which we had come. They stuck with us all the way to the sea and until we embarked.

More than half the trees of this island are of dyewood as good as that of the East.

From this island we went to another ten leagues distant, and we discovered a very large population, who dwelt in houses having foundations that had been built in the water, like Venice, with much ingenuity. ["Veneçuela," or "Little Venice"—the resemblance was apparent at once to an Italian. The island was Aruba, fifteen miles from the mainland and forty-five miles from Curaçao.] Marveling at them, we approved of the idea of going and looking into them. Since the inhabitants were in their houses and determined to prevent our entering any of them, they were given proof that the sword cuts; they then found it advantageous to let us in. We discovered that they kept their houses full of the finest cotton, and all the beams of their habitations were of dyewood. We took away a great deal of cotton and dyewood and returned to the ships. You must know that wherever we landed we found much cotton, and the plains were filled with cotton trees, so that all the ships throughout the world could be loaded in those regions with cotton and dyewood.

Finally we sailed another three hundred leagues [counting from the neighborhood of "Puerto Flechado"] along the coast, continuously finding valiant people and very often battling with them. We seized twenty of them, who were using among them seven languages, not one of which was understood by those who used the others. It is said that in the whole world there are not more than seventy-seven languages, but I declare that there are more than a thousand. I alone have heard more than forty.

After having sailed along this coast seven hundred leagues or more, without counting the great number of islands we had explored, we judged the ships to be unseaworthy, because they leaked endlessly and we could hardly reduce the water with two pumps going constantly. The men were worn down with fatigue and hardship, and the provisions were growing short. Since we found ourselves, according to the reckoning of the pilots, opposite and within one hundred and twenty leagues of an island which they call Española, discovered by the Admiral Columbus six years before, we determined to proceed to it; and, since it is inhabited by Christians, to repair our ships there and to rest the men and refit the stays; because from this island to Castile are thirteen hundred leagues of open water without any land. In seven days we reached this island.

We remained there about two months. We trained the ships and procured provisions. We agreed together to go in a northern direction, where we discovered more than a thousand islands [Bahamas] and found many naked inhabitants. They were all timid people of small intellect; we did what we liked with them. This last region that we discovered was very perilous to our navigation because of the reefs and shoals which we found in it. We often ran the risk of being lost. We sailed in this sea for two hundred leagues towards the northward. [It is possible that he may have touched the coast of the mainland west or northwest of the Bahamas. "In this sea" implies the contrary. The "two hundred leagues" was during, not before, the return to Castile. Writing in retrospect, Vespucci interrupts chronological order to mention the total distance he sailed toward the north.]

Since the men were worn out from having been nearly a year at sea and were rationed down to six ounces of bread a day to eat and three small measures of water to drink, and the ships were becoming dangerously unseaworthy, the crew cried out that they wished to return to Castile to their homes and that they no longer desired to tempt fortune. Therefore we agreed to seize shiploads of the inhabitants as slaves and to load the ships with them and turn toward Spain. We went to certain islands and took by force two hundred and thirty-two persons,[13] and then set our course for Castile.

In sixty-seven days we crossed the ocean and arrived at the islands of the Azores, which belong to the king of Portugal and are three hundred leagues from Cadiz. Here, having provided ourselves with refreshments for the passage to Castile, we encountered contrary winds and were compelled to go to the Canary Islands, and from the Canaries to the island of Madeira, and from Madeira to Cadiz. [Spanish ships could not sail close to the wind, but only before the wind or on the wind when it was nearly abeam.]

We had been thirteen months on this voyage, having run into most awful dangers and discovered a very large country of Asia, and of islands a great plenty and for the most part inhabited. I have many times made calculations with the compass, which show that we sailed about five thousand leagues; that is, twenty thousand miles. In conclusion, we crossed the equator and went six and a half degrees to the south of it, and later returned by way of the north, going so far that the north star was at an elevation of thirty-five and a half degrees above our horizon; we sailed eighty-four degrees [on the return voyage] in meridian distance from the city and harbor of Cadiz. We discovered a vast country and beheld an immense number of people, all naked and speaking various languages. Inland we saw many wild animals and various species of birds and an unlimited wealth of trees, all aromatic. We brought away pearls and virgin gold; we brought two stones—one the color of emerald, the other of amethyst, very hard, half a span in length, and three fingers thick. Their Majesties esteem them highly; the sovereigns have set them among their jewels. We brought a large piece of crystal which some jewelers say is beryl, and according to what the Indians told us they had a great abundance of it. We brought fourteen flesh-colored pearls that greatly pleased the queen; and for ourselves many other stones that seemed beautiful to us. We did not bring all these things in quantity, because we did not stay long in any one place, but were sailing continuously. When we arrived at Cadiz, we shared our slaves. We found that we had two hundred of them alive, the others that made up the total of two hundred and thirty-two having died at sea. Having sold them all, the profit that we had above the cost of the ships was five hundred ducats, which had to be divided into fifty-five shares, so that each of us received little. However, we contented ourselves with having arrived in safety with our lives, and we rendered thanks to God that on the whole voyage, of the fifty-seven Christian men whom we had, none died save two, whom the Indians killed.

Since my arrival I have had two quartan agues. With confidence in God I expect a speedy recovery, for they do not continue long and are without chills.[14]

I underwent many experiences worthy of note, but in order not to be prolix, all of them are reserved for the pen and are stored up in memory. The king is fitting out for me three ships to the end that I may go again to discover. I believe they will be ready by the middle of September. May it please our Lord to give me health and a safe journey! In due course I hope to bring back very great news and discover the island of Taprobana, which is between the Indian Ocean and the Gulf or Sea of the Ganges. And thereafter I intend to return to my own country and look forward to the days of my old age.

Most excellent Lorenzo, as I have given you an account by letter of what has happened to me, I have determined to send the picture of the world in two forms composed and arranged by my own hand and knowledge. There will be a map on a plane surface and a map of the world in spherical form, which I expect to send you by ship by means of one Francesco Lotti, a Florentine met here. I believe they will meet with your approval, especially the globe, since I made one not long since for the king, and Their Majesties esteem it highly.[15]

My resolution was to come with them, but the new decision to take another turn at discovery gives me no opportunity or time. Men are not lacking in your city who understand the map of the world, who may perhaps correct something in it; nevertheless, whatever is to be corrected, let them await my coming, since it may be that I shall successfully defend my map. I believe Your Excellency will have heard of the many countries visited by the fleet which was sent two years ago by the king of Portugal to discover the country of Guinea. [The expedition of Vasco da Gama.[16]] Such a voyage as that I do not call a discovery, but a going to discovered regions, because, as you will see by the map, their navigation was continuously in sight of land, and they sailed around the whole southern part of the continent of Africa, which is by a route spoken of by all the cosmographical authors. It is true that the navigation has been very profitable, which is what is nowadays judged great, especially in that kingdom where enjoyment of possessions reigns inordinately. I understand that they passed beyond the Red Sea and over the Persian Gulf and arrived at a city which is called Calicut, which is situated between the Persian Gulf and the Indus River. And now the king of Portugal is again arming twelve ships, returned from sea very richly laden, and is sending them to those countries, and I believe they will do a big business if they arrive safely. [Expedition of Pedro Alvares Cabral.]

This is the eighteenth of July, and there is no other news. May our Lord give Your Excellency length of days and continued health! This is the prayer of

Amerigo Vespucci in Seville.

Chapter Six

CHANGING FLAGS

During the thirteen months of Amerigo's absence from Europe, Portugal had triumphed over Spain in the race to India. Vasco da Gama had sailed around Africa, to the famous ports of the East. He had been to Calicut, Pandarane, Mangalor, and Goa and had returned to Lisbon in safety with shiploads of spices, well repaying the Portuguese for what the opening of their route had cost.

Amerigo's reaction to the Portuguese triumph echoed his disappointment in the results of his own voyage and showed that he had been swept with more than a twinge of jealousy. At the same time, his reaction was characteristic of the new man he had become, for he not only decried the world's standard of judging success by the financial profit of an undertaking, but he upheld the banner of the explorer by denying that there was any feat of exploration in a coastal voyage around Africa, since that was only a repetition of what had been done in ancient times.

There was maritime news, less important than the voyage of Da Gama. Peralonso Niño and Cristóbal Guerra, who had sailed a month after Amerigo did, had returned to Spain on April 6, having accomplished nothing new, but having merely duplicated part of the third voyage of Columbus. Within a few days of April 6, Hojeda and La Cosa had also arrived in Castile, two months before Amerigo. Vicente Yañez Pinzón, who had sailed in November, had not yet returned. But Diego de Lepe, who had sailed from Spain in December, had just returned that very month of June, and had reported having made a landfall at four degrees south and having thence sailed north.

When Amerigo had finished his business in Cadiz, he set out for Granada to report to Their Majesties, arrangements having been made for a royal interview. Ferdinand and Isabella no doubt asked him questions, hoping that he would resolve the doubts raised by the many conflicting reports from across the western ocean. In all probability he used this opportunity to explain something of his work in attempting to determine longitude and talked of the stars and of the motions of the moon and the planets. He not only told the King and the Queen about the immense coastline he had explored, which appeared to be an eastward and southward extension of Asia, but he also told them of the latitudinal and longitudinal positions of the farthest points on it which he had reached. When he descended from his exposition to description and presented Their Majesties with stones the color of emerald and of amethyst and with fourteen flesh-colored pearls, they were like children, frankly delighted. He told them that he had not brought home more of such precious objects, because, as he said, a land that could produce such things would be the source of great riches, and rather than pause to accumulate, he had chosen to continue sailing in order to explore.

Their Majesties did not fail to appreciate the fact that he had discovered for them more leagues of territory than all that had been discovered hitherto, although Alonzo Hojeda and Juan de la Cosa had preceded him in exploring the middle portion of the long coastline. "Señor Vespucio" had seen it all as one, however, and had learned the position as well as the great length thereof. Here was a man who more than justified his having been appointed one of the pilots a year ago and now must be recognized as a successful explorer. The king therefore declared that he would immediately provide Amerigo with three ships with which to undertake further discovery. Soon after this, Amerigo wrote a letter (July 18, 1500) to his former patron, Lorenzo di Pier Francesco de' Medici, in which he gave an account of his voyage and mentioned the king's offer of ships and the rush of preparations already begun for another voyage.

Three ships provided by royal order! How the courtiers must have flocked around him to congratulate him! Everyone assumed, of course, that he would jump at the chance of sailing in command of three ships to be fitted out by the royal treasury. Why should he not? The offer was indeed flattering, and he must have felt pleased that he had grown into a position of leadership in navigation. It was a cause for pride and satisfaction that he would be able to start out again that very year to continue exploration beyond his farthest south, beyond that point where he had been compelled to turn back by the force of the ocean current.

But for the moment there was the joy of being at home again in Seville; there was the pleasure of recounting his adventures to his former business associates; there was also the hope, whose futility he did not know, of complete recovery from the attacks of malaria which had commenced soon after his return to Cadiz.

Now he had leisure to correspond with his friends and to make a globe and a plane map. Because he was eager to defend his new map of the world against the scholars in his native city who might attack it, and because he loved a good argument, he wrote to his patron Lorenzo that he had planned to come to Florence with the maps he was sending, but as "the new decision to take another turn at discovery" gave him no opportunity or time, he asked that those who disagreed with his maps should await his coming, since it might be that he could prove his maps to be essentially right. He was concerned with the larger implications of his discoveries, by which he would dare to uphold against all the famous cosmographers certain notable innovations in world geography.

For one thing, the direction and extent of the coastline he had explored upset the preconceptions of the scholars. All the old maps of Asia were inaccurate, since none of those maps placed correctly any of the islands or gave any such extension of Asia eastward as Amerigo now believed he had found. The puzzle was intensified by the report of Vicente Yañez Pinzón, who returned to Spain in July and declared that he had made a landfall in January at ten degrees south and thence followed the coast to the north, but without discovering any strait. What, then, was the latitude of the strait into the Great Sinus? Could it be farther south than the eight and a half degrees south that Ptolemy led one to expect?

Amerigo wrote also to Lorenzo: "If God grants me life and health, I hope to return at once to that hemisphere, and not come back without identifying the pole." He meant, identifying the celestial south pole in relation to the stars near it, for the benefit of all future navigators. So intense was this ambition that he wanted to devote his life to it, and was willing to lose his life if need be.

Both his ambition and the king's proposal constrained him to postpone his contemplated trip to Florence. So after he had sent off his letter to Lorenzo he began preparations for another voyage and with renewed fervor pursued his astronomical studies for the more accurate determination of longitude. During the succeeding months he observed conjunctions of the moon and the planets every night that weather permitted, in order to increase his knowledge and improve his technique. He mentioned this labor in a letter written in June of the following year at the outset of a new voyage: "In the endeavor to ascertain longitude I have lost much sleep, and have shortened my life ten years, but I hold it well worth the cost, because if I return in safety from this voyage, I have hopes of winning fame throughout the ages." Well he knew the value of his contribution to mankind in devising a practicable method of determining longitude, as surely as he knew that it was the basis of his own work as an explorer. He was meeting the Ptolemaic challenge, something which no other man of his time was doing, and he believed his work in determining longitude would immortalize his name.

While continuing his observations he no doubt inquired of astrologers, for they placed great significance upon conjunctions, to learn from them the actual time as observed at Cadiz, and perhaps in Italy, of the conjunction which had occurred on September 15, 1499, when he had been at his farthest west. This inquiry, if he made it, revealed the extent of error in Regiomontano's almanac, upon which he had relied while on his first voyage. Or it may have been from his own observations at this time that he discovered the inaccuracy in Regiomontano. In any case, we have reason to believe that he became aware of an exaggeration in his estimate of his farthest west longitude. We know that the conjunction of the moon with Jupiter on September 15 occurred in Italy, not after high noon, or in "Hour 1," as Regiomontano had foretold, but during the hour before noon, and that here was an error of an hour which should be subtracted from his estimate of his farthest west. Whether he became directly aware of this error or deduced its equivalent from various observations and computations, it appears that he must have made a substantial subtraction from his estimate of his farthest west longitude, for this is the only conclusion compatible with a statement made by him in June, 1501, that a league was "four and a half miles" (ogni lega è quattro miglia e mezzo). It will be remembered that repeatedly in his letter of July, 1500, he declared the length of a league to be four miles: "a width of four leagues, which is sixteen miles"; "three leagues or twelve miles"; "twenty-four thousand miles, or six thousand leagues." But eleven months later he declared that a league is "four and a half miles." This statement that he now considered a league longer than he had formerly conceived it was made to Lorenzo without being accompanied by any compensating reduction in the number of leagues in a degree, and it is incredible that if he had made this other change he would have omitted mentioning it to Lorenzo; for while the number of miles in a league was a matter of popular dispute, the number of leagues in a degree seemed to fall within the field of scholarship. The implication is unavoidable, and it must be accepted unless proof can be adduced to the contrary, that during the year following his Spanish voyage Amerigo was compelled by astronomical data to adopt the conception that a degree is longer than he had at first believed. Since the longitudinal distance or number of degrees from Cadiz to his farthest west had been less than he had supposed, the length of each degree must be greater; and "giving to each degree sixteen and two-thirds leagues," as he thought Ptolemy and Alfragano did, each league must be longer.

His revised estimate was stated after he had spent considerable time in Portugal. If there had been a tendency in Portugal toward accepting a smaller number of leagues for a degree than were acknowledged in Spain, we might suspect that Amerigo's conception that a league was larger was only an attempt to compensate. But the tendency was actually in the opposite direction, toward increasing the number of leagues in a degree, and this was the case both in Spain and in Portugal. Encisco, a Spanish geographer, who published his work in 1519, and Ruy Faleiro, a Portuguese astronomer, who published his in 1535, both held that there were sixteen and two-thirds leagues in a degree. The scholarly Varnhagen, in trying to determine at what meridian the Line of Demarcation should have been drawn by agreement between Spain and Portugal, made his calculations with sixteen and two-thirds leagues to a degree, the measure common to both countries before 1520; but he said that at about that date the measure of seventeen and a half leagues to a degree was first introduced into the Iberian Peninsula and that later it came into general use there.[1]

Therefore it is clear that Amerigo held to sixteen and two-thirds leagues to a degree, while he now adopted his conception of four and a half Roman miles as the length of a league. In this he found himself in disagreement with the Portuguese, whose league was four Roman miles. But sixteen and two-thirds leagues at four and a half Roman miles each, fitted the facts of his corrected astronomical observations. He was committed to faith in his method of determining longitude, and he chose to follow the evidence of the celestial bodies as against the traditional conceptions of the time-honored authorities.

If, as seems a perfectly valid thing to do, we revise his computations on his first voyage in the light of his new measure of the league, we find a convincing explanation for his surprising treatment of the Spanish King's offer of three ships. His ultimate decision in the matter turned upon his estimate of his longitudinal position on July 24, 1499, at his farthest east on the long coastline he had explored. Was that farthest east a position to the east or west of the Line of Demarcation?

He obtained his answer to that question somewhat as follows: The Line of Demarcation set by the Treaty of Tordesillas was 370 leagues west of the Azores or of the Cape Verde Islands. The Azores, he wrote, were "300 leagues from Cadiz." By this he naturally meant that the island of the Azores nearest to Cadiz was 300 leagues west of that city. The westernmost of the Azores, the island of Flores, was six degrees or about 100 leagues farther west in equatorial distance, and we may assume that Amerigo's estimate of that farther distance was not far wrong. The Cape Verde Islands were, he thought, farther than the westernmost of the Azores, since he said the Cape Verde Islands were "beyond every other meridian toward the west." Hence, in his opinion the Line of Demarcation was 370 + 300 + about 100 + = about 770 + leagues west of Cadiz.

In order to compute where his farthest east on July 24 had been in relation to the Line of Demarcation, he had to assemble and to revise his data and to work out the problem backward. That is to say, he had to begin with his estimate of the longitude at his farthest west in September, and from that he had to subtract his estimate of the east-west distance between his farthest west in September and his farthest east on July 24. It was a simple problem in arithmetic, which we shall follow through with some assurance that while we cannot duplicate his figures exactly we can keep close enough to them to make certain of the conclusion he drew from them.

He estimated his farthest west in September as eighty-two and a half degrees west of Cadiz. At the time of his Spanish voyage that meant thirteen hundred and seventy-five leagues, but his conception that a league was four and a half rather than four miles compelled a revision downward of the number of leagues in the proportion of four divided by four and a half, or eight-ninths of thirteen hundred and seventy-five, which was twelve hundred and twenty-two. He gave "seven hundred leagues or more" as the total length of coastline he had explored, and this was in a direction between northwest and west. The seven hundred leagues might be considered as the hypotenuse of a right-angled triangle with the two sides unequal, the longer of the two sides being the east-west distance traveled while he followed the coast. This meant approximately five hundred and fifty leagues. He therefore believed that about five hundred and fifty leagues, subject to revision downward to eight-ninths of that number, or about four hundred and eighty-eight leagues, was the east-west distance between his farthest west and his farthest east on that coastline. Subtracting four hundred and eighty-eight from twelve hundred and twenty-two leagues left seven hundred and thirty-four leagues, his approximate longitudinal distance from Cadiz at his farthest east on July 24. This was well to the east of the seven hundred and seventy leagues west of Cadiz estimated for the correct location of the Line of Demarcation and meant that at his farthest east on July 24 he had penetrated into a region belonging to Portugal.

He had done this unwittingly. He had become aware of the fact only in retrospect. Not until several weeks later, after he had established his farthest west longitude, was data available from which only now he derived evidence of that trespass in July. Now he saw that it would help Spain to maintain pacific relations with Portugal if the data that indicated that the trespass had been unintentional and unwitting were made available to the court. The daily northwestward run of his ships while at sea from July 24 to August 4 was recorded while he was sailing out of and away from the region belonging to Portugal, and therefore was evidence that might prove to be of great political importance. If the figures for each day's run during those twelve days were placed on the elaborate official map which Juan de la Cosa had been commissioned to make for Their Spanish Majesties, they would tend to remove any suspicion that his Spanish expedition had deliberately explored land belonging to Portugal.

Juan de la Cosa was now at Puerto de Santa Maria, near Cadiz, drawing a world chart upon an oxhide nearly six feet long and more than three feet wide. The map was to show all the territory up to date (1500) which had been discovered for Spain, and also what Giovanni and Sebastiano Caboto had discovered for the English. La Cosa was placing upon it all the islands which Columbus had found. It was to show the outlines of the island of Trinidad and the land called Parias, the Gulf of Parias, and the Gulf of Pearls, which had all been discovered and named by Columbus and visited by Hojeda and by La Cosa himself. La Cosa was persuaded that it would be politic to record on his map the number of leagues sailed each day on the northwest course covered by Amerigo's two caravels.

Upon one thing Amerigo and La Cosa could not agree. La Cosa thought the best place to look for the sea passage into the Great Sinus was west of Cape de la Vela, while Amerigo clung to his idea that the strait must be beyond the Cape of Catigara to the south of the equator.

Therefore Amerigo now found the king's offer of three ships embarrassing to him, for he was concerned with something more than adding leagues to the territory of Spain. If he were to pursue his original purpose, sharpened by the success of Da Gama; if, as he expressed it, he were "to bring back very great news and discover the island of Taprobana, which is between the Indian Ocean and the Gulf or Sea of the Ganges," it could not be with the ships of Spain. His first voyage had proved that fact conclusively; for even if there were doubt that he had any more than reached the border of Portuguese territory when he was at his farthest east in July, it was certain that the coast which he had seen extending for many leagues farther to the east, which he had not been able to follow because of the strength of the ocean current, was east of the Line of Demarcation and was not under Spanish jurisdiction. That eastern end of the land most assuredly belonged to Portugal, and since he would have to sail around that eastern end and work southward to whatever might be the latitude of the Strait of Catigara, it could be only with the permission of Portugal that he could pursue the exploration he had in mind. Since the Portuguese would refuse permission to a Spanish expedition, the obvious thing for him to do was to enter the service of Portugal.

We do not know by what steps he declined the Spanish king's offer and opened negotiations with the Portuguese, but all the facts we have seem to justify the guess upon which we shall now venture. It is most probable that quite privately he opened his mind to a Florentine friend who was on business bound for Lisbon and suggested that one of the Florentine merchants in Lisbon present his case to the ear of the Portuguese king.

He had the best moral and legal justification for communicating with Portugal, for an official convention of Spanish and Portuguese pilots, astrologers (astronomers), and mariners in July, 1495, had decided that if either Spain or Portugal found land where the Tordesillas Treaty Line of Demarcation ought to fall, word was to be dispatched immediately to the other party to the treaty, which within ten months after having received word should send an expedition to mark the Line.[2] It was agreed also that all maps thereafter must contain the Line of Demarcation. No policy of secrecy, if there was any, on the part of the Spanish government could under the circumstances have been binding upon a man in Amerigo's position. Because the Spanish had been the first to discover that there was land beyond the ocean on the Line of Demarcation or to the east of it, it was Portugal's duty and privilege to send the expedition to mark the Line. Furthermore, since accurate marking of the Line was beyond the ability of dead-reckoning navigators, and since Amerigo had devised an astronomical method for determining longitude, he was of all men the one best fitted for the scientific task that Portugal would want performed.

That there was land beyond the western ocean belonging to Portugal could not be concealed by the Spaniards. With so many sailors in Cadiz and Seville gossiping about the recent voyages, there could be no deceiving the Portuguese spies. Portugal would soon hear about it, investigate, grasp what belonged to her, and prohibit further Spanish exploration in her territory. So Amerigo must have thought, but the situation was quite the opposite. Actually, the Portuguese were keeping secret from the Spanish the fact that they had already learned of the land that was theirs to the west —had learned of it even before he had brought his news of it to Spain. The Portuguese were not asleep. The twelve ships about which he had written to Lorenzo, which he had heard that the Portuguese king was refitting to be sent on a second voyage to India, had already sailed, with several additional ships, under Pedro Alvares Cabral in the month of March, 1500, and late in April they touched land beyond the western ocean at about eighteen degrees south. News of this discovery had been brought directly to Lisbon by a ship sent back for that purpose, and in the report brought by that ship the king was advised to look in his archives at an old map by Pedro Vaz Bisagudo, on which, he was told, he would find indicated the location of this land which had just been rediscovered. All this King Emanuel I of Portugal was keeping hidden from Spain.

Amerigo was honor bound not to reveal to the Portuguese any of Spain's legitimate secrets, but in telling them what he knew of land belonging to them, he would be acting in loyalty to an international agreement to which Spain had given assent. While explaining his project to the Portuguese, he would properly withhold from them all detailed information concerning the Spanish section of the land, but he would pledge himself to advance their knowledge of that portion which was theirs. He would be faithful to both Spain and Portugal. Having discovered land belonging to each, he would make correct assignment of it to each. Portugal would trust the Florentine gentleman after he had served Spain; Spain would trust him while he served Portugal; he would serve both countries so that both would honor him.

While he had the best of reasons for making his next voyage with a Portuguese commission, he did not know that at the same time the Portuguese king had a good reason for wanting to use him. The land along which he had coasted so extensively and the "island" whose discovery the Portuguese expedition under Cabral had privately reported to King Emanuel were very possibly connected. Amerigo intended sailing into the latitudes where Cabral had found land, and King Emanuel, possessing secret knowledge that Amerigo would there find land belonging to Portugal, naturally welcomed the idea that Amerigo's voyage should be under his aegis rather than Spain's. Just as certainly as that Amerigo knew that he should make the voyage for Portugal, the Portuguese king knew it also.

Whether it came about because King Emanuel sent Amerigo an invitation to come to Lisbon, or because Amerigo offered himself for service under the flag of Portugal, he was given a commission to sail with a Portuguese expedition of three ships. There can be little doubt that he was appointed to take directional charge of the expedition—that is, to plan the route which the captains were to follow. The King of Portugal would not have offered him a position inferior to that which he had held on his Spanish voyage, nor would he have offered him a smaller number of ships than had been promised him by the King of Spain; and it is improbable that Amerigo, under the circumstances, would have condescended to accept anything less than the directional command. His acceptance of the Portuguese offer obligated him to present an explanation to King Ferdinand, probably through Bishop Fonseca, who was continuing to direct all affairs relating to the Indies. Perhaps he asked the bishop to point out to the king that while the Cape of Catigara must be presumed to be in Portuguese territory, it was possible that the strait into the Great Sinus lay so far to the west as to be in Spanish territory, and that if he discovered it to be so, he would most assuredly make a report of that fact to Their Spanish Majesties.

A portion of the funds for Amerigo's Portuguese expedition may have been provided in the same way in which they had been provided in Spain—through Amerigo's banker friends. The leading banker in Lisbon was Bartolomeo Marchioni, a Florentine, who had numerous relatives in various countries and was in position to act as intermediary between the Medici and the king when the latter borrowed money. Marchioni shared the profits of voyages, representing foreign merchants at Lisbon for trade with the Indies. The ship *S. Tiago* in the fleet of Vasco da Gama belonged to Marchioni, as did also a ship captained by a Florentine in the fleet of João da Nova, in 1501, and a ship in the fleet of Albuquerque. He had at least one ship in every fleet that was sent to India. He was also, through his agents, a sort of master spy for Portugal, keeping an eye on what went on in Spain. He must have been cognizant of Amerigo's consistent purpose, and he probably assisted in financing the new expedition.

It was not, however, to be an expedition of private initiative, merely permitted by the king. Peter Martyr bore testimony to the fact that "Amerigo Vespucci, the Florentine, sailed at the command and in the pay of Portugal" (auspicio et stipendio Portugalensium). Nor was the expedition commercially inspired, for it was stipulated otherwise. It was to be for geographical purposes, to acquire information, an important feature of the work being to establish, if possible, the location of the Line of Demarcation. The terms were, as Amerigo later wrote, "solely to make discoveries, with a commission to that effect, and not to seek for any profit."

In Lisbon, during the months of preparation for his voyage, his situation was in sharp contrast with that of Columbus, who, except for his misadvertised second voyage, had always to sue and beg and wait for ships. The king and queen had violated the exclusive contract of Columbus by permitting other men to undertake expeditions. Fortune hunters over whom he could not exercise authority had poured in upon the admiral, despoiling his empire. Now the last injustice had been done him. Robbed of even the semblance of control over his possessions, he had been made prisoner on the island of Española, and in October, 1500, had been brought home to Spain in irons. His case was indeed pitiful. True, the shackles had been promptly struck off as soon as Their Majesties had been made aware of his condition, and Their Majesties had given him promises in an effort to make amends. But the mistreatment at the hands of Bobadilla, royal commissioner to Española, had left scars upon his memory as well as upon his limbs.

Columbus was a problem to his associates. In November he had quarreled violently with La Cosa, because La Cosa called Cuba an island and so represented it on his map. Columbus was angry at this defiance of his affidavit that Cuba was part of the mainland of Asia. La Cosa probably quoted the reports of natives. He no doubt reminded Columbus that when they were together on their first voyage along the north coast of Española, they had been informed by the natives that "the island of Bohio was larger than that of Juana, which the inhabitants called Cuba," and that Bohio, unlike Cuba, "was not surrounded by water, but as nearly as could be understood from them, was a continent, and situated behind Española, which they called Caritoba." But Columbus was never disposed to admit what he had chosen to forget. La Cosa doubtless attempted to point out to Columbus that "behind Española," when they were on the north coast of it, must have meant that part of the mainland which lay to the south of it; he and Hojeda and Amerigo Vespucci, as well as Columbus himself, had in part explored it, and they all agreed that it was an eastern extension of the continent of Asia. When Columbus was in a state of rage, however, he would listen to no arguments. He had made up his mind about Cuba, and with him it was not a question of knowledge, but of willingness to believe.

In Lisbon, Amerigo found that the Portuguese had been more enterprising and far more successful than the Spanish, more consistently progressive and more intrepid and daring. He was to learn how mistaken he had been in calling them coasthuggers. In Lisbon harbor he undoubtedly became acquainted with Gaspar Corte-Real, who the year previous had crossed the western ocean toward the northwest and had visited the coast of what the Portuguese were to call "Terra Corte-Real," which the world generally was to know by the name "Newfoundland"; for Gaspar Corte-Real's ships were making ready for a second voyage, upon which they set forth two days after Amerigo sailed. He found that King Emanuel displayed much more interest in exploration than did the war-making politician King Ferdinand. The work of Prince Henry the Navigator had established a royal tradition of direct supervision of fleets and voyages, and the kings of Portugal found that it paid them well to give personal attention to maritime affairs. King Emanuel the First, who had ruled since 1495, had already tasted the first fruits of the monopolistic overseas trade with India, and was on the eve of becoming the most prosperous monarch in Europe. Men called him "Emanuel the Great" or "Emanuel the Fortunate." He assumed the title: "Lord of the Conquest, Navigation and Commerce of India, Ethiopia, Arabia and Persia," in which expansive but justifiable appellation he was confirmed by Pope Alexander the Sixth.

With respect to equipment, the Portuguese had ships that were larger and faster than Spanish ships and able to sail closer to the wind. Some of them were a hundred feet in length, with a twenty-five foot beam, and some of them much larger, with a capacity of hundreds of tons. Amerigo must have been well content to have Portuguese ships when he remembered the force of that current below the equator, which his Spanish ships had been unable to stem.

Discipline on Portuguese ships was very strict. A ship's clerk was liable to branding on the forehead, the loss of his right hand, and the forfeiture of his property, if he wilfully made a false entry in his bookkeeping. A sailor who fell asleep on watch was put on a diet of bread and water; but if the offense should occur in enemy waters, he would be stripped, flogged by his messmates, and ducked thrice. If he were an officer, he would have a pail of water flung over his head, and water was unpopular in the nonbathing centuries.

In seamanship the Portuguese were unexcelled among Mediterranean peoples, even if they were not yet acquainted with some of the most common sea terms. For example, the steersmen on some Portuguese ships in 1505 were unfamiliar with the terms "larboard" and "starboard," and so a bunch of onions was hung up in the rigging to mark the larboard, and a bunch of garlic on the starboard. For once, mariners could steer by smell, if not by a sense of humor.

Amerigo was the first explorer in the service of Portugal who definitely planned to cross the ocean to the southwest, Cabral's discovery of land across the ocean in that direction having been accidental. He wrote to Lorenzo on the eighth of May, in a letter that has been lost, that he was "ready to depart." He considered it his duty to keep Lorenzo informed of his movements, and no doubt Lorenzo transmitted news to Amerigo's family and friends and business associates.

Before we follow Amerigo on his Portuguese voyage, however, we shall do well to note a sensational consequence of his enlarged conception of the length of the league, and thereby prepare ourselves for better comprehension of what he achieved on that voyage.

The circumference of the earth according to Columbus was twenty thousand four hundred Roman miles, and according to Ptolemy it was twenty-two thousand five hundred, although Amerigo thought Ptolemy made it twenty-four thousand Roman miles.

But Amerigo's astronomical work proved these various estimates wrong. His acceptance of four and a half miles as the length of a league, with sixteen and two-thirds leagues in a degree, made a degree of longitude on the equator seventy-five Roman miles, and the circumference of the earth twenty-seven thousand Roman miles. This enlarged conception of the earth was quite individual and was a daring break with tradition. Amerigo took this step because all his nighttime studies confirmed the larger view.

His 27,000 Roman miles at 1,620 English yards to the mile were 24,852 English miles—*only fifty English miles less than the actual circumference*, which is 24,902 English miles. The accuracy of his estimate is so obvious, it is astonishing that it has never before been pointed out.

Amerigo was closer to the correct measurement than anyone before him had ever been. He was closer than Toscanelli and closer than was ever claimed for Eratosthenes, even when that ancient physicist was credited with the forced results of the most favorable computations based upon intentionally chosen data. The best any misguided enthusiast ever did for Eratosthenes was to bring him from his actual error of more than four thousand English miles to about one hundred and fifty miles. But scholarship can allow no such approach to accuracy in Eratosthenes.

In the absence of any evidence that Amerigo made any other changes in his linear measurements at the time he changed the length of a league from four to four and one-half miles, arithmetic leads to only the one conclusion. His estimate in 1501 was the closest approximation to the correct measurement of the circumference of the earth ever made, so far as is known, by anyone previous to modern times. Unless it can be proved that in 1501 he changed his conception of the number of leagues in a degree to compensate for having changed the number of miles in a league, the honor must remain his.

Chapter Seven

THE VOYAGE FOR PORTUGAL

On May 13, 1501, Amerigo sailed from Lisbon with three caravels. His voyage was "commenced with the aid of the Holy Spirit," which as generally interpreted means the spirit of understanding and truth.

He kept the Canaries in the offing and passed southward beyond them and approached Cape Verde. At Cape Verde (Dakar) his three ships were met by two ships of the expedition of Cabral, who was returning from India. One of these was the property of the Florentine, Bartolomeo Marchioni, no doubt with some of Amerigo's fellow countrymen on board. Since Amerigo was supplied with fresh provisions, he was able to give the weary returning mariners a hearty welcome and to regale them with European food such as they had not tasted for many months. They repaid him with gifts of spices from the Orient and with information.

On one of Cabral's ships was a most widely traveled man, Guaspare, a Jewish refugee from Posen. He had worked his way from land to land on Arabian ships in the Red Sea and the Persian Gulf, and eventually to Goa in India, where he remained with Iussuf Adil Chan, the Sabayo of the Portuguese. When this ruler sent him to Vasco da Gama, he was suspected of deceit and was seized and tortured. Accepting baptism through fear of worse treatment, he received the name Da Gama from the man who had thus converted him, and he served that navigator with fidelity as an interpreter. He was taken to Portugal by Da Gama and was sent with Cabral again to India. As a man who had thus been twice to India and had sailed for three hundred leagues up a river in India and had crossed the Indian Ocean four times, Guaspare da Gama was as well acquainted with the East as was any man in the service of Portugal. He was Amerigo's chief informant. He talked freely of all that he had seen on his voyage with Cabral, revealing far more than King Emanuel would have permitted.

Amerigo at once had high hopes that Guaspare would tell him with some definiteness of the latitudinal and longitudinal position of Taprobana Island, and of the entrance to the Gulf of the Ganges. But he learned to his astonishment that the name "Taprobana" was unknown to the people of India. He was therefore practically forced to identitfy it with Ceylon or with Sumatra.

He was trying to harmonize the classical geography of Ptolemy with this new and direct information. He could not doubt Guaspare's sincerity and accuracy, since all Guaspare said was corroborated by another man on Cabral's ships, an Italian named Gherardo Verdi, brother of one of Amerigo's men. No! Guaspare was not to be doubted, yet Amerigo had never before been confronted with such fallacies in Ptolemy. Place names of the East, it appeared, passed through some mysterious transformation before they got to Europe. Must a cartographer repudiate Ptolemy's authority? It began to look as though the facts would compel him to do so.

What he heard of everything east of the Cape of Good Hope seemed so distorted, according to his Ptolemaic preconceptions, that he became intensely depreciative of the directors of Cabral's voyage. He was disgusted when he found there was "no cosmographer or any mathematician" on board the two ships he had met. He made the mistake of assuming there had been none on the whole expedition and became hypercritical. But he was conscious that he was in danger of becoming a stickler for his own ideas, so earnestly did he believe that navigation should be conducted with strict attention not only to latitude but to longitude, and so he prayed, "May God not ascribe my ambition to arrogance."

Actually, when Cabral sailed from Portugal, he had with him one of the most famous cosmographers, Duarte Pacheco Pereira. Other men he had with him, such as Jean the Physician and Guaspare da Gama, were not savants, but experienced technicians. He had no "mathematician" in Amerigo's sense of the term; that is, no one who could by astronomical means determine longitude.

Pedro Alvares Cabral had sailed from Lisbon on the ninth of March, 1500, with a total of sixteen ships, thirteen of them powerfully armed. Two of the ships did not accompany him beyond the

Cape Verde Islands. His was the second Portuguese expedition to India, and he was sent forth as a conqueror, to avenge the mistreatment Vasco da Gama had received and to establish trading posts by force if necessary. In addition to merchants, he carried with him Franciscan friars and skilled gunners to encourage each other and to supplement each other's work. He had with him Bartolomeu Dias, his brothers Diogo and Pero, and several old sailors who had been to India, such as Pero Escobar, Alfonso Lopes, and Nicolau Coelho.

The presence of these men had a bearing on the route Cabral took, for it meant that he had the benefit of accumulated experience and that his course from the Cape Verde Islands a little south of west for a great distance into the ocean before attaining the latitude of the Cape of Good Hope was by deliberate intention, not the result of a storm or haphazard navigation.

There was distinct continuity of experimentation in the three Portuguese voyages: those of Bartolomeu Dias, Vasco da Gama, and Cabral. Dias had followed the coast of Africa until within a few degrees of the Cape of Good Hope and had then found himself compelled by winds and currents to leave the coast and fetch a course to the southwest and then south in order to attain latitude, and then had gone east beyond the cape, without sighting it. Da Gama was guided by the same chief pilot, Pedro de Alemquer, who had directed Dias. He was accompanied by Bartolomeu Dias as far as Cape Verde, and Diogo Dias was clerk on his flagship. Da Gama, however, did not follow the course Bartolomeu Dias had taken. He was well advised not to do so. Instead, to avoid dangerous winds from the west blowing toward Africa near the Cape of Good Hope, he sailed a little south of west from the Cape Verde Islands to mid-ocean and then attained latitude, but not enough, for he came up to the west coast of Africa some distance short of the cape and thence only by much traverse sailing in the face of terrible gales was able to get around the cape.

Cabral's ships, in turn, followed instructions prepared for them by Vasco da Gama:

> When they have the wind behind them they should make their way to the south. If they must vary their course let it be in the southwest direction. And as soon as they meet with a light wind they should take a circular course until they put the Cape of Good Hope directly east.

And from then on they are to navigate as the weather serves them, and they gain more, because when they are in the said parallel, with the aid of Our Lord, they will not lack weather with which they may round the aforesaid cape. And in this manner it appears to him that the navigation will be shortest.

Cabral, thus advised by Da Gama to sail southwest to the latitude of the cape, sailed to the south of west from the Cape Verde Islands much farther than Da Gama had done; so far, indeed, and with such fair winds that in less than a month he reached the coast of Brazil at about eighteen degrees south. This landfall was on the twenty-second of April, 1500. He erected a cross, naming the land "Santa Cruz." He immediately sent one of his fourteen ships back to Lisbon with news of his discovery. He followed the coast northward until he reached a place where the fleet could ride at anchor in safety, a well-protected harbor which he called "Porto Seguro." He took on fresh water and wood; on Easter Sunday, April 26, named a high elevation "Monte Pascoal"; and on the second or third of May left the Land of Santa Cruz and sailed southeast toward the Cape of Good Hope on his way to India. While running down the easting, five of his ships, including the one commanded by Bartolomeu Dias, sank in a storm with all hands. The navigation of Cabral was important, for it advanced man's knowledge of the western ocean and of the prevailing winds and currents. His was the first crossing of the Atlantic south of the equator.

Amerigo was eager for every scrap of information he could acquire from the men on Cabral's ships, and he painstakingly recorded all that he was told about the East. He was more immediately concerned, however, with what lay to the west. Cabral's men, of course, were under orders not to divulge to anyone except the king the sailing directions for the eastward route to India. In fact it was not until three and a half years later that King Emanuel permitted reproduction of the itinerary of the India fleet. But the westward route was a different matter. Amerigo was already acquainted with the main fact of the discovery of Portuguese land to the west, and since he was in command of ships of Portugal and was headed for India by way of the west and, as seemed inevitable, would soon revisit places Cabral had visited by a route which would take him near to the land which had been named Santa Cruz, the men of

Cabral's expedition gave him all the data which might help him in his westward navigation.

They discussed with him the possibility that the coastline of Cabral's Land of Santa Cruz was continuous with the land which he had explored two years before. They gave its distance westward by dead reckoning, and he adduced his own revised computations as to its longitudinal position, according to which his farthest east on his Spanish voyage had been less than three hundred and seventy leagues in longitudinal distance west of the Cape Verde Islands. He believed Cabral's landfall had not been far from the longitude of his own farthest east. The latitude of Cabral's brief touching of the coast had been from something under eighteen degrees south to about sixteen degrees south. Amerigo believed that he himself had gone to at least six degrees south. Vicente Yañez Pinzón had explored the coast at ten degrees south and for some distance northward. It seemed probable that the various known portions of coastline were continuous, except possibly for the strait which Amerigo sought.

He began to question whether he might not have to look for that strait further to the south than he had previously thought. One of the Ptolemaic maps located the southern tip of Asia at about six degrees south, and another, in which Amerigo probably placed most confidence, indicated that eastern Asia presented a continuous coastline at least as far south as Catigara, beyond eight degrees south.

All this confusion, however, tended to strengthen the supposition that Cabral and he had explored different portions of the same land. And so he came to a conclusion on the matter, and wrote to Lorenzo on a ship that rode the high seas off Cape Verde: "This was the same land which I discovered for the King of Castile and which I wrote you about in my other letter, only their landfall was farther to the east."

His letter was probably carried privately by Cabral's man, Gherardo Verdi. It would have been confiscated by the Portuguese government had its contents been known, even though it was not for Spanish eyes, but was addressed to someone in far-off Florence, for it mentioned Cabral's discovery in the west and that was something which King Emanuel had been concealing for nearly a year.

Two months after Amerigo sailed, however, the king himself

divulged the news of Cabral's discovery. The arrival in Lisbon of the first ship of the Cabral expedition returning from India seems to have precipitated the king's action, for doubtless some of the crew upon their arrival and before they came into the presence of the king, not considering it incumbent upon them to withhold details of information now fourteen months old, naturally talked about the discovery. The king, becoming aware of this and perceiving that soon all Europe would know of it, realized that he must act quickly before his royal cousins in Spain heard of it by roundabout and unofficial channels, lest they justly charge him with lack of confidence in themselves and with not being aboveboard in matters pertaining to the treaty by which the pope had divided the world between them. And so, on July 29, 1501, King Emanuel wrote about Cabral in a letter to King Ferdinand and Queen Isabella:

> My aforesaid Captain sailed from Lisbon with thirteen ships on the 9th day of March last year. During the octave of the Easter following he arrived at a country which he first discovered and on which he bestowed the name of Santa Cruz. In it he found the people naked as in the days of primal innocence, mild and peaceable, and it would appear that our Lord intended that that country should be miraculously discovered, for it lies most conveniently and is indeed necessary to the voyage to India for the repair and watering of ships. Because the voyage which he had to make was long, he did not delay for the purpose of obtaining information regarding the country, but he sent back a ship thence to me informing me that he had discovered it.

Amerigo, meanwhile, was on his way across the Atlantic. His conception of a longer league than he had previously accepted, compelled the assumption that the circumference of the earth was larger, and led to the rising conviction that the land to the west, which he had accepted as an eastward extension of Asia, was at a very great distance from the Gulf of the Ganges. Nevertheless, he clung to the hope that he might find the strait which he sought. So much confusion now existed as to its probable latitude, that as he escaped from the doldrums and approached the land, he appears to have followed the same sort of plan which Hojeda and he had carried out two years before. It was most reasonable, certainly, for him to call together the captains of his three ships and to propose that two of them remain in consort, while the third take a more southerly course in order to make a landfall at or near the latitude of that secure harbor, Porto Seguro, which Cabral's fleet had found. This one ship would explore the coast northward from its landfall and come straightway to meet the other ships in case it found the strait of Catigara, or else return and wait at Porto Seguro for their arrival. He himself, with two ships, naturally wanted to make a landfall at the latitude of what he believed to have been his farthest south on his Spanish voyage so that his two voyages would overlap. By the time his three ships were reunited, they would have explored more than ten degrees of latitude with maximum effectiveness and speed. The knowledge that there was such a harbor as Porto Seguro, where ships might ride at anchor in safety, had been welcome news. It made feasible the separation of his fleet, since it provided a definite rendezvous.

After sixty-four days at sea, with little wind and sometimes no wind at all, but with a mind that went faster and farther than any navigator's mind had ever traveled, he made his landfall with two ships about August 15, at or not far from five degrees south. Finding himself on an east coast, he sailed northward and found the turn of the coast which he named "Cape S. Rocco" (Cape São Roque) at 5° 26′ S. on August 16. Perhaps he ventured a little beyond this cape, where the current close to shore was not strong enough to prevent his returning; but it is more probable that he did not, because of his previous experience with the strong offshore current flowing toward the northwest. But the turn of the coast must have satisfied him that he was close to his farthest east on his Spanish voyage, so that he soon turned southward toward Porto Seguro.

Meanwhile, judging by the dates of place names on the earliest maps of the coast, the third ship made its landfall at or near "Rio Sta. Lena" (S. Elena, August 18) at about fifteen degrees south. This was a little north of Porto Seguro (the present Baia Cabralia at 16° 20′ S., the name "Porto Seguro" having been shifted to a harbor five miles farther south). Obedient to orders, the ship sailed northward. It named "Rio S. Augustino" on August 28, and thereafter, no doubt, left a signal flag at a headland with a message for the other ships, before it retraced its course to fifteen degrees south. From Rio Sta. Lena it continued on its way to Porto Seguro, naming "Rio dos Cosmos" on September 27, and "Rio de Vergine" on October 21.[1]

Amerigo, with his two ships, sailed southward and named Cape St. Augustine on August 28. He landed there and accurately determined the latitude as about eight degrees south, for he had gone far enough into the Southern Hemisphere to be able to identify the South Pole. In the Process del Fisco, official Spanish hearings on legal claims based upon discoveries, both Giovanni Vespucci and Sebastian Cabot affirmed that Amerigo Vespucci had determined the latitude of Cape S. Augustine as eight degrees south. Nuño García de Toreno testified under oath: "Américo, who had maps in his house, told me many times that the cape was at eight degrees." Cape St. Augustine is at 8° 21′ S., just south of the modern Pernambuco.

Amerigo probably remained at Cape St. Augustine through September 3, to observe a conjunction there for longitude. Thence he proceeded southward, exploring the coast in detail. He entered rivers and observed the life of the natives and studied the flora. His two ships did not always keep together. The crew of one of them named "Sam Michel" on September 29, and "Rio de S. Francesco" on October 4, while the other ship, in advance of it, named "Rio de S. Ieronimo" on September 30. They entered the "Baie de Tuti li Santi" (All Saints Bay—Bahia) on November 1. In November the three ships were reunited at or in the neighborhood of Porto Seguro, and thereafter kept together, following the coast to the south and southwest, naming capes, mountains, rivers, and bays until they were distant from Cape S. Rocco "about eight hundred leagues."

In his letter to Lorenzo written after his return to Lisbon the following year, Amerigo did not dwell so much upon the distance he had gone as upon the beauty of the country, its healthfulness, "the fragrant smells of the herbs," and "the savor of the fruits and the roots." He wrote, "I fancied myself near the terrestrial paradise." He was conscious that he had fancied it, but did not actually believe it. As he said, "I am one of those followers of Saint Thomas, who are slow to believe." His mind presented the sharpest contrast with the romantic, credulous mentality of Columbus.

He was most of all interested in "the inhabitants and the animals and the plants and the other things . . . of general usefulness to human living." The racial types of the various native tribes found in this immense land especially presented matter for speculation. He no longer called them "Indians," as he did on his Spanish voyage. Whatever they were, they were not Asiatics, and therefore they were deserving of independent study.

What were the customs and ideas of the cannibals? He was so eager to find out, that, as he wrote, "for twenty-seven days I ate and slept among them." To eat and sleep among man-eating savages for purposes of research was, to say the least, in advance of his day. So also was his natural kindliness, which caused him to purchase ten poor creatures from the cannibals to save them from being victims of a ritualistic slaughter.

Amerigo Vespucci had the scientific passion and too questioning a mind to have been approved of by the heresy hunters of his day had they directed their attention to him. He wrote to Lorenzo that among these cannibals, without laws or religious faith, the administration of justice was unnecessary, *because they had no ruler or private property*. He added as his personal opinion that "private property," "sovereignty of empire and kingdoms," and "lust for possession; that is, pillaging or a desire to rule . . . appear to me to be the causes of wars and every disorderly act." This was written in the year 1502, and in the Iberian Peninsula!

The earliest picture of American Indians was a German wood engraving of 1505, believed to have been printed by Johann Froschauer of Augsburg. There was such a close resemblance between the inscription accompanying it and Amerigo's description of the natives among whom he had lived that the inference is unavoidable that the wording of the inscription was derived from what he had written and the picture itself inspired by his account. The German inscription said:

This figure represents to us the people and the islands which have been discovered by the Christian King of Portugal or by his subjects. The people are thus naked, handsome, brown, well shaped in body. Their heads, necks, arms, private parts, feet of men and women are a little covered with feathers. The men also have many precious stones in their faces and breasts. No one else has anything, but all things are in common. And the men have as wives those who please them, be they mothers, sisters, or friends, therein make they no distinction. They also fight with each other. They also eat each other even those who are slain, and hang the flesh of them in the smoke. They live to be a hundred and fifty years old. And have no government.

EARLIEST WOODCUT OF AMERICAN INDIANS, 1505

The picture showed a man with a bow who seemed to be considering the ritualistic shooting of a mother and her children. As Amerigo put it, "They set before them a mother with all the children she has, and with certain ceremonies they kill them with arrow shots and eat them." The picture showed also the construction of the "very large cabins" with "no iron or indeed any metal," which Amerigo called "truly miraculous houses." And it showed how, as he said, "the men have a custom of piercing their lips and cheeks" so that "most of them have at least three holes, and some seven, and some nine." It showed how "in their houses human flesh hung up to smoke." He wrote that the natives were "entirely naked, the men, like the women, without any covering of their shame." German pudicity required the feathers at the waist.

Some of the place names used on Amerigo's voyage, which appeared on the map of Canerio in 1502, the year of his return to Lisbon, were: "Vazio baril" (empty cask—"vazia" on the map being a misspelling for "vazio"); "Rio de Perera" ("pereira" meaning pear tree and being also a Portuguese family name); "Rio de Caxa" ("caxa" meaning chest or box); "Monte Fregosso" (craggy mountain); "Rio de Sam Iacomo" (Saint James—the name being probably Vespuccian in origin, although the date in the church calendar, July 25, was too early); "Rio de Vergine" (named for the virgin Saint Orsola, or for the Feast of the 11,000 Virgins, the date October 21 being somewhat less certain than those of the other place names); "Rio de Sam Ioam" (St. John the Baptist, June 24, the Protector of Florence—a name that might have been given by a Florentine without referencé to the date—probably used by Amerigo in gratitude for the safe reunion of his three ships near or at Porto Seguro); "bareras vermeias" (red claybanks); "barossa" (misspelling for "barrosa," clayey); "Serra de Sam Tome" (Cape Saint Thomas, "serra" meaning saw or serrated mountain, named for the patron saint of Portugal, December 21); "Alapego de Sam Paullo" ("alapego" meaning at the main sea, or at the ocean); "Rio da Refens" (River of the Hostages); "Baie de Reis" (Bay of the Kings, Epiphany, January 6—the bay of Rio de Janeiro); and "Pinachullo Detencio" (Craggy Pinnacle–descriptive of the scenery in the harbor of Rio de Janeiro, particularly of the peak now called

"Corcovado"). Amerigo was the first man in history to roll down to Rio.

At twenty-five degrees south Amerigo entered a port which he named "Cananor." Years later this name was corrupted to "Cananea." Cananea might seem to refer to the widow of Canaan, but would have been without meaning in its application. The earliest maps of South America, those of Canerio, 1502, Waldseemüller, 1507, and Ruysch, 1508, had "Cananor," not "Cananea." "Cananor" was the name Amerigo used.[2]

"Cananor" was not an abbreviation of the Latin "cananorum," which would have pointed to the date February 24, nor did it have reference to any date in the church calendar, nor was it an American Indian name. We can deny categorically these suggestions of various writers. "Cananor" was taken directly from what Amerigo heard from the men on the ships of Cabral at Cape Verde, when they spoke of the port and city of Cananor in India, north of Calicut.[3]

King Emanuel wrote in his letter to the Spanish kings in regard to Cabral:

> When he was in that Kingdom of Cochin . . . there came a message to him from the King of Cananor and one from the King of Colum which adjoins it, inviting him to come to them because he would find a more profitable market there. . . . He made his way to the Kingdom of Cananor, to one of the kings. . . . The king ordered so much spicery delivered to the ship that there was sufficient for a cargo if the ships had been empty, and it was given in order that he might bring it without payment as a present to me.

Cabral took in 100 bahars of cinnamon at Cananor, and on January 16, 1501, he sailed for home. Beyond a doubt Amerigo was allowed to taste some of that cinnamon at Cape Verde.

Cananor was Cabral's last port in India. When Amerigo, voyaging southwestward along the coast of the western continent, came to what his estimate of longitude told him was the Line of Demarcation and the western limit of the territory which Portugal might claim, and to the last port therein, he sought a suitable name for it and recalled that Cabral's men had said that their "last port" was Cananor. He thus gave it a name which the Portuguese would appreciate, which would have meaning to them, and which was at the same time a compliment to Cabral. Since it marked the western limit of the Portuguese lands on the continent, Amerigo took formal possession of Cananor in the name of the King of Portugal. It must have been Amerigo who at the entrance of the barra of Cananor on the continental side, on the top of a cliff, erected a *padrão* of

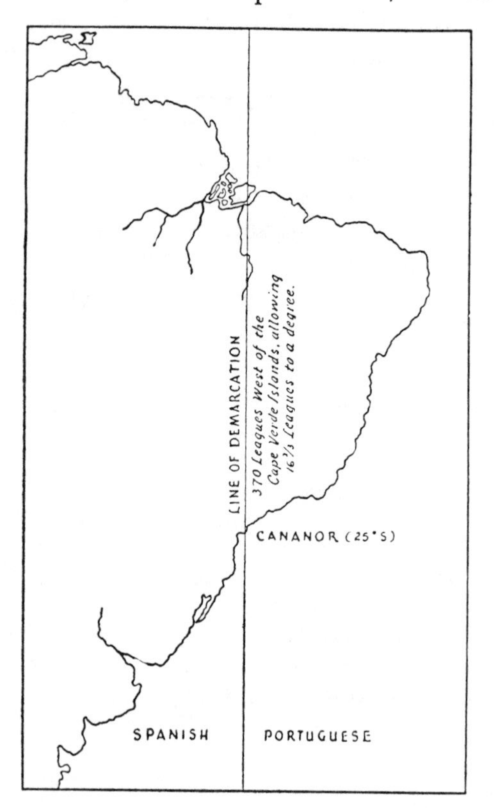

CANANOR AND LINE OF DEMARCATION

European marble two palms in height, two in breadth, and one in thickness, bearing the arms of Portugal without the castle.[4]

His recognition that Cananor was the last port which the Portuguese could legally claim, that it was in fact on the Line of Demarcation, reveals the astonishing success with which on this occasion he determined longitude. The Treaty of Tordesillas allowed the Portuguese "three hundred and seventy leagues" west of the Cape Verde Islands and three hundred and seventy leagues, at sixteen and two-thirds leagues to the degree, meant twenty-two and one-fifth degrees, or 22° 12′. Cananor was precisely 22° 10′ west of San Antonio, the westernmost of the Cape Verde Islands! Or, to put it another way—San Antonio in the Cape Verde Islands is at longitude 25° 40′ west of Greenwich; and 22° 12′ (representing three hundred and seventy leagues) added to that longitude gives 47° 52′ west of Greenwich. The actual longitude of Cananea (Cananor) west of Greenwich is 47° 50′. In a distance of fifteen hundred miles Amerigo was correct within two minutes of longitude, or about two miles!

There was no other instance of such accurate determination of longitude as that of Cananor in all the Great Age of Discovery. Within two degrees would have been remarkable. Finding the correct longitude, with the limitations under which he labored, involved the element of accident, of course; but it was the sort of accident that happens to a man who by valid means works painstakingly toward perfection. It has been generally assumed that in the early sixteenth century the Spanish and Portuguese governments did not know where the Line of Demarcation should be drawn, but Amerigo obviously had a very clear idea of it. Certainly no other man of his time was so well qualified to fix that Line and thus to carry out what seems to have been one of the specific purposes of his Portuguese voyage.

In naming Cananor as the last port belonging to Portugal (and it was the last place name which appeared on the maps of Canerio, 1502, Waldseemüller, 1507, and Ruysch, 1508, and indeed on maps for almost another generation), Amerigo gave positive evidence that while he had enlarged his conception of the length of the league, he had not revised his conception of the number of leagues in a degree.

From Cape S. Rocco at five and a half degrees south to Cananor at twenty-five degrees south, as long as he was on the coast of what belonged to Portugal, Amerigo took time to explore carefully and in detail. He gave five and a half months to these twenty degrees of latitude, or eight days to a degree. As soon as observations of longitude showed that the line of the coast had carried him west of what belonged to Portugal and that he was in territory that Spain would claim, he went as rapidly as possible, in fairness to the King of Portugal, who had commissioned him. The long continuous coastline had exploded his theory of the location of the Ptolemaic strait into the Great Sinus. He now would have to seek the southern end of the continent to get around it to India. In consequence, he followed the coast from Cananor southwestward with much greater speed, giving little more than one day to a degree. The season of the year, advanced summer in the Southern Hemisphere (ten days earlier or more advanced in the Old Style calendar), was a contributing factor in his decision to progress rapidly.

While the place names stop with Cananor on the early Portuguese maps and on maps stemming from them, "the map of 1523 of the Royal Library of Turin," to quote Magnaghi,

> gives several additional names, all of Portuguese origin, which would accord with the continuance of the voyage of Vespucci toward the south. Formerly it would not have been easy to explain how the Florentine navigator had spent his time from the twenty-fourth of January to the twenty-second of July, the date of his return to Lisbon, and no place names taken from the Church calendar fit into the time scheme of the return voyage. The map of 1523 has Portuguese nomenclature along the coast of Brazil to the River Plata, whence recommences the Spanish nomenclature conforming to the data of the expedition of Magellan; and since, as has been said, we have no certain evidence of any Portuguese voyage after that of 1502, it may be that this [map of 1523] has utilized material left by Vespucci, so much the more likely since this is probably the work of Giovanni Vespucci who was in possession of Amerigo's diary.

Beyond Cananor there was a change in the character of the place names—only two or three names of saints and for the most part names descriptive of the obvious features of a coast as it might be seen from the deck of a passing ship which did not pause to explore details. The names that were given were in any case not the concern of Portugal, but were withheld by Amerigo for the Spanish, to whom the territory belonged. Between Cananor and Rio de S. Francisco he applied the names "arvoreda" (grove of trees) and "palmar" (grove of palms, or, in Brazil, a village); and after "Rio Cerado" (Closed River), he named "Rio del Gado" (alagado?—cattle of any sort—sheep, goats, and so forth). "Rio de S. Francisco" was São Francisco at 26° 20′ S. "Rio dos Dragos" (River of Dragons) was followed by "Golfo do Estremo Repairo" (Gulf of the Last Repairs)—indicating that here for the last time (perhaps on his return northward) the ships were beached and heeled over so that the bottoms could be scraped and refitted and caulked and put into condition for the remainder of the voyage. "Rio dos Voltas" was a river within the Golfo do Estremo Repairo and the actual site of the repair work. "Voltas" means turn about, return home, and to undergo alteration. "Golfo dos Patos" means gulf of ducks, and "Seco" means arid land. In "Golfo de S. Maria da Peña," "peña" means sorrow. The date of Saint Mary the Sorrowful is June 17. The name may have been used without thought of the date, for this saint was apparently an early saint, patroness of seafaring people. On many ships a wooden image of this saint was carried under the bowsprit. "Costa de Acoa" was probably intended for coast of water (agoa). "Costa Baxa" was low coast, and "P. Daracife" was bridge of reefs. "C. de S. Maria de bo Deseo" was Cape Saint Mary of Good Desire—the desire, of course, being to find the end of the continent. It was at the same latitude as the Cape of Good Hope. The name was later shortened to "Cape Santa Maria."

It seems that "Rio Giordan" was the name Amerigo gave to the River Plata, unless there is utter confusion with a river not far south of Rio de Janeiro, which may have been named in reference to the Baptism of Jesus, on January 13. On the map of Canerio, 1502, "Rio Jordam" was placed at thirty-four degrees south, which was almost the exact latitude of the mouth of the River Plata (a degree north of the entrance to the estuary); while "Cananor," the last name on his map, was confusedly placed south of it. On the map of 1523 in the Royal Library of Turin, "Rio Jordam" was retained at that latitude of thirty-four degrees south, while "Cananor" and names close to "Rio Jordam" on the Canerio map were placed on the map of 1523 at approximately their correct latitudes. On a map of the sixteenth century in the library of Palermo was written: "This River Plata, or River of Silver, was discovered by the Florentine Amerigo Vespucci in the year 1501."

Some time after 1526 the Portuguese claimed this river as theirs, because it had been discovered by Vespucci with Portuguese ships. On two sixteenth-century maps the estuary of this river was called "Mare Ameriacum" (American Sea). It was not in character for Vespucci thus to use his own name, but the fact that others did so use it was corroborative evidence that he was the first discoverer of the great river of Argentina, as he had been of two of the greatest rivers of Brazil. There was no possibility that in following the coast he could have crossed the estuary without being aware that here was a great river, for the water was discolored with mud for a hundred miles out to sea. The freshness of the water also would have convinced any mariner who turned to the westward from Cape St. Mary that his good desire would not here be fulfilled, and that he was not entering a strait or opening into another sea, but a huge river estuary. Its very size would suggest that he was not even near the end of the continent. From the estuary, therefore, Amerigo pushed on with the utmost dispatch, perhaps not attempting to name the capes and bays. If he explored the River Plata at all, he did so upon his return northward.

The name "Porto di San Giuliano" (at 49° 21′ S.) was first used on the map of 1523, and there appeared in its Italian form. Previous to the making of that map the only recorded voyages to this latitude were those of Vespucci and Magellan. The most widely accepted date for Saint Julian was February 27, a date which fits perfectly into the time scheme of Amerigo's voyage. While there are several "Julian" saints' days in the church calendar, there are none on or near March 31, the date when Magellan entered the Port of St. Julian.

Original sources of information give no basis for the oft-repeated assumption that Port St. Julian was named by Magellan. A Genoese pilot who accompanied Magellan stated in his account of the voyage that Magellan's expedition named Port St. Antony, Cape St. Apelonia, Shoals of the Currents, Bay of St. Mattias, the Island of St. Matthew, and the Bay of Labours; but he did not say anything about naming the Port of St. Julian. He merely wrote, "arrived at the Port of St. Julian, which is at forty-nine and one-third degrees." The statement by Pigafetta, Magellan's secretary, substantiated this negative: "We remained at this port, which was called the Port of St. Julian." The logbook of Magellan's voyage told of naming the Bay of St. Mattias: "On Feb. 24 at 42° 51′ we were to the right of a very large bay, to which we gave the name of Bay of St. Matthew, because we found it on his day"; but of the Port of St. Julian the logbook said merely: "We did not take the sun again until we entered a port called St. Julian." The narrative of a Portuguese who was with Magellan was to this effect:

> We found ourselves near the river [river of Solís, the River Plata]. We named it the River of Saint Christopher. From this river we sailed sixteen hundred and thirty-eight miles southwest by west, where we found ourselves at the point of the Lupi Marini, which is in forty-eight degrees of south latitude. And from the point of Lupi Marini we sailed southwest three hundred and fifty miles where we found ourselves in the harbor of Saint Julian. . . . From this harbor of St. Julian . . . we sailed [southward and then] westward one hundred miles where we found a river to which we gave the name of River of Santa Cruz.

The implication of all these statements which tell of naming other places but avoid saying anything of naming Port St. Julian is that Port St. Julian had been named previous to Magellan.

On October 23, 1522, in a discourse on Magellan's voyage, Gian Battista Ramusio, who had not taken part in the expedition, said, "not till the last day of March of the following year did they reach a bay, to which," he carelessly added, "they gave the name of Saint Julian." This was the first appearance of this error.

Amerigo estimated his whole coastal voyaging from Cape S. Rocco as being "about eight hundred leagues." At four and a half Roman miles a league, this was thirty-three hundred English miles, the distance from Cape S. Rocco to the River Plata. From five and a half degrees south to fifty degrees south ("until the South Pole stood above my horizon at fifty degrees, which was my latitude from the equator") along the eastern coast of the continent was about four thousand English miles. It would be in keeping with all the statements in Amerigo's account of the voyage and in keeping with all other evidence to assume that from the River Plata he sailed southward at some distance off shore, until he put in at the port which he named St. Julian.[5]

Though he had not found the end of the continent, immediate return was advisable because of the lateness of the season, which was near the close of summer. He sailed back northward along the coast in March, April, and early May, taking time for more detailed exploration at least as far as the Golfo do Estremo Repairo at about twenty-eight degrees south, and perhaps to Cananor. He was "in"

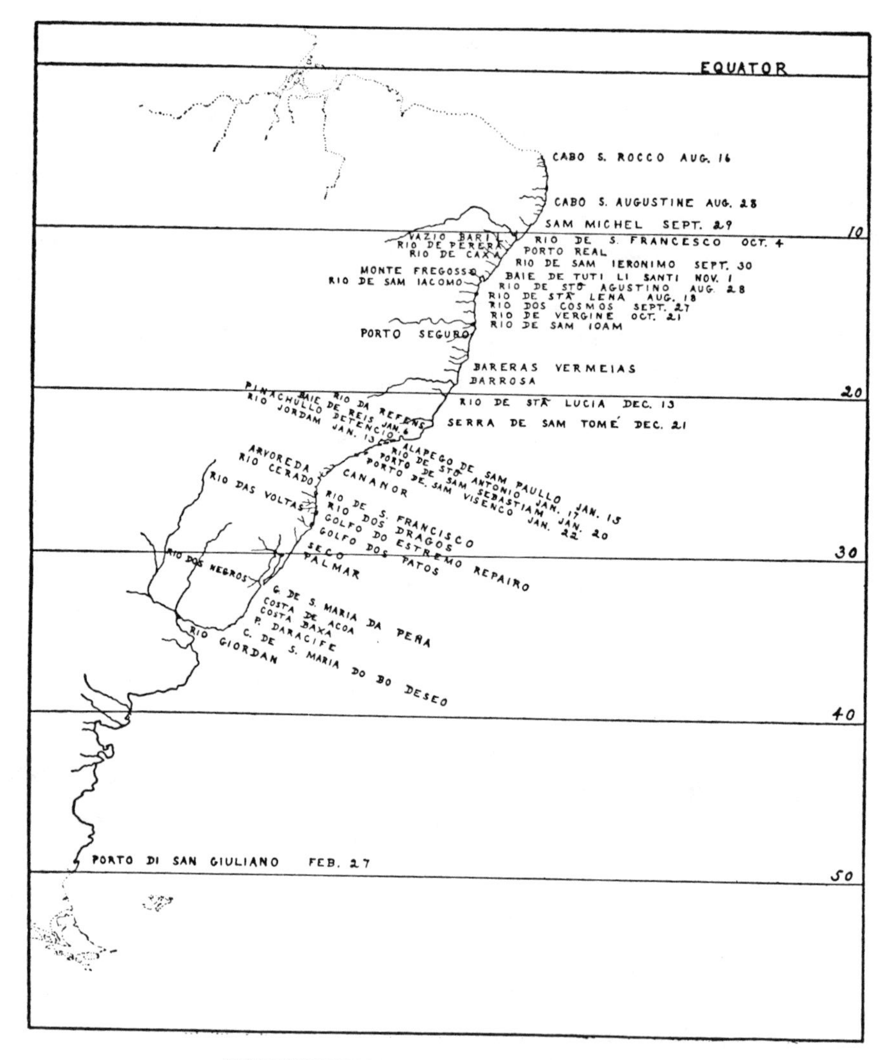

PORTUGUESE VOYAGE OF VESPUCCI

the land for "ten months," or from mid-July, 1501, to the middle of April, 1502. He recrossed the equator in mid-ocean about April 27, having crossed it going westward about the first of July. He wrote to Lorenzo, "We navigated in the Southern Hemisphere for nine months and twenty-seven days."

Good fortune had attended him in his explorations. When voyaging for Spain he had discovered some land that belonged to Portugal; voyaging for Portugal, he had discovered much that was Spain's. One voyage perfectly complemented the other, with no wasted effort or needless duplication. Both had been achieved without the loss of a ship; and though during the Spanish venture two men had been killed by Indians, this time he was bringing home all his men alive and well. The fates had been kind to him, as though they had recognized the purity of his motives.

He had been ambitious to be the first to identify the celestial south pole. Perhaps he had achieved that ambition when he drew a careful diagram of the stars near it. But his "hopes of winning fame throughout the ages" had been based chiefly upon his work in determining longitude by lunar distances. Now, however, as an outgrowth of his study of longitude, he had indeed made a discovery that would, he clearly saw, win him lasting renown. He had made a geographical discovery that surpassed any ever made by any man in all human history. He himself was in awe of its immensity. What it was, other men had not even suspected, and he was bringing home conclusive proof.

Chapter Eight

VESPUCCI'S LETTERS FROM CAPE VERDE, 1501, AND LISBON, 1502

[To Lorenzo di Pier Francesco de' Medici, July 4, 1501]

Your Excellency, My Patron:

My last letter to you was written on May 8 in Lisbon, when I was ready to depart. On this present voyage, which I have commenced with the aid of the Holy Spirit, and thinking I would not have any more to write to you until my return, it appears that chance has given me one more opportunity to write, this time not far from shore, on the high seas.

You have been given to understand, Lorenzo, both from my letter and from the letter of our Florentines of Lisbon, how I was summoned, while I was residing in Seville, by the king of Portugal, who entreated me to prepare myself to serve him by this voyage, upon which I embarked at Lisbon the thirteenth of last month. We set our course to the south and sailed within sight of the Fortunate Isles, which are now called the Canaries. We passed them in the offing, holding our course along the coast of Africa and sailing until we arrived at a cape which is called Cape Verde. This is the beginning of the province of Ethiopia. It is located in the meridian of the Fortunate Isles, and is fourteen degrees from the equator. [Cape Verde is at 14° 41′ N. and is in the same meridian with Gomera in the Canaries.]

There by chance we met with two ships of the king of Portugal, which were returning from the East Indies. These were ships which went to Calicut in an expedition of thirteen vessels, fourteen months ago. [The expedition of Cabral sailed fifteen months earlier, from Lisbon; fourteen months earlier, from the Cape Verde Islands.][1]

I have had full discourse with them, not so much about their voyage as about the coast along which they sailed and the riches they found and what they had possessed themselves of. As to the course they followed, let me briefly mention to Your Excellency that it was not a course of cosmography. In this crowd there was no cosmographer or any mathematician. That was a great mistake! What they related to me was so distorted that I have corrected more than a little in accordance with the cosmography of Ptolemy.

This great outfit of the king of Portugal departed from Lisbon in the month of April, 1499. [An error in the month, as explained above. Cabral sailed from Lisbon March 9, 1500, which was in 1499 according to the Florentine calendar, in which the year began on March 25.] They sailed southward to the Cape Verde Islands, which are about fourteen degrees from the equator and beyond every other meridian toward the west. [The southernmost of the Cape Verde Islands is at about fourteen and a half degrees north. The Portuguese used San Antonio, the westernmost of these islands as their prime meridian, although it is at almost the same longitude as São Miguel, one of the easternmost of the Azores.] These islands are six degrees, a little more or less, farther west than the Canary Islands. You know well how Ptolemy and most of the schools of cosmography place the Fortunate Isles at the extreme western limit of the inhabited world. The latitude of these islands was determined by the astrolabe and the quadrant, and I myself found it to be so.

The longitude is a more difficult thing, which only a few know how to determine, except through much night work, and observation of the conjunctions of the moon with the planets. In the endeavor to ascertain longitude I have lost much sleep [in Spain, during the preceding year], and have shortened my life ten years, but I hold it well worth the cost, because if I return in safety from this voyage I hope to win fame throughout the ages. May God not ascribe my ambition to arrogance! All my labor is consecrated to His holy service.

Now I return to my subject. As I was saying, the above-mentioned thirteen ships set their course toward the south of the Cape Verde Islands.[2] They sailed on the wind, which they say was between south and southwest.[3]

And then having sailed in twenty days a distance of about seven hundred leagues, a league being four and a half miles,[4] they set foot upon a land where they found people who were light complexioned and naked.

This was the same land which I discovered for the king of Castile, about which I wrote you in my other letter, only their landfall was farther to the east. There, they say, they secured every refreshment, and thence departed and set their course toward the Orient. They sailed on a southeast wind and worked eastwardly. And when they were free from that land, they were so storm-driven with wind from the southwest, and it was so hazardous, that five of their ships were driven under and sank with all hands. God have mercy upon their souls! The other eight ships, they said, ran under bare poles, that is to say, without sails, for forty-eight days and forty-eight nights with mountainous waves. They ran so far that they found themselves blown beyond the Cape of Good Hope. This Cape is on the coast of Ethiopia and is ten degrees south of the Tropic of Capricorn; that is to say, it is thirty-three degrees south of the equator [actually, 34° 22′ S.]. Taking into account the difference in meridian distances at different parallels, they estimated that this cape is in longitude seventy-two degrees, a little more or less. We can say that it is in the same meridian as Alexandria.[5]

From it they then sailed north by northeast, continuing to follow the coast.

[At this point let us summarize a portion of the letter which has no direct bearing on Vespucci's own voyage. Vespucci names many ports visited by Cabral's fleet on the east coast of Africa and in the Red Sea and along the coasts of Arabia and Persia. A remark characteristic of the man is: "This is as much information as I was able to get about the Red Sea. I leave it to him who knows it better." After naming several ports in the Persian Gulf, he says: "I believe there will be many more which I shall recall, which in truth were told me by a man worthy of credence, whose name is Guaspare, who has been working on ships between Cairo and a distant region which is called Molecca and is situated on the shore of the Indian Ocean." But as to the reported wealth of the Persian Gulf, Vespucci is cautious: "This Persian Gulf is, so they say, very rich, but one does not have to believe everything, and therefore I leave this matter to the pen of someone who will more nearly present the truth." He makes another reference to Guaspare, "who knew many languages, and the names of many countries and cities. As I say, he is a most trustworthy man, for he has twice made the voyage from Portugal to the Indian Ocean." Vespucci then names many ports on the coast of India and says, the scientist in him speaking: "As far as this the fleet of Portugal sailed, although they did not compute the longitude and latitude of this navigation. That was doing an impossible thing, to anyone who does not have much familiarity with navigation. It can establish belief in falsehood. I hope on my present voyage to see for myself the above-named and to run a large part of the course through the above-named regions and to discover much more; upon my return I shall give a valid and real account of everything. May the Holy Spirit go with me!" Vespucci gives it as his opinion that the Ptolemaic "Taprobana Island" may be identified with one or the other of the islands mentioned by Guaspare, with "Ziban" (Ceylon) or "Stamatara" (Sumatra). He describes Chinese junks as they were described to him by Guaspare. While writing his letter, he says, a third ship of Cabral's "just at this moment has arrived here at this cape." Of the three ships he has met at Cape Verde, he says:]

That which the said ships carry, coming loaded, is a great quantity of cinnamon, fresh and dried ginger, much pepper, cloves, nutmegs, mace, musk, agallochum, stomax, delicacies, porcelains, cassia, mastic, incense, myrrh, red and white sandalwood, wood aloes, camphor, amber, canes, much lacquer, mummy wax, indigo, and tutty, opium, hepatic aloes, India paper, and a great variety of drugs, which would be too lengthy a matter to relate. Of jewels I do not know the rest, except that I saw many diamonds, rubies, and pearls, among which I saw one ruby in a round piece of most beautiful color, that weighed seven and a half carats. I do not wish to expatiate further, because the motion of the ship will not let me write. You will hear the news from the Portuguese. In conclusion, the king of Portugal holds in his hands an immense trade and great riches. May the Lord make it prosper! I believe that the spices will come from these parts to Alexandria and to Italy, after the quality is cheapened. So goes the world. [Three years later, in 1504, no spices were obtainable in Alexandria or Beirut, for none were brought by the old overland routes. All available supplies in Indian ports had been bought by the Portuguese.]

Believe me, Lorenzo, that what I have written up to this point is the truth. And if the provinces and kingdoms and names of cities and of islands do not agree with those of the ancient authors, it is a sign that they are well altered as they come into our Europe, so that it is by a miracle that a single ancient name is heard. And for better evidence of the truth, Gherardo Verdi is at hand, brother of Simone Verdi, of Cadiz, who is accompanying me and presents his respects to you.

This voyage which I am now making is perilous, to the limit of human courage. Nevertheless, I am doing it with bold resolution to serve God and the world. If the Lord is served by me, He will give me courage, as long as I am prepared to do His will. Likewise, may He give eternal repose to my soul!

[To Lorenzo di Pier Francesco de' Medici, 1502]

Your Excellency, My Patron Lorenzo,

after due salutations, etc.

The last letter written to Your Excellency was from the coast of Guinea from a place which is called Cape Verde. In it you learned of the beginning of my voyage. By this present letter you will be informed in brief of the middle and end of my voyage and of what has happened up to now.

We departed from the above-mentioned Cape Verde very easily, having taken in everything necessary, such as water and wood and other requirements essential for putting to sea across the ocean wastes in search of new land. We sailed on the wind within half a point of southwest, so that in sixty-four days [delayed by the doldrums] we arrived at a new land which, for many reasons that are enumerated in what follows, we observed to be a continent. ["Arrived at a new land" is an unexpected statement, since he had been aware, as he previously wrote, that it was the same land which he had visited two years before. His discovery of the existence of a new continent was thus quietly announced.] We ran the course of that land for about eight hundred leagues, always in the direction of southwest one-quarter west. ["About eight hundred leagues," at four and a half Roman miles a league, was a distance of about thirty-three hundred English miles.]

We found the land thickly inhabited. I noted there the wonders of God and of nature, of which I determined to inform Your Excellency, as I have done of my other voyages. ["My other voyages" —plural. In addition to his Spanish voyage, he had made voyages between Italy and Spain. Bandini said that Vespucci, as a young man, had voyaged to the Levant and to England.]

We coursed so far in those seas that we entered the Torrid Zone and passed south of the equinoctial line and the Tropic of Capricorn, until the South Pole stood above my horizon at fifty degrees, which was my latitude from the equator. We navigated in the Southern Hemisphere for nine months and twenty-seven days [from about August 1 to about May 27, which were the approximate dates when he crossed the equator], never seeing the Arctic Pole or even Ursa Major and Minor; but opposite them many very bright and beautiful constellations were disclosed to me which always remain invisible in this Northern Hemisphere. There I noted the wonderful order of their motions and their magnitudes, measuring the diameters of their circuits and mapping out their relative positions with geometrical figures. I noted other great motions of the heavens, which would be a tedious matter to write about.

But [6] the most notable of all the things which occurred to me in this voyage I collocated in a small work, to the end that when I reside at leisure I may apply myself to it, to win renown after my death. I was intending to send you an epitome, but His Serene Highness retains my work. When he returns it to me I will send a summary. [The summary has not survived the centuries. There is no compelling reason to believe that the king permanently retained Vespucci's notes, in order to withhold them from the Spaniards and the rest of the world. Amerigo was confidently expecting that they would be returned.]

To conclude, I was on the side of the antipodes; my navigation extended through one-quarter of the world; my zenith direction there made a right angle, at the center of the earth, with the zenith direction of the inhabitants of this Northern Hemisphere in the latitude of forty degrees. This must suffice.

Let us describe the country and the inhabitants and the animals and the plants and the other things I found in their habitations which are of general usefulness to human living.

This land is very pleasing, full of an infinite number of very tall trees which never lose their leaves and throughout the year are fragrant with the sweetest aromas and yield an endless supply of fruits, many of which are good to taste and conducive to bodily health. The fields produce many herbs and flowers and most delicious and wholesome roots. Sometimes I was so wonder-struck by the fragrant smells of the herbs and flowers and the savor of the fruits and the roots that I fancied myself near the Terrestrial Paradise. What shall we say of the multitude of birds and their plumes and colors and singing and their numbers and their beauty? I am unwilling to enlarge upon this description, because I doubt if I would be believed.

What should I tell of the multitude of wild animals, the abundance of pumas, of panthers, of wild cats, not like those of Spain, but of the antipodes; of so many wolves, red deer, monkeys, and felines, marmosets of many kinds, and many large snakes? We saw so many other animals that I believe so many species could not have entered Noah's ark. [A heretical and quite dangerous doubt; long experience with the limited space on shipboard helped to make him skeptical.] We saw many wild hogs, wild goats, stags and does, hares, and rabbits, but of domestic animals, not one.

Let us come to rational animals. We found the whole land inhabited by people entirely naked, the men like the women without any covering of their shame. Their bodies are very agile and well proportioned, of light color, with long hair, and little or no beard. I strove a great deal to understand their conduct and customs. For twenty-seven days I ate and slept among them, and what I learned about them is as follows.

Having no laws and no religious faith, they live according to nature. They understand nothing of the immortality of the soul. There is no possession of private property among them, for everything is in common. They have no boundaries of kingdom or province. They have no king, nor do they obey anyone. Each one is his own master. There is no administration of justice, which is unnecessary to them, because in their code no one rules. They live in communal dwellings, built in the fashion of very large cabins. For people who have no iron or indeed any metal, one can call their cabins truly miraculous houses. For I have seen habitations which are two hundred and twenty paces long and thirty wide, ingeniously fabricated; and in one of these houses dwelt five or six hundred persons. They sleep in nets woven out of cotton, going to bed in mid-air with no other coverture. They eat squatting upon the ground. Their food is very good: an endless quantity of fish; a great abundance of sour cherries, shrimps, oysters, lobsters, crabs, and many other products of the sea. The meat which they eat most usually is what one may call human flesh a la mode. When they can get it, they eat other meat, of animals or birds, but they do not lay hold of many, for they have no dogs, and the country is a very thick jungle full of ferocious wild beasts. For this reason they are not wont to penetrate the jungle except in large parties.

The men have a custom of piercing their lips and cheeks and setting in these perforations ornaments of bone or stone; and do not suppose them small ones. Most of them have at least three holes, and some seven, and some nine, in which they set ornaments of green and white alabaster, half a palm in length and as thick as a Catalonian plum. This pagan custom is beyond description. They say they do this to make themselves look more fierce. In short, it is a brutal business.

Their marriages are not with one woman only, but they mate with whom they desire and without much ceremony. I know a man who had ten women. He was jealous of them, and if it happened that one of them was guilty, he punished her and sent her away. They are a very procreative people. They do not have heirs, because they do not have private property. When their children, that is, the females, are of age to procreate, the first who seduces one has to act as her father in place of the nearest relative. After they are thus violated, they marry.

Their women do not make any ceremony over childbirth, as do ours, but they eat all kinds of food, and wash themselves up to the very time of delivery, and scarcely feel any pain in parturition. [This statement that Indian women wash themselves during pregnancy was most startling to Europeans, who believed in the superstitious custom of unclean motherhood.]

They are a people of great longevity, for according to their way of attributing issue, they had known many men who had four generations of descendants. They do not know how to compute time in days, months, and years, but reckon time by lunar months. When they wished to demonstrate something involving time, they did it by placing pebbles, one for each lunar month. I found a man of advanced age who indicated to me with pebbles that he had seen seventeen hundred lunar months, which I judged to be a hundred and thirty-two years, counting thirteen moons to the year.

They are also a warlike people and very cruel to their own kind. All their weapons and the blows they strike are, as Petrarch says, "committed to the wind," for they use bows and arrows, darts, and stones. They use no shields for the body, but go into battle naked. They have no discipline in the conduct of their wars, except that they do what their old men advise. When they fight, they slaughter mercilessly. Those who remain on the field bury all the dead of their own side, but cut up and eat the bodies of their enemies. Those whom they seize as prisoners, they take for slaves to their habitations. If women sleep with a male prisoner and he is virile, they marry him with their daughters. At certain times, when a diabolical frenzy comes over them, they invite their kindred and the whole tribe, and they set before them a mother with all the children she has, and with certain ceremonies they kill them with arrow shots and eat them. They do the same thing to the above-mentioned slaves and to the children born of them. This is assuredly so, for we found in their houses human flesh hung up to smoke, and much of it. We purchased from them ten creatures, male as well as female, which they were deliberating upon for the sacrifice, or better to say, the crime. Much as we reproved them, I do not know that they amended themselves. That which made me the more astonished at their wars and cruelty was that I could not understand from them why they made war upon each other, considering that they held no private property or sovereignty of empire and kingdoms and did not know any such thing as lust for possession, that is, pillaging or a desire to rule, which appear to me to be the causes of wars and of every disorderly act. When we requested them to state the cause, they did not know how to give any other cause than that this curse upon them began in ancient times and they sought to avenge the deaths of their forefathers. In short, it is a brutal business. Indeed, one man among them confessed to me that he had shared in the eating of the flesh of more than two hundred corpses, and this I assuredly believe. It was enough for me!

As to the nature of the land, I declare it to be the most agreeable, temperate, and healthful, for in all the time that we were in it, which was ten months, none of us died and only a few fell ill. As I have already said, the inhabitants live a long time and do not suffer from infirmity or pestilence or from any unhealthy atmosphere. Death is from natural causes or from the hand of man. In conclusion, physicians would have a wretched standing in such a place.[7]

Because we went solely to make discoveries, and departed from Lisbon with a commission to that effect, and not to seek for any profit, we did not trouble ourselves to search the land or look for any gain. Thus we did not perceive in it anything that would be profitable to anyone; not because I do not believe that the land might not produce every kind of wealth, from its wonderful nature and from the climate of the region in which it is situated. It is not surprising that we did not at once become sensible of everything there that might make for profit, since the inhabitants value neither gold nor silver nor precious stones—nothing but feathers and the previously mentioned ornaments made of bone. I hope that this Serene King will send an expedition now to inspect it and that before many years pass it will bring to this kingdom of Portugal a handsome profit and a yearly income.

We found an endless growth of very good dyewood, enough to load all the ships that nowadays sail the seas, and free from cost. The same is true of the cassia fistula.[8]

We saw crystals and a great variety of savory and fragrant spices and drugs, but their properties are not known. The natives told us of gold and other metals and many miracle-working drugs, but I am one of those followers of Saint Thomas, who are slow to believe. Time will reveal everything.

The sky was clear there most of the time, and aglow with many bright stars, and I made notes on all of these, with their circuits. This is only a brief outline and a mere list of the things I saw in that country. Many things have been omitted, in order not to be wearisome and because you will find them in complete detail in my account of the voyage.

As yet I am remaining here at Lisbon awaiting that which the king may determine for me. Please God that what follows hereafter for me may be to promote His holy service and the salvation of my soul!

Chapter Nine

THE DISCOVERY OF A CONTINENT

Soon after disembarking in Lisbon, Amerigo wrote to Lorenzo: "We arrived at a new land which, for many reasons that are enumerated in what follows, we observed to be a continent." From the variety of its inhabitants and fauna and from its size, indicated by his observations on two voyages of the extent of its coastline and the volume of its rivers, he knew it to be "a continent"; and from its longitudinal width at the north and its continuance so far to the south, he knew it to be, not as everybody had thought an eastern extension of Asia, but a "new land."

Here was an entirely new, hitherto-unsuspected continent. Here was a continent unknown to the ancient geographers; for while they had believed in a land south of the equator, they had said it could not be inhabited; but his voyage had demonstrated that the southern continent in which they had believed had been only imaginary, because this land was inhabited. Thus, by rigorous logic it was a new continent. And if so, it was more than a new continent. It was proof of the existence of a Western Hemisphere [1] unguessed-at by any of the geographers. It was a New World.

All this Amerigo had perceived before he sailed back into the port of Lisbon. This was an idea of breath-taking magnitude, of concern not merely to the Portuguese and the Spanish, but to men of all countries. This was an idea big enough to compensate for his failure to find the Strait of Catigara and for his disappointment in not reaching India.

No other man of his day was so well prepared for making this discovery. He was prepared to interpret the findings of his own voyaging. He was like Leverrier who discovered Neptune by calculations based upon eccentricities in the orbit of Uranus. Given the data of both of his voyages, which only he was cognizant of (and it is uncontroverted that he explored much of the northern and the eastern coasts of South America and was the only man who had done so previous to his presentation to Lorenzo of the idea of a New World in the summer of 1502), and given a knowledge of cartography and cosmography such as few men had, he became aware of the inconsistencies between the accepted notions

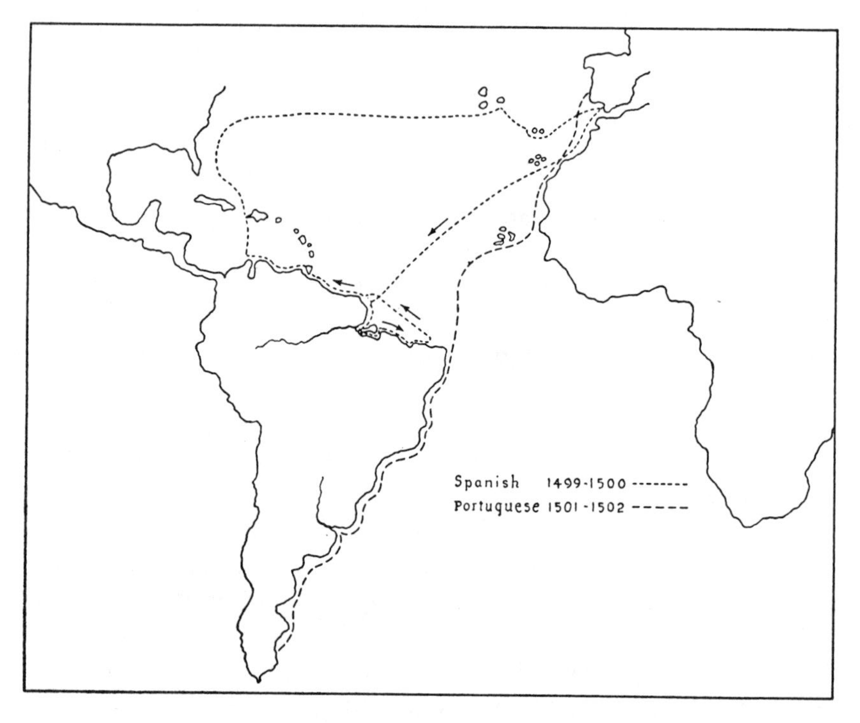

MAP SHOWING BOTH VOYAGES OF VESPUCCI

of traditional geography and the facts he had observed. He had discovered a new continent in the only way it was possible at that time to discover it, by extensive exploring coupled with well-grounded deductions in line with a remarkably near-to-accurate conception of the circumference of the earth.

And so he made his announcement of the greatest geographical fact ever revealed by any one man—a new continent. A New World! A Western Hemisphere! An astounding enlargement of the habitable earth! As though he were presenting mankind with half a planet! There is much more to this earth than Europe and Asia and Africa. There is also a New World, a new half of the earth, a never-before-dreamed-of Western Hemisphere. There is a whole new continent waiting for the men of Europe to explore and possess and thereon to begin a new civilization.

This was the most stupendous fact the Old World had ever encountered. In sheer magnitude the new continent was an astonishing gift. It was twice the size of Europe. It was fourteen percent of the land surface of the globe. While it was a discovery dependent not solely upon the Portuguese voyage but upon the Spanish voyage as well, the idea of it was brought to Europe on a Portuguese ship; [2] and since it was upon Amerigo's Portuguese voyage that he found the new idea, that voyage may be called, in view of this result, the most dynamic in its consequences of any ever achieved.[3]

He arrived in Lisbon with the knowledge that what Columbus had led men to was a new and separate hemisphere that blocked the way to Asia by the western route, unless there could be found a passage through it—a passage that was thousands of miles distant from the strait into the Gulf of the Ganges. Between Columbus, who thought he had reached Asia, and Magellan, who sought a passage through the New World to Asia, there was an intervening step, and that step was taken by Amerigo, who showed what lay between the Atlantic Ocean and the Far East.

He revolutionized geography, for his discovery of the new continent carried the unavoidable corollary that between the New World and Asia there was another ocean to cross, an ocean of which Columbus never dreamed, larger than the one in which Columbus navigated. Amerigo broke with the old theory that there was one single ocean which surrounded the land masses of the three old continents. His discovery smashed that theory for all impartial students. Columbus, it is true, still clung to it blindly and obstinately, and so did his brother Bartholomew; but they were in the rapidly dwindling minority.

Bartholomew's map of the world showed the findings of Columbus, including those of his last voyage. It omitted Cuba, or rather included it in the continent of Asia, for the Admiral would never admit that Cuba was an island. The map by Bartholomew Columbus, in agreement with the geographical conceptions of Christopher Columbus, was drawn in three sections on the margins of three separate pages of a copy of the Florence edition of the Admiral's letter from Jamaica of July 7, 1503, which was a description of his

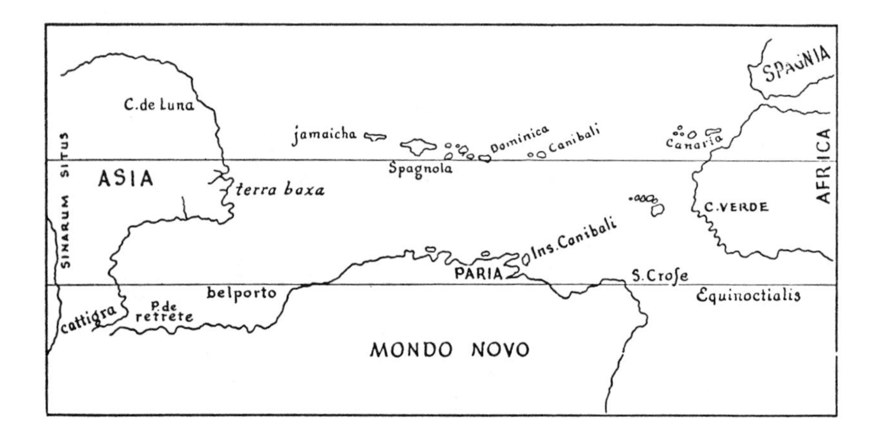

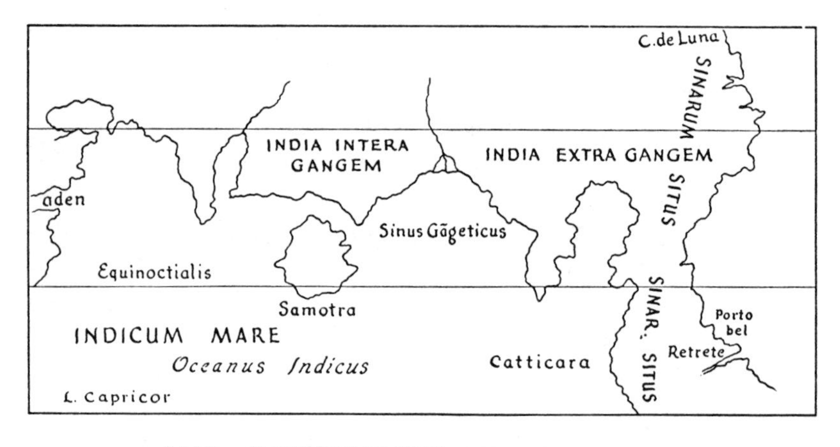

MAP—BARTHOLOMEW COLUMBUS, 1503

fourth voyage.[4] The term "Mondo Novo" (New World) used by Bartholomew and Christopher Columbus meant to them the recently-discovered, hitherto-unsuspected, and hence "new" part of Asia extending to the east. It did not mean to them a new and separate continent.[5]

The realization that there was a New World was no gradual dawning in the minds of Europeans, although the full consequences of the fact that there was a New World were only gradually perceived. The realization came with sharp suddenness ten years after 1492, borne by the evidence presented by Amerigo in 1502. The Portuguese court, merchants, scholars, and map-makers were the first to receive it, but it was common knowledge throughout Europe within a very short time.

Before the year was out in which Amerigo had returned to Lisbon, cartographers began to incorporate his great idea into their maps; for example, in the Portuguese portolano of 1502, in the world chart of Nicolo de Canerio Januensis, and in the chart which Alberto Cantino, envoy in Portugal of the Duke of Ferrara, procured in Lisbon for the duke.[6] On the portolano of 1502 the coastline of the new continent was shown in two sections, not connected, apparently because there was a gap between Amerigo's exploration for Spain along the north shore of Brazil in 1499 and his exploration for Portugal of the eastern shore of the continent. But the shape of half the continent was indicated. The southern section of coastline stopped a little below the latitude of the southern tip of Africa, since Amerigo in fairness to Spain withheld from the Portuguese knowledge of the coastline to the west of the Line of Demarcation. The map showed two equators on the new continent, for which the least lame explanation would seem to be that the map-maker was confused by the actual gap between Amerigo's two voyages, when theoretically there should have been an overlapping, since Amerigo's estimate of his farthest north on his Portuguese voyage (about five degrees south), as computed in relation to the accurately determined latitude of Cape St. Augustine, was more than a degree to the north of his farthest south on his Spanish voyage (six and a half degrees south—an erroneous estimate caused by refraction and lack of information as to the latitudes of the stars). Amerigo and the map-maker were too honest to force an agreement between two sets of incompatible data. The portolano gave no solution to the problem as to whether Cuba was an island or an eastern extension of a northern continent, but it left no doubt that Cuba was not part of Asia.

This portolano had far-reaching significance. Amerigo's concep-

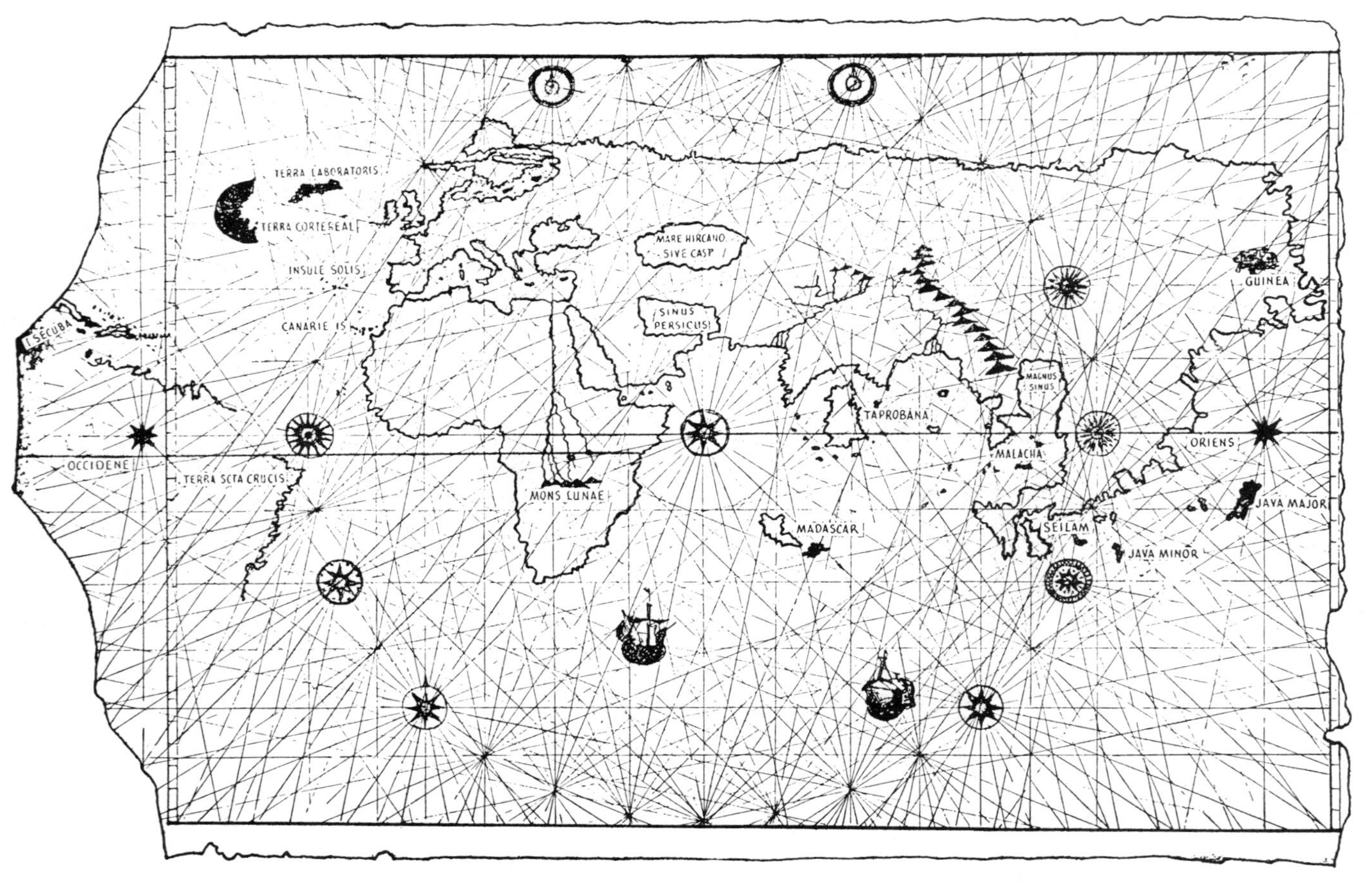

PORTOLANO OF 1502

tion of the western continent as a separate continent, a New World, was revealed by the right-hand section of the map, where eastern Asia ended clear of the margin, showing that another ocean, not the Atlantic, lay between the New World and Asia. Contrast the implications presented by this portolano of 1502, and the fixed convictions of Columbus as indicated by his brother's map.

The belief of Columbus that he had reached Asia was stated in an inscription on the map of Bartholomew along the west coast of Africa, to the effect that from Cape St. Vincent in Portugal going eastward to Catigara was two hundred and twenty-five degrees. To Columbus, therefore, the distance from Portugal to Catigara going westward was this number of degrees subtracted from three hundred and sixty, or one hundred and thirty-five degrees. Since he stated that "a degree measures on the equator fifty-six and two-thirds miles," he thus believed that the longitudinal distance from Portugal westward to Catigara was seven thousand six hundred and fifty Roman miles. Having persuaded himself that Española was about half as far to the west, he believed with subconscious deception that he had navigated so much farther westward on his fourth voyage (witness the map) as to be very near "Retrete," or the eastern end of the Strait of Catigara. He not only very greatly underestimated the size of the earth, but by exaggerating the number of degrees to the end of Asia going eastward, he correspondingly further underestimated the distance from Portugal to Asia going westward.

On the other hand Amerigo professed to follow Ptolemy, and Ptolemy, in the *Cosmographia* of 1482, for example, gave the longitudinal distance to Catigara from the Fortunate Isles as one hundred and eighty degrees, which would be eastward or westward the same. According to Amerigo's revised estimate of seventy-five Roman miles to a degree, this meant thirteen thousand five hundred Roman miles at the equator and was from a meridian several degrees west of Cape St. Vincent in Portugal. Thus he came to the conclusion that Catigara was more than six thousand miles farther west than Columbus thought it was.

Since Ptolemy placed Cadiz at six degrees east of the Fortunate Isles, the distance going westward from Cadiz to Catigara was one hundred and eighty-six degrees. Since Amerigo must have reduced his estimate of his farthest west in 1499 on his Spanish voyage from eighty-two and a half to about seventy-three degrees west of Cadiz, to compensate for his new conception of the length of a league, he now believed that from his farthest west on that voyage he was seventy-three less than a hundred and eighty-six, or one hundred and thirteen degrees from Catigara; and with his longer degree, this was eight thousand four hundred and seventy-five Roman miles, or far more than what Columbus believed to be the total distance between Portugal and Catigara.

Arguments as to longitudinal distances were more than theoretical. "To whom does the new continent belong?" was the practical and immediate question that concerned Portugal and Spain. Amerigo's discovery established a new field of competition between the two countries. The Treaty of Tordesillas became more important than ever. Amerigo's placing of the Line of Demarcation at the meridian of Cananor was of the greatest interest and significance to the rival powers. By naming Cananor and thus indicating the last port belonging to Portugal on the coast of the new continent, he gave Portugal all to which she was entitled. When the Portuguese later expanded their colony in the New World and occupied land west of the meridian of Cananor, they did so to the detriment of the rightful claims of the Spanish and in violation of the treaty.

The Old World to which Amerigo had brought the great idea had not progressed very much during his absence. The events of greatest moment to him were those connected with the voyages of other men. Juan de la Cosa had undertaken a fourth voyage in 1501 and had returned safely from a port he named "Retrete," escaping a hurricane in a ship of the fleet in which Rodrigo de Bastidas was returning. His escape had occasioned great rejoicing in Spain, especially since he brought home with him considerable treasure. In Lisbon sailors were still talking of the return in October of one of the two caravels which His Most Serene Majesty had sent the past year under the command of Gaspar Corte-Real, which had come home without that leader. And in the spring his brother Miguel sailed in search of him, but men were doubting whether Miguel himself would ever be seen again. The one caravel which did return reported having explored between six hundred and seven hundred miles of coastline of a country more than two thousand miles distant to the west and northwest of Portugal.

Amerigo did not remain long in Portugal. An Italian named Piero di Nofri di Giovanni Rondinelli, writing in connection with the return to Lisbon in September of four Portuguese caravels from Calicut, stated as much in a letter dated October 3, 1502. After recounting the gains of those who had ventured into the new and successful trade with India, Rondinelli wrote from Seville that "Amerigo Vespucci will be here in a few days, a man who has endured labor enough and has had little profit." [7]

Amerigo had his own good reasons for returning to his home in Seville. There is no ground for assuming, as some have done, that his departure from Portugal was occasioned by some injustice there received. Even if, contrary to his expectations, the King of Portugal permanently retained his ship's record and the charts he had made, in accordance with the Portuguese law that forbade the exportation of maps, he was not being discriminated against. Nor was he being suspected by the Portuguese government of crooked intentions. Unlike Juan de la Cosa, who was sent to Lisbon the next year to find out all he could about the plans of the Portuguese, Amerigo was not being treated as a spy. There is no reason to believe that he fled from Portugal or that he was asked to leave.

He returned to Spain because he had explored all the coastline of that portion of the new continent which belonged to Portugal, without finding any passage through it toward India. He now knew that such a passage would be entirely separate from the Strait of Catigara and that it could be found only in some region farther west, on the Spanish side of the Line of Demarcation, either far to the south, beyond fifty degrees south, or else in latitudes north of the new continent. He had no wish to remain in Portugal, since his discovery of the new continent showed that all the yet-unknown coastline in the West would belong to Spain. Here was the consideration that motivated him. His aim had been single and undivided from the beginning and continued so throughout his double shift from the service of Spain to the service of Portugal and back again. He wanted to find a western route to India. Now that the finding of it promised to be more difficult than ever, he was keen to return to the only country in whose service he could pursue the search.

The atmosphere in Spain was more congenial to one of Amerigo's temperament. Spain was less suspicious and less fearful than Portugal, because she felt she had less to lose, now that Portugal was growing rich through her monopolistic trade with India. Spain was inferior to Portugal on the sea and was therefore making a great effort to surpass her rival. When the Moors were driven out, national energies were released, and a new Spain was being built. Salamanca University was re-endowed by King Ferdinand, and the University of Alcala was established by Ximénez. Some of the nobles took to a show of learning, and Queen Isabella began to collect books, since printing had made possible a new hobby for the wealthy. In scholarship there was no jealousy of foreigners. Lucio Marineo was brought from Sicily, Antonio and Alexander Geraldino from Tuscany, and Peter Martyr, of Anghiera, from Arona. Spain was ready to appreciate the accomplishment and the capacity of Amerigo Vespucci.

Back to Seville, therefore, Amerigo went, eager to be at home again. He was weary from voyaging and had not shaken off the malaria, which had become a chronic enemy. He needed physical rest. But his physical condition and his whereabouts were of little importance, whether in Portugal or in Spain, for his idea of a New World was marching into all Europe. That great idea could not be stopped by any national boundary. It was advancing into the consciousness of all mankind.

VESPUCCI ON SHIPBOARD

Chapter Ten

THE FORGERIES

Destiny had been kind to Amerigo on his voyages, and in four years of adventuring he had accomplished enough in practical navigation, in study of the southern sky, and in geographical discovery to satisfy the loftiest ambition. But what the storms of the sea and the perils of an unknown coast did not do to engulf him, the greed of men was to effect. He became the victim of an unparalleled fate. Many men have suffered from active slander or from passive misunderstanding, from deliberate enmity or from a sometimes more dreadful indifference. Upon Amerigo Vespucci, however, was inflicted a unique injury; for he suffered almost irreparably, not at first by direct vilification, though that came later in heavy measure, but by misrepresentation. By forged quotation, by libelous exaggeration, he was made to appear as a boaster, a liar, a quack navigator. Thus, excess of fame defamed him.

What happened was this. Lorenzo di Pier Francesco de' Medici died in June, 1503. The loss of his friend and patron was a severe loss to Amerigo personally, but worse than that it opened the way for irresponsible men who proceeded to do something which was bound ultimately to besmirch Amerigo's character. Lorenzo had treasured Amerigo's letters describing his voyages and had often proudly shown them to his visitors, who in turn started much talk about them throughout Florence. Now that their recipient was dead, they were part of an estate, in the possession of executors, and they were read by various persons who had no qualms against embroidering upon them and circulating their contents in a garbled form. Amerigo's scrupulousness in truth telling, his reliance upon careful observation and upon reason, could not be appreciated by the general public of his day. Knowledge could be preserved in purity only if it were kept from vulgar misrepresentation; not if it were cheapened, sensationalized, made extravagant to suit the taste of the populace.

Thus, while he was in the Iberian Peninsula his letters in far-off Florence were unprotected from pirating and misquotation. He had told his fellow Europeans something which electrified them, that there was a New World beyond the western ocean. Neither Columbus nor Da Gama nor any other navigator had brought home a fact of such great publicity value. The news was so exciting that men were not satisfied with merely passing it to one another by word of mouth. There were no newspapers to flourish headlines, but the printing press nevertheless was available. Any account of the New World supposedly written by Amerigo Vespucci would command the widest attention.

And so the printing press was called into play, and the first of the forgeries was born: *Mundus Novus* (New World) in August, 1504, purporting to be a letter by Amerigo Vespucci addressed to Lorenzo di Pier Francesco de' Medici, now translated from the Italian and printed in Latin in Vienna.[1]

Mundus Novus was based partly upon correct data, but in a confused form. It was an amplification of some of the material in the letters of 1501 and 1502 from Cape Verde and Lisbon, and may have been in part based upon some work Amerigo was himself preparing but, as far as we know, never published. *Mundus Novus* correctly ascribed to Amerigo the discovery of a new continent:

> Those new regions which we found and explored with the fleet, at the cost, and by the command of this Most Serene King of Portugal . . . we may rightly call a New World. Because our ancestors had no knowledge of them, and it will be a matter wholly new to all those who hear about them. For this transcends the view held by our ancients . . . that there was no continent to the south beyond the equator, but only the sea which they named the Atlantic. . . . In those southern parts I have found a continent more densely peopled and abounding in animals than our Europe or Asia or Africa. . . . Part of this new continent lies in the torrid zone beyond the equator toward the antarctic pole, for it begins [its most eastern point, Cape St. Augustine] eight degrees beyond the equator.

Mundus Novus restated Amerigo's assertion that he had followed the coast of the new continent to fifty degrees south. "We sailed along this coast until we . . . found the antarctic pole fifty degrees higher than the horizon. We advanced to within seventeen and a half degrees of the Antarctic Circle." The Antarctic Circle is at 66 ° 32 ′, and "to within seventeen and a half degrees" of that circle was to beyond forty-nine degrees south.

Along with much undeniably correct data, along with Amerigo's diagraming of the stars of the Southern Hemisphere, *Mundus Novus* contained patent absurdities, such as the author's statement that he had written "at some length" of his voyage, and then within a few sentences, that he was sending to the same person a brief outline of it—"only capital matters." *Mundus Novus* contained contradictions, such as an unbending coast with a bend in it: "That land . . . stretches forth in the form of a very long and unbending coast. . . . We reached a bend." It contained also the confusion in arithmetic: "We cruised for the space of two months and three days before any land appeared," and "of the sixty-seven days of our sailing." It made Amerigo a small-minded boaster: "I was more skilled than all the ship-masters of the whole world."

Whoever wrote *Mundus Novus* seemed to have been ignorant of Amerigo's Spanish voyage, yet *Mundus Novus* was supposed to have been addressed to the same person to whom he had written of his Spanish voyage in his letter of July 18, 1500. On one page of *Mundus Novus* was the statement that this was a "first voyage," and on another page the incompatible statement that there had been "two other voyages."

The voyage in *Mundus Novus* was impossible:

> Following the coast of this continent toward the east . . . we sailed along until at length we reached a bend where the shore made a turn to the south; and from that point where we first touched land to that corner it was about three hundred leagues, in which sailing distance we frequently landed and had friendly relations with those people.

This was impossible, for it is certain from various corroborating sources that Amerigo was at Cape Verde on June 4, 1501, the date of his meeting with ships of Cabral's expedition and of his letter to Lorenzo. If he sailed from Cape Verde the very next day, June 5, "sixty-seven days of sailing," as *Mundus Novus* had it, carried him to August 11. Amerigo named Cape S. Rocco on August 16, five days later. Five days was insufficient time to have sailed three hundred leagues, even if he had not "frequently landed." Even if he had reached the continent "on the seventh day of August," or "two months and three days" after June 5, the nine days from August 7 to 16 would have been insufficient time to have made good "a shortage of fire-wood and water" and to have sailed three hundred leagues with frequent stops to have "friendly relations" with the natives.

There were numerous inconsistencies in *Mundus Novus.* As C. Manfroni has said, *Mundus Novus* contained such "vulgarisms," such "scientifically inexact affirmations," that it is "absolutely inadmissible" that he wrote it. It is indeed "alien to his character."

Most impossible of all was the last paragraph of *Mundus Novus:*

> Jocundus, the translator, is turning this epistle from the Italian into the Latin tongue, that Latinists may know how many wonderful things are daily being discovered, and that the audacity of those who seek to scrutinize heaven and sovereignty and to know more than it is licit to know may be held in check; inasmuch as ever since that remote time when the world began, the vastness of the earth and what therein is contained has been unknown.—Master John Otmar, Vienna, printer, August, 1504.

One may, like Shakespeare, have little Latin, but enough to see the "joker" in "Jocundus." No man who had written such a work as *Mundus Novus* purports to be would have stultified himself by giving the manuscript to a translator with permission to publish it as an example of sacrilegious audacity.

The Jocundus paragraph was evidence that the great idea was tremendously disturbing to the traditional schoolmen. To their minds diagraming the positions of the stars in the Southern Hemisphere was impious for the same reason that diagraming the northern stars by Hipparchus had caused Pliny to censure Hipparchus for his "almost impious daring in attempting to catalogue the fixed stars and to determine the place of each so that future astronomers may note whether any changes really occurred in them." Here is a key to the Jocundus paragraph. The astronomical portion of *Mundus Novus* challenged the fixed ideas of some of the philosophers.

Another forgery was published in September, 1504, a month later than *Mundus Novus.* This was a longer work purporting to be an account of four voyages of discovery and was often known as *Letter from Amerigo Vespucci to Piero Soderini, Gonfaloniere, the Year*

1504. This Soderini letter we shall call by the more descriptive title, *Four Voyages.*[2]

The four voyages presented were:

1) 1497, for the Spanish kings, ascribing to Vespucci priority of one year over Columbus in reaching the coast of South America, and making him the first European to reach the continent of North America (Central America, Mexico, Florida, and so forth).

2) 1499, for the Spanish, to South America, exploring from five degrees south to fifteen degrees north. This was based upon Vespucci's actual voyage of that year.

3) 1501, for the Portuguese king, to five degrees south on the coast of South America, and thence to thirty-two (fifty-two?) degrees south. This was based upon Vespucci's actual voyage for the Portuguese.

4) 1503, for Portugal, to eighteen degrees south on the coast of Brazil.

When it became evident that Columbus had been in error in maintaining that he had landed on the shores of Asia and that Amerigo Vespucci's contributions to geographical knowledge were accurate and of consummate significance, some men for a time belittled the importance of the initial success of Columbus. Since the discredited Columbus had made four voyages, some people were prone to assume that Amerigo had made at least as many. This assumption was supported by patriotic enthusiasm, Florence desiring to outshine her rival Genoa. Such psychology shaped the forgery of the *Four Voyages.*

The forgery was motivated also by rivalry in another direction. Amerigo had written of his travels in letters to his friend and former employer, Lorenzo di Pier Francesco de' Medici. Now in 1504 the Gonfaloniere of Florence was Piero Soderini, the political boss or ruler of the city. He had newly risen to power above the Medici, whom he had temporarily downed, and was jealous of the Medici as potential political rivals. When Lorenzo di Pier Francesco de' Medici, of all men in Florence, had received first news of the discovery of a New World, Soderini was envious; and when the *Four Voyages* was published, flatterers of the new political boss planted in it the implication that it was addressed to Soderini, to enhance his prestige. They made it appear that this Soderini letter was an advance notice or prospectus of a large detailed work not yet ready for publication and that Amerigo had told Soderini more than he had told Lorenzo; thus the addition of the two extra voyages received further motivation. All this was obviously false to those who knew the character of Piero Soderini, a man who was "feeble and timorous, unequal to the moment," certainly not the kind of man the adventurous Amerigo would hold as a close friend to be made the recipient of letters descriptive of his work as an explorer. Soderini was not only in the opposite political camp to Amerigo's patron, Lorenzo, but there was definite antagonism between the Vespucci and Soderini families, as evidenced by the fact that Giovanni Vespucci, Guidantonio's son, took part in a plot against Piero Soderini.

The *Four Voyages* thus carried patent evidence of forgery, as though the lies in the text of it were not enough. The first edition, or earliest known edition, of the letter describing the four voyages was addressed to the Gonfaloniere Soderini in language identifying him, but without naming him and without any dedication. Printed works were almost invariably dedicated in that day. The absence of dedication was prima-facie evidence of forgery. The early editions of the *Four Voyages* were printed without date and with every characteristic of spurious writings.

The dates given in the *Four Voyages* for the "first" voyage were May, 1497, to October, 1498, thus conflicting with the period of Amerigo's presumable activities as Berardi's successor in Andalusia from mid-April, 1497, to the end of May, 1498, while preparing the ships for the third voyage of Columbus. One text of the *Four Voyages* made him return from the "first" voyage on October 18, 1498. Another made him return from that voyage a year later, on October 1, 1499. Still another gave the date as October 15, 1499. Throughout the *Four Voyages* there is a confusion of dates and duration of voyages. Contemporary letters to Florence from various Florentines living in Lisbon and Seville frequently gave the actual dates of sailings and arrivals. In the face of this knowledge possessed by his countrymen and the certain knowledge of the Spanish government, Amerigo could not have ventured to falsify dates, as he would have had to do if the *Four Voyages* were genuine.

The *Four Voyages* presented a further confusion in latitudes. On the "first" voyage the landfall was made at sixteen degrees north.

The only possible identification of this landfall was Cape Gracias a Dios on the coast of Honduras, at fifteen degrees north. Thence, according to the "first" voyage, the ships proceeded along the coast always in the direction of northwest for more than eight hundred and seventy leagues, or for thirty-one hundred English miles—in other words, in a direct line from Honduras across Mexico and Arizona to somewhere in California.

Columbus had discovered and named the Land of Parias in 1498 on his third voyage, so that the reading "Parias" in the alleged "first" voyage of Amerigo, in 1497, not only raised the issue of priority between the two explorers, but identified the geography of the "first" voyage as certainly not northwest from a landfall at sixteen degrees north. Absurd as all this was, people persisted for many years in accepting the "first" voyage as genuine, because as partisans they could not bear to relinquish the pleasing fantasy that Amerigo reached the continent of North America several days before John Cabot. A careful comparison, however, of the *Four Voyages* with the genuine letter of July 18, 1500, would have shown that the alleged "first" and "second" voyages in the spurious letter to Soderini were based upon the two parts of the complete voyage, and actual voyage, of 1499–1500, first to the northwest along the coast of South America, and second, from Haiti (Española) north to latitude thirty-five and a half degrees north before returning to Spain.

The earliest version of the *Four Voyages* was written in a barbaric jargon with ignorance of correct forms. It contained serious language errors, including many words that were a corrupt and bastard sort of Spanish-Italian. Amerigo was incapable of these ignorant hispanicisms, which were such as no Florentine of the time wrote from Seville or Lisbon. He had lived in his native Florence until he was nearly thirty-eight, and at that age a man's linguistic habits are formed. Thereafter, in Spain, Amerigo had kept in constant contact with his fellow countrymen. He was a man capable of expressing himself in correct Latin, in perfect Italian, and in good Spanish. Whoever composed the *Four Voyages* could not write intelligently in the language of Tuscany. The work was obviously a forgery by someone who knew some Spanish, but no Portuguese. Amerigo had been for two years or more with the Portuguese.

As for the alleged "fourth" voyage, no definite record was made of Amerigo's whereabouts in 1503–1504. He may have been at sea, but there is no evidence to substantiate the assertion that he was. At any rate, the "fourth" voyage was not important enough to evoke controversy, for it added no further geographical knowledge to what was related in the "third" voyage, which was itself in part copied from *Mundus Novus*.

The demand in Amerigo's day, as in ours, was for spiced-up narratives. Amerigo's genuine letters had been too dispassionate, and he had presented too calmly his startling, revolutionizing idea of a New World. He had been too truthful. He had told no tales of prodigies, of stone giants, pygmies, one-eyed cannibals. No hermaphrodites, double-headed men, dog-headed men, half-men with heads below their shoulders, no tailed tribes, no sea-serpents. With so tremendous an idea as a new continent, men felt his story should be correspondingly sensational.

All printers (there had been two hundred and sixty-eight printers in the city of Venice alone) faced the competition of an overstocked book market. The composers of the *Four Voyages* did their best to attract readers. Amerigo had written in a letter to Lorenzo that he had slept among the natives. The *Four Voyages* made him say that he slept with native women; it made him tell how the natives defecated; it made him suggest things he dared not tell. The first consideration with the forgers was to produce a booklet of succulent fare, juicy enough to sell. They put in a storm and a shipwreck—well-intentioned improvements. With pious enthusiasm they made their hero boast of his superiority as a navigator. We have seen how they increased the number of his voyages and how with innocent exaggeration they told of voyages he never took and could not have taken and how they confidently gave him priority over Columbus. What difference could it make to his great idea if they threw in some ingenious contradictions, or tossed in some guileless absurdities, or an idiocy such as, "near the equator, where in the month of June it is winter"? What harm could it do if they mixed up the directions of the compass, or put words into his mouth that made him a fool? It seemed a legitimate speculation in literature to profit upon curiosity with regard to the New World—no damage to the great idea. There was a New World, a "Mundus Novus," and people in all lands wished to be entertained in reading about it.

Thus the forgeries were born. Printed in Latin and Italian, then frequently reprinted in various languages as the demand grew, thus they were disseminated. The man himself was in Spain and could not stop them. Nothing, indeed, could have stopped them, for they perfectly fitted the popular fancy. The uncovering of nakedness was the most shocking and the most provocative conception of Amerigo's day, and whereas in his private letters he had written that to dwell upon the nudity of the natives "would be entering upon obscenity" and that it was "better to keep silence," it was as follows that the forged *Four Voyages* [3] dwelt upon it:

We neared the land, and before we reached it, observed many people running along the shore. . . . We saw that they were a naked race. . . . What we learned concerning their manner of life and customs was that they go entirely nude, men as well as women, without covering any shameful part, just as they issued from their mothers' wombs. . . . They have no hair on the body, except long black hair on the head. . . . They do not let hair grow on the eyebrows, in the eyelashes, nor in any other part of the body except the head; for they conceive of hair as ugly. . . . They sleep in large nets made of cotton, suspended in the air. . . . They are neat and cleanly of person, since they wash themselves constantly. When, pardon my mentioning it, they evacuate the bowels, they do it with utmost concealment; and the more cleanly and modest they are in this, the more filthy and shameless they are in making water. Even while speaking to us, without turning their backs or showing any shame, they let go such nastiness. . . . They do not practise marriage: each man takes all the women he desires; and when he wishes to discard them, he repudiates them without discrediting himself or disgracing the woman; for in this the woman has as much liberty as the man. They are not very jealous, and are excessively libidinous and the women much more than the men; for I refrain out of decency from telling you of the art with which they gratify their immoderate lust. They are very prolific, and do not avoid work during pregnancy. They give birth so easily that the following day they walk around everywhere, and especially to wash themselves in the rivers; and they are sound as fish. They are so lacking in affection and so cruel that, if they become angry with their husbands, they immediately by artificial means destroy the embryo within the womb, and bring about an abortion. . . . They are women of charming person, very well proportioned, so that their bodies show no ill-shaped part or limb. And although they go about completely nude, they are fleshy women, and that part of their sexual organ which he who has never seen it may imagine, is invisible; for their thighs conceal all save that part for which nature provided no concealment, and which is, speaking modestly, the *mons veneris*. In short they are no more ashamed of displaying their sex organs than we are in showing the nose and mouth. Very rarely will you see low hanging paps on a woman, or a belly shrunken from too much childbearing, or other wrinkles; for all look as though they had never born a child. They made it obvious that they desired to copulate with us Christians. . . . The greatest mark of friendship which they show you is that they give you their wives and their daughters, and fathers or mothers feel highly honored when they bring you their daughter, even though she be a virgin, if you sleep with her. In this practice they express the fullest hospitality. . . . Three leagues from the coast we came to a village. . . . Here we spent the night. They offered us their women in such a way that we could not refuse them. After we had been there that night and half of the next day, countless numbers of people came out of curiosity to see us. And the elders invited us to come farther inland to other villages, indicating their intention of doing us very great honor; wherefore we decided to go; and it would be out of the question for me to tell you all the honor they did us.

The fact that his private letters to a friend were pirated, misquoted, and that new ones were forged, printed, translated, reprinted, in a day when there was no copyright law, was altogether beyond Amerigo's control. His letters showed how consistently he sought for accuracy and validity. Yet this honest man—so painstaking in his observations, so scrupulous in relating as true no more than he had himself verified—this lover of truth was made to appear as a cheap and vulgar falsifier. The printing of books, which had been begun in Europe in the year of his birth, which was the principal gift to progress in his time and was coming to be valued as an indispensable invention for the dissemination of knowledge, now in this first notable instance revealed the destructive force inherent in its misuse. To have the spurious *Mundus Novus* and *Four Voyages* foisted upon readers in Europe must have galled and exasperated him beyond measure.

The publication of the forgeries must have taken out of his mouth the pleasant taste of news that the *signoria* of Florence, which had honored him after his Spanish voyage by ordering that the house in which he was born should be illuminated three nights and by decreeing that the Vespucci family were to be allowed to attach a beacon or lighthouse to their dwellings, had again organized a public fête in his honor. Only in Spain, where the truth was known as to what he had done and had not done, only where he could personally correct the false impression created by the forgeries, only in the Medici household and among his friends and those who knew his honesty, could the tide of misrepresentation be stemmed.

Ferdinand, the natural son of Columbus, who began to be a collector of printed books some time after returning from his father's fourth voyage, procured a copy of *Four Voyages.*[4] It is apparent that he knew it to be a forgery, else he would have protested, in the legal proceedings that were held to establish his father's rights, the attempt in *Four Voyages* to overthrow his father's priority. The true dates of Amerigo's voyages were too well known in Spain and Portugal for the *Four Voyages* to be accepted there; but those dates were not known in Italy, France, the Low Countries, and Germany, where the pamphlets were being printed. *Four Voyages* did not sell well in Florence, probably because many there knew it to be false, but it was selling well elsewhere. And so the clouds of misrepresentation began to rise about Amerigo, though they did not obscure his true stature immediately. "Truth always gets above falsehood as oil above water," was a Spanish proverb that might have given him comfort, but not if he could have foreseen the centuries that would intervene before the truth would triumph. The world would someday know that he had nothing to do with the writing of *Four Voyages,* but until then their shadow would lie upon his deeds, upon his scientific contributions, upon his reputation, upon his character. The forgeries came to be accepted as genuine; and then, to explain the false statements, men said he was a liar. In the ensuing confusion men lost sight of the fact that Amerigo, though physically he had reached the continent later than Columbus, had been mentally first in realizing what it was. Only long afterward did anyone begin to question the authorship of the forgeries. Thus for generations he was distrusted as a charlatan, and most people got into a fog as to what he had actually accomplished, though they did retain an instinctive feeling that it must have been something important, because the repercussions of the first presentation to Europe of the idea of a New World could not be lost, even after men had become so accustumed to it that they forgot what a tremendous idea it had been.

The first man to suggest that *Four Voyages* was a forgery was M. F. Force, who said in 1879:

The only way I see out of the difficulties which surround these letters is to say they were not written by Vespucci. There is some warrant for this conclusion in the absolute inattention and indifference to these letters among the contemporaries of Vespucci in Spain. If any person in Spain supposed that this narrative had been written by Vespucci, if any person in Spain supposed that Vespucci ever claimed to have visited the coast of South America in 1497, there would have been some mention of it in the case of the heirs of Columbus against the crown, where the government strained every nerve to restrict the extent of the actual discoveries made by Columbus; and the friends and partisans of Columbus would have shown some resentment against Vespucci. But the friends and opponents of Columbus alike ignored, as if it did not exist, this narrative that was flooding France and Germany. . . . Only after the *Four Voyages* were in the literature and belief of Europe in all countries outside of Spain and Portugal, did Las Casas attack the veracity of Vespucci.

The *Mundus Novus* and the *Four Voyages*, for four hundred years accepted as the published works of Vespucci, have been used as a stock puzzle in graduate study in the history of exploration, geography, and cartography. No satisfactory solution to the problems they present has ever been obtained on the strength of their retention as genuine. In 1926 Professor Alberto Magnaghi, of Palermo, whom Professor Charles E. Nowell, of Fresno State College, called the "reputed foremost living authority on Vespucci," [5] presented his thesis (*Amerigo Vespucci, studio critico*) that both the *Mundus Novus* and the *Four Voyages* are spurious. Of this scholarly piece of work C. Manfroni says: "In freeing Vespucci from paternity of the *Mundus Novus* and the *Four Voyages*, all, or practically all, contradictions are eliminated."

Either *Four Voyages* and portions of *Mundus Novus* are spurious, or the letters to Lorenzo di Pier Francesco de' Medici are. They could not be by the same man. If this assumption be correct, then we need to compare the rival documents as to their tone, their air of genuineness, their agreement with established facts. Of the unanimous verdict on that comparison there can be no doubt. It is credible that the printed versions were pirated from the letters to Lorenzo di Pier Francesco with amplifications added to make a best seller. It is incredible that the letters to Lorenzo were handwritten forgeries copied from a widely published work.

As for philological evidence, let an authority speak. Professor George Tyler Northup in an exhaustive study of the texts of the various versions of the Letter to Piero Soderini,[6] presents textual evidence which corroborates the view of those who have denied that the first voyage was authentic.

> Much of the material found in the first voyage of the Soderini Letter also appears in the *Mundus Novus* which has to do with the third voyage. . . . There is nothing inherently improbable in the assumption that the Soderini Letter may have had an antecedent Spanish form. . . . A Spanish origin seems to be confirmed by the numerous hispanicisms.

Professor Northup states the theory of those who seek to account for these hispanicisms:

> Vespucci had lived so long in Spain and Portugal, had sailed on so many voyages with cosmopolitan crews, that he had virtually forgotten his own language and had come to speak and write a sort of *lingua franca* in which it had become as natural for him to employ a Spanish or a Portuguese as an Italian word.

Then, in answer to this argument, Professor Northup refers to the autograph letter of Vespucci's dated December 9, 1508, and says:

> This letter is written in Vespucci's hand throughout. . . . We should not be surprised if the document revealed traces of Italian idiom. But nothing of the sort is apparent. The language is pure Castilian. We are asked, then, to believe that an educated man, capable of expressing himself in good Spanish, was incapable of writing intelligently his mother tongue. . . . The dilemma is unavoidable: either Vespucci, the gifted navigator and astronomer, who wrote good Castilian, was a hopeless illiterate in his mother tongue, or else the errors in the Soderini Letter, of the sort mentioned, must be ascribed to a translator. The present writer cannot accept the first supposition.
>
> Then there is the evidence of the so-called apocryphal letters. . . . On purely historical grounds Luigi Hughes and Uzielli contended that these letters were authentic. There is a growing tendency among scholars to accept them. . . . They offer evidence, with all allowance made for italianization in copying, that Vespucci was capable of writing intelligible Italian. . . . Whatever the difficulties in the way of ac-

cepting the theory of the existence of a Spanish original for the Soderini Letter, I cannot but feel that greater difficulties confront the critic who would contend that Vespucci himself wrote the absurd jargon found in the Italian versions.

In the light of the above, Professor Northup's subsequent opinion is most interesting. In a letter dated January 31, 1941, from which he has given the writer permission to quote, Professor Northup writes:

> I saw so many Hispanisms shining through the bad Italian that I thought I had to do with a clumsy translation out of a Spanish original. I now consider this a mistake. . . . I now think that there was no Spanish original. This is probably another strange example of the lingua franca hispanized Italians used.
>
> Certainly the Four Voyages arouse much suspicion. There are suppressions and probably deliberate falsifications. . . . To attempt to plot the Vespucci voyages from such a source is sheer nonsense.

Thus the philologist Professor Northup supports the major contention of Force, Magnaghi, and Manfroni.

While the forgeries were being disseminated, Amerigo was busy with matters pertaining to navigation and was formulating plans which he hoped to persuade the government to adopt. But the whole enterprise of further exploration received a temporary setback from the death of Queen Isabella in November, 1504, and from the country's preoccupation with a war being successfully waged in southern Italy, at the price of temporary paralysis of movements in other fields.

Columbus had returned (November 7, 1504) from his last voyage, not in chains as from his third voyage, but ill, worn out from months of privation while stranded on the coast of Jamaica. He had explored the coast of Nicaragua, Costa Rica, Veragua, and the Isthmus of Panama, but he had sailed on this voyage under the same prohibition against landing on his own island Española, which he had himself tried to enforce against competitors, and he had met with misfortune. He had been shipwrecked, and rescue had been delayed. Now, back in Spain, he was wretchedly poor, living upon borrowings, embittered by his struggle against an unsympathetic world.

Early in February, Amerigo visited him in Seville, and knowing what Columbus had suffered because of court intrigues, he brought what cheer he could. Columbus, in an unhappy state, was in a mood to complain against his enemies, rail against the men who had dispossessed him of his contract rights in the West Indies, and most feelingly express his disappointment over his own son, the spoiled courtier Don Diego, who had squandered most of his father's money and given no love in return. Not to be relished was the reflection that he had spent his life seeking wealth and power for a son who was a wastrel. Now, deprived of everything except his title, there was little consolation in the assurance that his name would be long remembered.

The government owed him money, which it must be made to pay. But he could not travel to the court to press his demands, for he could not walk, and the army had commandeered all the mules. Fortuitously, Amerigo Vespucci was going to the court, and so Columbus asked Amerigo to speak a word in his behalf and use all his influence. This Amerigo promised to do.

We may well believe that on this occasion Amerigo asked Columbus whether he had found or heard rumors of any strait in the region which he had visited on his fourth voyage and had named Veragua, for Amerigo never gave up the hope that he might some day discover a strait through the land in the Western Hemisphere. We do not know whether Columbus told him the definite location of the coastline he had so recently discovered, between the latitudes of sixteen degrees north and nine degrees north, or whether he was as secretive as he had been when he wrote:

> Let the pilots make known, if they themselves know it, the location of Veragua! I say that they cannot give other information or account except that they went with me to some lands where there is much gold and to insist that they did this; but if they are ignorant of the route by which to return there and if they want to go there, they will be obliged to make a new discovery of it!

There was no justification for such secretiveness, since he had failed to find the "much gold" which he said was in Veragua, nor in all probability did he really believe there was much gold where he had seen so little in the hands of the natives. His reason for concealing the location of Veragua was his desire to thwart others who might hope to enrich themselves in a land which he felt belonged to him, its discoverer. As for gold, his finding so little of it in Veragua and the Isthmus and the islands of the West Indies had made him fancy that there must be more gold south of the equator than north of it. No doubt he was surprised to learn that Amerigo had not become wealthy through his voyage for Portugal into the Southern Hemisphere.

Columbus remained to the end unyielding in his conviction that the large territory south of Española, which Amerigo called a New World, was only an extension of Asia. After his discoveries on his fourth voyage he wrote that "the countries bordering on the Great Sinus stand in relationship to Veragua as Tortosa is to Fuentarabia, or as Pisa is to Venice." He believed it would take a ship only ten days to sail from Española to the River Ganges, because he thought it was only a thousand miles.

Amerigo bore to Don Diego the letter [7] which Columbus importuned him to carry:

To my very dear Son, Don Diego Colón, at the Court.
My dear Son,

Diego Mendez departed here on Monday, the third of this month. Since his departure I have talked with Amerigo Vespucci, the bearer of this letter, who is going to court on some business connected with navigation. He has at all times shown a desire to serve me, and he is an honorable man. As with many others, fortune has not treated him kindly, and his labors have not been as rewarding as he deserves. He is going with a sincere desire to procure a favorable turn of affairs for me, if it is in his power.

I know not, here, what instructions to give him that will help my cause, for I am ignorant of what will be required there. He goes determined to accomplish for me everything possible. Find out what can be done there to help, and go to work on it, so that he may be fully informed and able to devote himself to presenting my case; and let everything be done with secrecy, that no suspicions may arise. I have told him all that I can concerning the business, and have informed him of all the payments which I have received and what is due.

This letter is intended also for the adelantado [Bartholomew, the brother of Columbus], that he may take advantage of any advice on the subject. His highness believes that the ships were in the best and richest region of the Indies, and if he desires to know anything more on the subject, I will satisfy him by word of mouth, for I cannot tell him by letter.

May our Lord have you in His holy keeping.

Done at Seville, February 5, 1505.

Thy father, who loves thee better than himself.

Christopher Colón

Amerigo delivered this letter to Don Diego, but was unable to effect any amelioration in the fortunes of the Admiral. Yet his own prestige was growing. In appreciation of his work as navigator and cartographer, Queen Joanna of Castile made him a citizen of Castile by a decree of April 5, 1505, and gave him the following royal letter of naturalization:

> Dona Juana by the Grace of God: In order to do the proper thing and show grace to you, Américo Vespucio, Florentine, in recognition of your fidelity and certain good services you have rendered, and which I expect that you will do from henceforward; by this present I make you a native of these my kingdoms of Castile and Leon . . . with all honors, courtesies, favors, freedoms, exemptions, prerogatives, and immunities . . . City of Toro, April 24, 1505.

He not only became a native, but he married one, a woman whose name was Maria Cereso. It may have been to some extent a love match, for she was by no means a rich woman. But according to Italian custom, marriage was considered an event of slight importance in a busy man's life, certainly not primarily a matter of sentiment. As Michelangelo put it: "A wife should be ten years younger than her husband, healthy, and of a good family." A woman's mind and heart were of small consequence, and beauty might be a dangerous distraction. In selecting a wife an Italian did not let himself be guided by his heart, but followed his reason and chose a thrifty housekeeper. All that is known in Amerigo's case is the name of his wife and the fact that after his marriage he continued to make his home in Seville.

In 1506 he received word of his brother Antonio's second marriage, and in May of that year that his nephew Bartolomeo had been appointed professor of astrology (astronomy) at the University of Padua. He heard also of the death of Columbus in Valladolid on May 20, 1506.

Unhappy Columbus, whose life of drama, of tragedy, made his poignant personal story a perpetually appealing one! How many difficulties he brought upon himself by his evasions, credulousness, and self-delusion! Commonly credited with extraordinary foresight, he was singularly lacking in prevision as to the workings of cause and effect in human relations and was in consequence repeatedly finding himself in situations from which prevarication seemed to offer the only escape from humiliation. What he had tried to do, all the world knew. What he said he did and what he thought he did and what he failed to do, were only partly clear to others and very dark to him. His claims in regard to his discoveries cried for a scientist to correct the errors. But in spite of all his romantic exaggerations, his tossing aside of obvious truths, his boasting, his thirst for power and glory, his obsession with gold, his lack of singleness of aim (desiring with equal ardor to find a western passage to India, to become a rich potentate, to be lord of his islands, and to rescue Jerusalem from the infidel) and despite his superstition and all his confusions, Columbus was an originator, a man whose faith gave him power, like one who walks on water, a mystic whose dream upheld him against all adversities.

Amerigo, on the contrary, never seemed to face embarrassing moments in which a lie seemed desirable. This was not by good luck, but because he was a realist who relied upon observation, was eager to receive new truth and willing to adjust his mind to it, and also because he never swerved from his single purpose, which was to add to man's knowledge of the earth and to man's ability to steer his course upon the face of it. The two navigators presented a contrast which most of their contemporaries failed to understand. In succeeding generations many thought Columbus to be as ingenuous as Amerigo Vespucci; many thought Amerigo Vespucci to be as incredible as Columbus.

Columbus, penniless, friendless, rejected, going from court to court, cheated, insulted—the world takes him to its heart. Amerigo Vespucci, the scion of a noble family, fulfilling his family obligations, a merchant among merchants, a successful business executive, fitting out ships for others to sail, until such time as it was convenient for him to go to sea—does not so swiftly touch the emotions. The quiet, the contemplative, the dutiful seem secondary. It is easy to enthuse over the wild, stormy, tortured soul who breaks himself against restraint and wins the laurel and the popular applause in history. A Gauguin, leaving the stock exchange in middle age and walking out on his family to take up painting, stirs the mind, but he never wins the heart as does a Van Gogh, whose life was misordered from start to finish.

Nothing can be claimed for Amerigo Vespucci that will win over to him a Columbus worshiper. Nor have we any wish to do so. But there are always a thousand burly vocal seamen milling around the King's court, storming the king's portals, and swarming over the wharves, mariners whose principal assets are determination and "nerve"—a thousand such for one like Amerigo, whose idea was the pursuit of knowledge. To the man pondering an idea, what he does or is forced to do because of external circumstances, does not matter much, so long as his mind is left spacious and fluid enough to nurture the idea—so long as the idea is not hurt. The idea is a ruling passion, but in reverse as compared with the urge of a man of conflict like Columbus.

From February, 1505, Amerigo had been in the service of the *Casa de Contratación*, or Board of Trade in Seville, (established January 20, 1503), as an expert in the provisioning of ships, the making of charts for shipmasters, and the planning of routes for the ships to take. Upon one occasion he handled the sum of five million maravedis, involved in the settlement of accounts in the matter of fitting out three ships. From May, 1505, to August, 1506, he was at Palos and Moguer, preparing an expedition. A royal letter dated August 25, 1506, showed that he was with Vicente Yañez Pinzón in a port of Biscay, fitting out a fleet of three ships, *La Magdelena* and two others, to go for spices. "To go for spices" meant to Amerigo's mind to go by way of the southwest, south of fifty degrees south, if only a strait could be found, or a passage around the southern end of the New World. But maritime affairs became involved because of the confusion in the political situation of the country.

When Queen Isabella of Castile and Leon made her will, she appointed her husband, King Ferdinand of Aragon, Regent of Castile until her grandson Charles should come of age, and only in case of the incapacity of her daughter Joanna, who had shown signs of insanity. After the death of Isabella, Ferdinand proclaimed Joanna Queen of Castile and acted as Regent, but after Joanna and her foreign consort Philip arrived, the nobles and populace compelled Ferdinand to retire from Castile to his own kingdom of Aragon. They preferred the consort of the mad Joanna, who assumed the throne of Castile as Philip the First. King Philip dismissed those who had held office under Ferdinand and appointed new administrators in all government departments. The wily old King Ferdinand immediately took steps to win back what he had lost, by intrigue and foul means.

The affairs of the Board of Trade in Seville, and with them the activities of Amerigo, were thrown into confusion. The Board of Trade did not know which monarch would be victorious in the struggle, and they were fearful of offending the winner. They did not know whether to let Amerigo continue his preparations for the expedition or to order him to desist. In their dilemma they placed their problem in the hands of Amerigo, trusting to his proved skill in diplomacy to solve it for them. On September 15, 1506, a few weeks after the accession of King Philip, they sent Amerigo to the court of Castile at Burgos. They provided him with three letters and with five memorials on the business of the Indies, with the understanding that he was to use such of the letters and to approach such persons at court as circumstances there might dictate. The president of the Board of Trade gave him the following written instructions:

> To the Captain, Américo Vespucio—You will take three letters: for the king, for Vila, his grand chamberlain, and for the secretary, Gricio. Also, five memorials: one upon the dispatch of the armament, two others received from Española concerning the tower which King Ferdinand commanded to be built upon the Pearl Coast, and the remaining two upon the caravels which are on service in Española, and concerning the things necessary for the fortress which is being built there. If Gricio is at court, and is in charge of the affairs of the Indies, give him the letter, show him the memorials, and he will guide you to the ear of the king and expedite the business. We are informed, however, that the king has intrusted the business of the Indies to M. de Vila, his grand chamberlain. If that is the case, go directly to him. What we principally desire is a full understanding of the agreement entered into between the king, our lord, and King Ferdinand, in order that we may be able to give to each prince that which is his.

The agreement between the kings was terminated by the speedy death of one of them. Ten days after Amerigo received his instructions, the ambitious old King Ferdinand simplified the politics of Castile by a stroke of treachery. While he was himself in Italy visiting his conquered city of Naples, his son-in-law King Philip I swiftly died, poisoned by Mosen Ferrer, a gentleman of the bedchamber, by order. By order also, Joanna was imprisoned on grounds of insanity. Ximénes, soon afterward made a cardinal, held Castile with a firm hand until his master, King Ferdinand, returned to become undisputed ruler through the nominal regency of his mad daughter.

With his prestige as an explorer who had discovered a continent, Amerigo found himself welcome in official circles. He was now called "Capitano" and was given an annual salary of thirty thousand maravedis. His practical application of astronomy to the Ptolemaic problem of longitude was soon to bring him high honor and a position of unique responsibility. Meanwhile, he was so busy with ships and navigation that he had little leisure to reflect upon the contrast between the fanatic, wholesale destruction by Cardinal Ximénes, as Inquisitor General, of priceless Moorish manuscripts of astronomy and mathematics, poetry, and medicine, and the unimpeded sale of many editions of the forgeries, which, if he did reflect upon it, must have forced his mind to the conclusion that the authorities were burning the wrong books. He would have shuddered if he had realized how almost impossible it is to kill the printed word.

~~~

Chapter Eleven

THE NAMING OF A CONTINENT

More than four years had elapsed since Amerigo announced the discovery of a continent, and as yet that new continent had no satisfactory name. It needed one that would be in keeping with the names of the other continents.

Natives of Española had called the great land to the south of their island "Bohio." The Portuguese used names Cabral had given: "Vera Cruz" and "Terra de Santa Cruz"; but a name of Portuguese origin was acceptable only to themselves, not at all to the Spanish, who rightfully claimed more than half the continent, and who had touched its shores two years before Cabral and had made extensive explorations of it the year before Cabral. The term used by some of the map-makers, "Land of Brasil," was confusing, for "Brasil" was the name of an imaginary island located somewhere in the Atlantic, according to popular belief, when there had been no thought of a continent. "Terra dei Pappagalli" (Land of Parrots) was a name only locally applicable to a part of the continent; "Parias" was the native name for a limited region near Trinidad; and "India Nova" (New India) was inaccurate. "Mundus Novus" (New World) was less a name than a description, though for several years that term had served. But now the fact that there was a new continent beyond the western ocean had become common knowledge throughout Europe, and there was everywhere a subconscious demand for an adequate name, a universally acceptable name.

That name was invented when a group of scholars decided to produce a revised edition of the Cosmography of Ptolemy to meet the urgent need for new maps, according to the new conception of the world made compulsory by the recent discoveries. It happened that in the Vosges Mountains in the little town of Saint-Dié, there was a college under the patronage of the studious Duke Renaud (René) II of Vaudemon, of Lorraine, the titular "King of Jerusalem
~~~

and Sicily," who was there resident. Walter Lud, Secretary to the Duke, and a wealthy man, had established a printing press at Saint-Dié in 1500. The duke and several professors in the college used this press in their geographical project.

One of their members, Matthias Ringman, Professor of Latin, went twice to Italy, eager to obtain information on the latest discoveries. Walter Lud recorded in his *Speculi orbis succintiis* that a French version of the Letter to Soderini, or *Four Voyages*, was sent from Portugal to Duke René. At Lud's request the *Four Voyages* was translated into Latin by a canon of Saint-Dié named Jean Basin de Sandecourt. Accepting this forgery as genuine, Lud and his colleagues used *Four Voyages* as the basis for their publication and reprinted it in full.

The preliminary epistle, or dedication, shows how uncritically the forgery was accepted, for its translator merely substituted for the name "Piero Soderini" in his French source the name of Duke René, retaining the words "His Magnificence" which were properly applicable to Soderini as Gonfaloniere, but were not applicable to the duke. Furthermore, the Duke René had not been (what Piero Soderini may have been) a schoolmate of Amerigo's in Florence studying grammar under Amerigo's uncle Giorgio Antonio Vespucci, as the preliminary epistle states; for René was educated at Joinville, and did not visit Italy until he was twenty-nine years of age.

It was not enough for the Saint-Dié coterie that no one except Amerigo Vespucci had been credited with bringing to Europe the idea of a new continent. As scholars, they welcomed corroborating evidence, or what they considered proof that he had a better right than anyone else to bring home that idea. Seeking for an argument to substantiate the claim that he should be credited with the discovery of the new continent, they believed they had found a conclusive one in *Four Voyages*, which erroneously gave him priority in setting eyes upon its shores.

Martin Waldseemüller, Professor of Geography at the college, prepared the treatise *Cosmographiae introductio*, which presented this description of itself: "An Introduction to Cosmography, together with some principles of Geometry necessary to the purpose. Also four voyages of Americus Vespucius. A description of universal Cosmography, both stereometrical and planometrical, together with what was unknown to Ptolemy and has been recently discovered." The *Cosmographiae introductio* was brought out as a small pamphlet on April 25, 1507.

Waldseemüller had a fondness for making up names, as we know from his signing himself "Hylacomylus," a hybrid composite of the Greek ὕλη, meaning "wood," equivalent to *Wald;* the Latin *lacus,* meaning "lake" or "See"; and the Greek μύλος, "mill." In a Latin preface to *Cosmographiae introductio* Waldseemüller indulged his name-coining propensity:

> Toward the South Pole are situated the southern part of Africa, recently discovered, and the islands of Zanzibar, Java Minor, and Seula. These regions [Europe, Asia, Africa] have been more extensively explored, and another or fourth part has been discovered by Americus Vespucius, as may be seen by the attached charts; in virtue of which I believe it very just that it should be named Amerige ["ge" in Greek meaning "land of"], after its discoverer, Americus, a man of sagacious mind; or let it be named America, since both Europa and Asia bear names of feminine form.

"Asia" was derived from "Asu," which meant "rising sun" or "land of light"; while "Europa" came from "ereb" or "irib," which meant "setting sun" or "land of darkness." "Africa" came from a local Carthaginian place name. The name "America" was a variant of the German "Amalrich," derived from "amal." In Greek it was Aimulos; in Latin, Aemelius. In all its forms the underlying meaning was that of work; as for example, the word for work in Hebrew is "amal," and in old Norse "aml," the consonant sounds of which were retained in the verb "moil." Amalrich, which literally meant "work ruler," or "designator of tasks," might be freely translated as "master workman." [1] A Frenchman said that Emeric meant "rich through work."

The name appeared in "Halmal," a semi-divine mythical forefather or ancestor of the Amelungen, or royal tribe of the Ostrogoths, which was called Ömlunger. German forms of the name were Amalrich, Almerich, Emmerich; the Spanish form was Almerigo; the French, Amalrie or Amaury; in England it was Almerick, or Merica in old families in Yorkshire. It appeared in feminine forms in Amelia, Emilia, Emily; its masculine forms were Amery, Aymar, Emeric, Emerique, Emery or Emmery. But as Charlotte Mary Yonge wrote in her *History of Christian Names,* it was the Italian form, Amerigo, which was destined to the most noted use . . . which should hold fast that most fortuitous title, whence thousands of miles, and millions of men, bear the appellation of the forgotten forefather of a tribe of Goths—Amalrich, the work ruler; a curiously appropriate title for the new world of labour and progress, on the other side of the Atlantic.

Waldseemüller prepared a globe and also an elaborate map of the world on a plane projection to accompany the *Cosmographiae introductio*. The woodcuts for this plane map were made at Strassburg, but printed at Saint-Dié.[2] It was for a long time supposed that all copies of Waldseemüller's map were irretrievably lost, but a well-preserved copy of Waldseemüller's plane map was found in 1901 in Wolfegg Castle, and then by comparison the so-called Hausslab globe was identified as Waldseemüller's work. The plane map widely influenced such cartographers as Schöner and Ortelius and had some bearing upon Mercator's invention of his famous projection. Waldseemüller designed his map to feature the work of two great geographers, presenting a picture of Claudius Ptolemaeus facing the East and of Americus Vespucius facing the West.

On the new continent of the new hemisphere the name "America" was used for the first time. It appeared on the main portion of the map, not on the small map, hereafter referred to as the inset map, between the stylized portraits of the two geographers.

Waldseemüller, in 1507, was aware of the work of Columbus and intended no denial of credit properly due to Columbus, for on his large map in twelve sections, covering a total of thirty-six square feet, which he called "A Map of the World According to the Traditions of Ptolemy and the Voyages of Americus Vespucius," he wrote on Section V: "These islands were discovered by Columbus, an admiral of Genoa, at the command of the King of Spain." On Section I of the map, commenting on the surprising fact of the existence of the new continent south of the equator "beyond the path of the year and the sun," he wrote, "Now finally it proves clearly to be true." He continued:

For there is a land, discovered by Columbus, a captain of the King of Castile, and by Americus Vespucius, both men of very great ability, which though a great part of it lies beneath the path of the year and of the sun and between the tropics, nevertheless extends about nineteen degrees beyond the Tropic of Capricorn toward the Antarctic Pole.

Instead of nineteen degrees he should have written twenty-nine which added to the twenty-three of the tropic, would have made the "fifty-two degrees" given in the "third" voyage as Amerigo Vespucci's farthest south. Since Columbus never went as far south as the equator, the words "it proves clearly to be true" are clothed with meaning only in the light of Amerigo's voyages into the southern hemisphere, not at all in the light of the "first" of the "four voyages," from which the dispute ultimately arose as to which could claim priority upon the shore of the new continent, Columbus or Amerigo Vespucci; for that "first" voyage, like all the voyages of Columbus, was entirely north of the equator. In other words, on his 1507 map Waldseemüller unmistakably showed that in his own mind he ascribed proof of the existence of the new continent to the Portuguese voyage of Amerigo (the "third" of the "four voyages"), and that it was acceptance of Amerigo's proof of its existence more than Amerigo's supposed priority which caused him to name the new continent "America."

The remarkable geographical features of the Waldseemüller map were more important than the giving of a name to one of them. In addition to the picturing of the new southern continent, with its approximately correct general contour, the inset map presented a portion of the northern continent as well, and the two were connected.[3] On the large map the two continents were separated by a hypothetical strait. Both the inset and the large map pictured another great ocean broader than the Atlantic, between the New World and Asia.

This close approximation to geographical actualities was a natural corollary of Amerigo's great discovery. One is tempted to lose sight of this revolutionary advance over the world conception of Ptolemy in contemplating the single feature that has made Waldseemüller's map so famous, the first appearance thereon of the name "America." For this reason the illustration from Waldseemüller's map on page 172 is not the large map of the southern continent showing the name "America," but part of the small inset map which clearly shows the more important geographical innovations for which Amerigo Vespucci was now recognized to be a geographical authority as worthy of acceptance as Ptolemy had been.

PART OF WALDSEEMÜLLER'S MAP, 1507

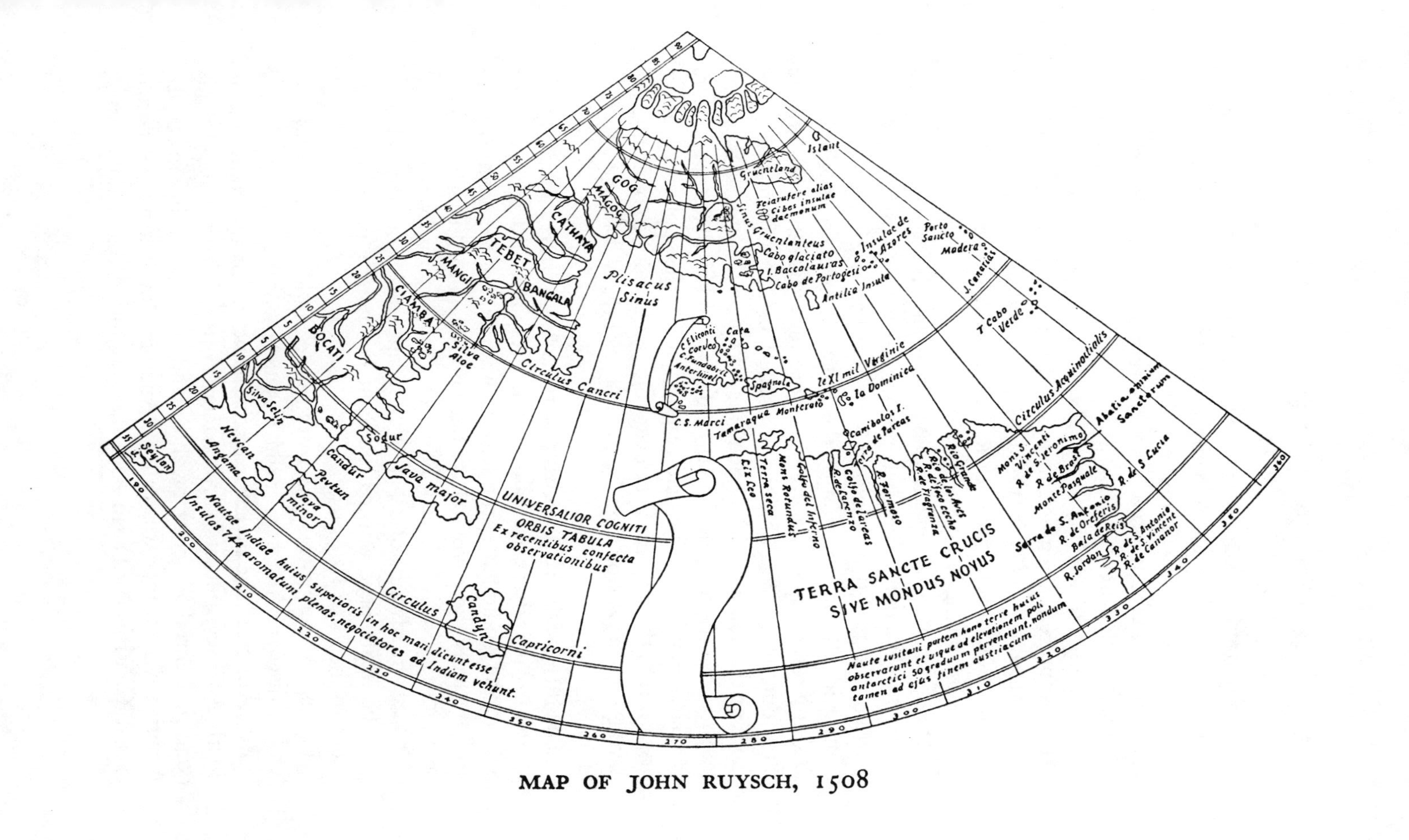

MAP OF JOHN RUYSCH, 1508

A successful name is a work of art. "America," so euphonious and so happily parallel with "Asia," "Africa," and "Australia" (meaning "southern," and applied to a mythical Antarctic continent before the actual Australia was discovered), was such an excellent choice that once it had appeared in print, nothing could destroy it. It "caught" immediately and irresistibly, spreading into universal usage with the force of the inevitable. Map-makers adopted it, so that in 1509 it appeared on a globe, in 1510 Glareanus employed it, in 1514 Stobnicza, and in 1515 it was used on several globes. Used at first for the southern continent of the New World, eventually it was applied to the whole Western Hemisphere.

The *Four Voyages* might have been speedily recognized as a forgery if Waldseemüller had not dignified it by using it to substantiate the fact that Amerigo Vespucci had discovered the new continent. His presentation of the *Four Voyages* in an edition of Ptolemy forced upon the attention of serious students of geography these questions: Did Vespucci precede Columbus in reaching the shore of the continent? Did he make a voyage in 1497, as the *Four Voyages* asserted that he did? If he did not and he therefore appears as a liar, should he not be held responsible for the application of his first name to the western continent? Should he not be condemned as having somehow stolen an honor that rightfully belonged to Columbus?

The fuel for the Vespuccian controversy was thus stacked up for burning. Men afterward said that if Vespucci had any sense of decency he would have protested the invention of the name "America." Actually there would have been no reason for his disapproving save modesty. It is believed, however, that Amerigo was not at all cognizant in advance of what Waldseemüller did in 1507. Had he been, he might have warned the Saint-Dié coterie not to give credence to the *Four Voyages*.

For us, the controversy narrows to the single question: Did Columbus discover America, or did Vespucci?

By "America" the inventor of the name meant the continent of South America, not of North America, nor did he include in his concept Central America or the islands of the Caribbean. South America was all that was called "America" until many years had passed. Controversy began with the assumption that whoever first reached the coast of the new continent should be credited with the discovery of it and that the application to the New World of the name of anyone who was not the first to reach the coast of the new continent was an error and an injustice to the one who did reach it first. Was this assumption valid?

Columbus was probably preceded in reaching the shore of South America by Phoenicians (c. 1000 B.C.) and certainly by natives of Guinea, who crossed from Africa in canoes from time to time,[4] and possibly also by the Portuguese, as is indicated by Andrea Bianco's map of 1448 which carried the inscription at the edge of the parchment to the southwest of Cape Verde: "Island authenticated is distant to the west 1,500 miles." This is further indicated by the reference at the time of Cabral's voyage to the ancient Portuguese map by Pedro Vaz Bisagudo, on which land found by Cabral had years earlier been drawn. Nevertheless, Columbus was the first European of unquestionable historical record to touch that continent. He approached it in 1498, caught sight of it from near Trinidad, thought it another island, saw all together perhaps two hundred miles of its coastline, and accepted it as mainland—as part of Asia. Was he not its discoverer?

The sole argument for calling Columbus the discoverer of America was based upon this priority. After Vespucci had been honored in the naming of America, Las Casas stated the complete thesis for Columbus:

> Others, besides these two (Pinzón and De Solís), say it is all one coast from Paria, though provinces have different names and there are also different languages. This, then, was declared by witnesses who had been there and knew it well by having used their own eyes, and now it would be needless to seek further for witnesses than in the grocers' shops in Seville. Thus it cannot be denied to the Admiral, except with great injustice, that as he was the first discoverer of those Indies, so he was also of the whole of our mainland, and to him is due the credit, by discovering the province of Paria, which is a part of all that land. For it was he that put the thread into the hands of the rest, by which they found the clew to more distant parts. Consequently his rights ought most justly to be complied with and respected throughout all that land, even if the region was still more extensive, just as they should be respected in Española and the other islands. For it was not necessary for him to go to every part, any more than it is necessary in taking possession of an estate, as the jurists hold.

The case for Columbus was at best a legalistic one. Even with the ironclad contract of Columbus and his undeniable priority, it was unreasonable to expect the Spanish Government to allow such far-reaching claims. According to the contract, the heirs of Columbus would have been governors of all countries, all territories and states, from Alaska to Patagonia. They would have enjoyed an inherited share in all the business and in all the commerce of all the nations of North and South and Central America. Thus to have extended the financial rights and the prerogatives of Columbus and his heirs forever, would have been absurd. It would have been equally absurd to have extended to Columbus credit for discovery of all the same wide territories. It would have been ridiculous to say that because he discovered some islands in the West Indies or because he discovered the Land of Parias, he was therefore also the discoverer of Mexico, Peru, and California.

Columbus was not the discoverer of what Waldseemüller meant by the word "America." He himself had denied it, by insisting to the day of his death that he had reached the mainland of Asia. Was there ever any justification for calling him the discoverer of all which the name "America" ultimately came to signify? Later, across maps of North America, which continent Columbus never saw, there was frequently printed the legend: 'In the year 1492, by Christopher Columbus." Was this not contrary to truth and reason?

It was no error and no injustice to name the new continent after the man who had discovered that it was a new continent. If someone has caught several lepidoptera, and if a scientist discovers that one of them is a new species of butterfly, the scientist gets the credit for the discovery of the new species and the new species is usually named for him, because he was the one who first brought knowledge to bear upon it. The word "discover" has two different meanings. If by "discover" is meant "to get first sight of," then Columbus was the discoverer of the continent that was named America, for his priority in landing on its shores during the fifteenth century cannot be challenged. But "discover" means also "to explore," "to lay open to view," "to bring to light by examination," "to disclose," as of some knowledge which one possesses and which one "brings to the knowledge of the world." Columbus could not bring America to the knowledge of Europe, because he had no faintest conception of what

America was or that there was any such thing as a New World. To be the first to see a thing with one's eyes was one kind of discovery; to be the first to perceive a thing in one's mind was another kind. Columbus saw a small piece of South America, but he did not understand what he saw. Amerigo Vespucci explored nearly two-thirds of the coastline of South America and got a God's-eye view of a new continent. To Columbus, priority; to Vespucci, understanding.

Strikingly parallel with the unwillingness of some to admit the propriety of bestowing Amerigo's name upon all of the New World is the reluctance that has been shown toward extending the use of the name of Lieutenant Wilkes of the United States Navy to the continent which he discovered. The Columbus of the Antarctica was Nathaniel Brown Palmer, Captain of the *Hero*, who in 1820 first saw Antarctica and sailed along the coast of it from sixty-two to sixty-eight degrees south. The region which Palmer saw was named by a Russian, "Palmer's Land," now the Palmer Peninsula. About twenty years later, in 1838–1842, Lieutenant Charles Wilkes explored seventeen hundred miles of the coastline of Antarctica and pronounced that land a continent. His report that he had thus "discovered" a continent met with opposition. His claims were controverted; he was court-martialed on the charge of having falsified; and his findings were disputed for more than seventy years. Not until 1912 was he vindicated. His right to be called the discoverer of the continent of Antarctica, although others had previously set eyes upon it, runs an exact parallel with Amerigo's discovery of the continent of South America, which Columbus had previously set eyes upon. The following quotation from an editorial in the New York *Times* [5] would, with change of names, apply perfectly to the case of Vespucci and Columbus:

> There is no little question that others before Wilkes had seen his "land," but it remained for him to regard it as a continent. . . . Yet there is still a tendency abroad to restrict the name "Wilkes Land" to a small part of the continent south of Australia. Full justice has not yet been done to a man who must go down in history with the great explorers of all time.

With his estimate of longitudinal distances Amerigo's discovery of a new "Fourth Part of the World" carried the conception of an entire western hemisphere. When, therefore, following the Vespuccian conception, the fifth part of the world [6] was revealed within the northern part of that hemisphere, there was more justification for extending the name "America" to that northern continent (as Mercator did in 1538) [7] than for naming it after Leif Ericson [8] or John Cabot,[9] who did not make known to the world what it was, though they did land upon its shores, or for naming it after Columbus, who never came within sight of it. The naming of America was no error, for the major premise upon which it was based was correct, that Vespucci discovered the fact that there was a new continent, even though the minor premise that he was the first explorer to reach its shores was not correct. The only mistake Waldseemüller made was his attempt in an edition of Ptolemy in 1513 to withdraw the name he had invented (having lost sight of the first and major one of his two premises, probably after having learned of the incorrectness of the second and minor one) [10] and to ascribe the discovery to Columbus on grounds of priority.

Several attempts were made in later years to apply the name of Columbus to the western world. One South American country called itself Colombia. Sporadic applications of his name appeared in scattered towns and in several American cities. However, while the residents of the various places known as Columbia or Columbus became proud of these names, the word "America" remained dearer to their hearts. Men loved the name "America." They clung to it, so that it lived and grew with irreducible vitality. It advanced until it covered the whole Western Hemisphere of which Amerigo had first conceived, until it covered two continents and many islands, one-third of the land surface of the globe.

Some have said that the New World should have been named "Ericsonia" in honor of the man who certainly preceded others in crossing the Atlantic. But the answer to that is clear. Leif Ericson's discovery awakened only a limited and temporary interest, and that only among Scandinavians; on the other hand, the discoveries made by Christopher Columbus and Amerigo Vespucci opened the way permanently and for all mankind. It is not being first, but being followed that counts.

If the rival claims for Columbus and Vespucci are submitted to this test, the question must be asked: Which of the two navigators sent to sea the greater number of subsequent explorers, adventurers, and colonists? Was it Columbus, who "proved" that one could cross the Atlantic to Asia, and so dotted the ocean with eager shiploads searching for the Spice Isles and treasure cities of India? Or was it Vespucci with the idea of the New World, which in offering free land with new opportunity for the ambitious as well as the oppressed and persecuted of all nations led to the emigration of many millions of Europeans and the establishment of the real America, that creation of the free spirit of men and women who had faith in themselves?

Between Columbus and Vespucci there need be no "recriminations in Hades." Columbus destroyed the conception that the western ocean was a vast and impassable barrier. He was the conqueror of the Atlantic, he was the "prince of promoters," "the founder of modern commerce." What he did, after all is said, was to perform the deed that led to the establishment of permanent communication between the two shores of the Atlantic. On the other hand, Amerigo Vespucci gave mankind the idea of a hitherto-unknown hemisphere. Which did more to enlarge man's conception of the earth? Here was their only rivalry. The planet is large enough for both.

Chapter Twelve

ORGANIZING NAVIGATION

Amerigo held to his ambition to sail again, his search now to be for a passage through the Western Hemisphere into the ocean that would lead to Asia. But his work for the *Casa de Contratación* had been occupying all his time, and the years were passing without his being able to arrange another voyage of exploration.

In all probability, however, as evidenced in two letters to the Venetian senate from diplomatic agents in Spain, he made two commercial voyages to the New World, in 1505 and in 1507, respectively, in the service of the Board of Trade. For at least one of these voyages there is corroborating evidence in the records of the *Casa de Contratación* that on one occasion Amerigo and Pinzón and Solís were charged with the safe conduct to the treasury in Seville of 6,000 ducats of gold from the "Indies." and each received 6,000 maravedis in payment for having performed this service. Participation in such commercial voyages was all in the day's work for Amerigo, but of no significance as compared with what he dreamed of doing.

The expert mariner, Juan de la Cosa, was also no longer engaged in exploration, but in commercial enterprises. After his first three voyages of discovery, two of which had been with Columbus and the third with Hojeda, La Cosa had in 1501 explored Darien and the Gulf of Urabá. Though he had gone to Urabá and Darien again in 1505, the voyage was merely in quest of gold; and in 1507 he had been sent on his sixth voyage to the New World, with two armed caravels to convoy treasure ships returning from the West Indies and to protect them from the Biscayan pirate Juan de Granada and from the Portuguese. He had indeed received honors and rewards for his services and was the pride of his country. The captain of the king's own ship described La Cosa as "a great seaman in the opinion of all, and in my own, not inferior to the Admiral himself." In 1503 La Cosa was given the title "Chief Constable of Urabá," which title was confirmed in 1508. He had also been granted a pension and certain special privileges and was recognized as the most distinguished of native-born navigators and the most skillful pilot.

The spirit of adventure, adversely affected by the death of Queen Isabella, seemed to be dying in Spain. That stimulating irritant, Columbus, was gone. For three full years after the queen's death, in November, 1504, exploration was neglected by the Spanish, in spite of the fact that King Ferdinand was more and more appreciative of the value of his western possessions as the stream of gold from them increased. But the income of the crown had been largely expended to further his ambition in the prosecution of the war in Italy. The king himself had been absent in Naples for more than a year, and there had been little money or energy left for voyages of discovery.

King Ferdinand fully realized the desirability of pushing the work of exploration. Amerigo's discovery of the existence of a New World had temporarily dimmed the promise of a direct western route to India, but the growing wealth of Portugal derived from trade with the East held an incentive before her jealous rival. About three months after his return from Naples, as soon as he could find time for it, King Ferdinand took steps to resume the search that had fallen into abeyance. On November 7, 1507, he issued a call to the four leading navigators in his service, Juan de la Cosa, Vicente Yañez Pinzón, Juan Díaz de Solís, and Amerigo Vespucci, to come to a conference with him in Burgos to formulate a policy for future maritime effort.

This conference of five men, well minded of their mutual purposes, could not have failed to note the fact that the western route to Asia was no longer a question of a short ocean voyage, as Columbus had thought, but that Amerigo Vespucci's revelation of a New World had put a new complexion on the matter, ushering in a second phase with regard to discoveries in the West. The problem was no longer to find the Strait of Catigara, but to search all the shores of the New World, from the frozen north to the storm-tormented south, for a passage through it or around it into that other ocean which must also be crossed before the ships of Spain could reach the Spice Islands.

Such a strait was to be sought wherever the coastline was not already known to be continuous, and that meant in three possible regions. For Amerigo Vespucci had searched the coast between ten degrees north and fifty degrees south, except that the beginning of his exploration for Portugal may not quite have overlapped the southern end of his exploration for Spain, but the intervening degree or one and a half degrees had been searched by Pinzón and Solís also. La Cosa had verified the continuity of the coastline to the west of the Cape de la Vela past Urabá to Darien, where Rodrigo de Bastidas had also been; and Columbus, on his fourth voyage, had seen the coast between Darien and sixteen degrees north. The Spanish may not have known with certainty what latitudes had been explored by the English under John and Sebastian Cabot, though La Cosa's map indicated that its maker had a fair conception of them. In all probability the Spanish understood that the Cabots had searched the coast of the New World from fifty degrees north to as far south as "the latitude of Gibraltar," as Sebastian Cabot said, or to about thirty-six degrees north. Thus, Spain must seek for a strait either to the north of sixteen degrees north and up to thirty-six degrees north, or to the south of fifty degrees south, or in a third region that might not be open to Spanish ships, since it was north of the latitudes explored by the English. The principal purpose of the conference was to decide which of these unexplored regions held forth the best promise of finding the desired strait.

We can only guess as to the arguments the conferees advanced. Perhaps it was pointed out that from all that was known of currents in the Atlantic and from what Amerigo had observed of currents among the islands which he had explored to the north of Española, it seemed likely that there was a continuous coastline between sixteen and thirty-six degrees north which caused the westward currents to turn and flow toward the north and then back toward the east. If so, the shape of that coastline would be in reality something like that which had been indicated on a map by Canerio in 1502, which showed a large peninsula on the mainland northwest of Cuba. This well-imagined peninsula, which had been called "Bimini," may have been, as George E. Nunn thinks it was, a mistakenly placed duplication of the eastern end of Cuba rather than a prefiguration of the not-yet-discovered Florida. A more valid argument would have been that the natives of Española and of the other islands in the Antilles, as well as the natives of Urabá and Darien, had never heard of a strait, yet some of them were in the custom of voyaging far in their war canoes. Furthermore, the reports of all natives must have tended to corroborate the map which showed the peninsula called Bimini.

For lack of evidence to the contrary, there seemed to be more reason for believing there was an opening through the New World or a passage around the end of it to the south of fifty degrees south. From the smaller size of the rivers beyond thirty-five degrees south and by analogy with the southern ends of Asia and Africa, Amerigo may have argued a narrowing of the southern end of the new continent.

In any case, it appears that the conferees decided that voyages of discovery ought to be continued along the coast of the new continent toward the far south. Following this decision, the king ordered four caravels to be rapidly fitted out and the "procuring of necessary stores assigned to Américo Vespucio, as he is well known to be experienced in such work." Pinzón and Solís were appointed to go as soon as possible with these caravels to seek for a strait to the southwest.

Amerigo began the work of provisioning the caravels for Pinzón and Solís, but before the ships were ready the Portuguese voiced opposition to the proposed voyage. Portugal objected strenuously to having Spanish ships sail past Portuguese territory into the Southern Hemisphere. A Spanish voyage to the southwest against Portugal's wishes would have been unwise, since Portugual had gone in for innovations in the form of cannon on the decks of her large ships. King Ferdinand consequently changed his plans and decided to send Pinzón and Solís elsewhere. They were now given revised orders to sail "westward, north of the equator, to seek for discovery of a strait not found by Columbus." They were to renew exploration to the west of the Caribbean Sea and to continue along the shore beyond the farthest north to which Columbus had gone on his fourth voyage. They were not to linger in any port more than necessary, but were to explore the coast, since this was the aim of the voyage. Whenever they landed, they were to take with them a writer, who was to keep a record of all they observed. They were to stop at Española to render account to the governor there, but must tell no foreigners at any time whence or whither they were bound.

While he was busy as ship chandler, Amerigo did not give up the idea of going himself to search for a passage to India, to the south of fifty degrees south, and he proceeded to make active plans for such an expedition. Francesco Corner wrote in July, 1508, the month in which Pinzón and Solís sailed, that Amerigo had declared "that he was going to provide good ships of Biscay, all of which he wished to cover with lead [to protect the hulls against teredo worms], and go west to find the lands which the Portuguese found by sailing east," and that he "will depart this month." The "depart" meant to leave Seville for some port where he would commence preparations. It is a natural deduction from the circumstances that Amerigo's plan was to seek a passage around the southern end of the continent he had discovered, because it would have seemed fruitless to him to explore in the latitudes to which Pinzón and Solís were going and thus merely duplicate their work.

But Amerigo's contemplated voyage was not to be, for it ran counter to the wishes of King Ferdinand. The king had considered in council the general ignorance of Spanish pilots and their lack of skill in navigation, which had caused grievous losses, and he had considered also Amerigo's skill in calculating degrees, and he desired that Amerigo should impart his knowledge to all pilots and masters of ships. In fact, the king had created a new office especially for Amerigo, an office which would give him opportunity to exercise his unique combination of talents. No other navigator of his day had equal qualifications for the work King Ferdinand wished him to perform. It was to be his province to examine, classify, and prepare all the pilots of Spain; to teach them piloting, navigation, and cosmography; to direct the construction of hydrographic charts; to correct these and keep them up-to-date; to inspect and to calibrate navigational instruments; to exercise control over the important problems of overseas navigation. To this extent he was to be responsible for all expeditions. Upon his knowledge and ability would depend the success of the maritime and colonial movements of Spain.

On March 22, 1508, he was named "Pilot Major of Spain," with a salary of fifty thousand maravedis, which was immediately increased to seventy-five thousand maravedis. Nevertheless, several months thereafter, as we have seen, Amerigo still had his heart set on another voyage of exploration. It was not that he did not realize the seriousness of his work as Pilot Major; the very creation of that position carried out a policy which he had advocated, but he had not foreseen the magnitude of the opposition which would arise against him.

When he first called in some of the pilots and attempted to teach them his astronomical method of determining longitude, they bluntly refused to learn. It was the usual sort of resistance with which conservatives in any profession greet new ways of doing things. Theirs was no superstitious opposition, like that which had been aroused by the introduction of the mariner's needle in the days of Friar Bacon; it was the stubborn antagonism of pilots who had always used the method of dead reckoning, as had their fathers before them. Each one of them prided himself on his skill in guessing the distance a ship had run. Each one of them boasted of the times when he had been nearly right, and all his rival pilots very wrong. What will happen to us, the Spanish pilots asked themselves, if we adopt the method this fellow Américo Vespucio is trying to teach? If longitude can ever be determined with anything like the accuracy with which mariners find their latitude, our practical experience as men who have followed the sea all our lives will count for nothing; our knowledge of wind and weather in relation to the speed of our ships and our intimacy with the sailing qualities of our ships will be of no value. We pilots must protect ourselves. This Florentine would destroy our vocation. Thus minded, the pilots combined in their resistance against the innovator.

Disgusted with the attitude taken by the pilots, whose noncompliance he was powerless to overcome, Amerigo had reason to ask himself what use there was in fitting out good ships for men who refused to learn how to determine longitude. And so he thought it better to go exploring. But the king understood the situation and, in order to strengthen Amerigo against the opposition he had met, issued Letters Patent which clearly defined Amerigo's duties and privileges as Pilot Major and granted him the powers necessary to compel all pilots to submit to his instruction. The terms of the royal mandate were impressive and were obviously a reflection of his personality and of what the Spanish government was convinced he was qualified to perform. King Ferdinand issued the Letters Patent nominally through Queen Joanna. They were as follows:

Dona Juana: It has come to our notice, and we have seen from experience that, since the pilots are not sufficiently skillful or acquainted with what they should know in order to be competent to direct and steer the ships that cross the ocean sea to our islands and mainland which we possess in the Indies, and since through their incompetence in not knowing how to master and steer, or in not knowing how to determine the altitude by the quadrant or astrolabe, or the methods for calculating it, many shipwrecks have occurred, and those who have shipped under their guidance have been exposed to great danger, by which our Lord hath been ill-served, as well as our royal exchequer; and likewise the merchants who trade with our Indies have suffered much damage and loss. And to prevent such disasters and since it is essential not only for that navigation but for other voyages by which, with the aid of our Lord, we hope to make new discoveries in other lands, that there should be more skillful navigators, better instructed in their knowledge of navigation, so that those who sail under their direction may voyage more safely, it is our will and pleasure and we command that all the pilots of our kingdoms and lordships who are now or shall hereafter be appointed as pilots in voyages to the islands and mainland that we possess in the regions of the Indies and in other regions of the ocean sea shall be taught the essentials of knowledge in the use of the quadrant and astrolabe, to the end that by combining theory with practice they may make able use of both in the said voyages to the said regions. Without such knowledge no one shall presume to pilot the said ships or receive pay as a pilot, nor may the masters receive them on board, until they have first been examined by you, Amerigo Vespucci, our Chief Pilot, and have been given each one by you a certificate of examination and approval. We order that those who obtain the said certificates shall be accepted and received as skilled pilots by whomsoever is shown them, for it is our pleasure that you shall be examiner of all pilots.

In order that those who are ignorant may learn the more easily, we order that you are to teach them, in your house at Seville, everything they need to know, you receiving payment for your work. And since now, at the outset, there may be a scarcity of approved pilots and some ships may be detained for the lack of them, causing loss and injury to the citizens of the said islands and to the merchants and those who trade there, we order you, the said Amerigo, and we license you to select the ablest pilots from among those who have been to our Indies, so that for one or two voyages or for a stated period they may serve as pilots, while the others receive the necessary instruction, with time to learn all the essentials.

Furthermore, we have been informed that there are many charts by various masters on which are delineated the lands and islands in our Indies, by our command recently discovered, and that these charts may give rise to confusion because they are very different from each other, both in the sailing directions and in the contour of coastlines.

For the sake of uniformity it is our pleasure and we order that there shall be made a general chart (*padron general*); and that this may be the more accurate, we order our officers of the *Casa de Contratación* (Trade Commission) at Seville to assemble all the best-qualified pilots that may be found in Spain at the time, and that in your presence, Amerigo Vespucci, our Chief Pilot, there shall be made a chart of all the lands and islands of the Indies that have hitherto been discovered belonging to our kingdoms and lordships; and that, after consultation and discussion with the said pilots and in accord with you, the said Chief Pilot, a general chart shall be constructed, which shall be called the *padron real* (royal chart) by which all pilots shall be directed and guided; and that this shall be kept in the possession of our aforesaid officers and of you, our Chief Pilot; and that no pilot shall steer by any other chart save one which has been copied from the royal chart, under penalty of a fine of fifty dobles to be devoted to the projects of the *Casa de Contratación* of the Indies at the city of Seville.

Furthermore, we order all the pilots of our kingdoms and lordships who voyage hereafter to the said lands of our Indies, discovered or to be discovered, that when they find new lands, islands, bays, harbors, or anything else, they make a note of them for the said royal chart and that upon arriving in Castille they shall give an account to you, the said our Chief Pilot, and to the officers of the *Casa de Contratación* at Seville, that all may be delineated correctly on the said royal chart, so that navigators may be more accurately instructed and may be made expert in navigation. Furthermore, we order that none of our pilots who navigate the ocean sea shall henceforth sail without his quadrant and astrolabe and the rules for working them, under penalty of being rendered incompetent to exercise the said employment during our pleasure and of being forbidden to resume such employment without our special license, and of paying a fine of ten thousand maravedis toward the projects of the said *Casa de Contratación* at Seville. Amerigo Vespucci shall use and exercise the said office of our Chief Pilot, and you are empowered to do so, and you shall do all the things contained in this letter, and which appertain to the said office; and by this our letter and by its copy attested by the public notary, we order the Prince Charles, our very dear and well-beloved son, the infantes, dukes, prelates, counts, marquises, *rico-hombres*, masters of orders, members of council, and judges of our courts and chancelleries, and the other priors, commanders, subcommanders, castellans of our castles and forts, the magistrates, officers of justice, knights, esquires, officers, and good men of all the cities, towns, and villages of our kingdoms and lordships, and all captains of ships, master mariners, pilots, mates, and all other persons whom our letter concerns or may concern, that they have and hold as our Chief Pilot, and consent and allow him to hold the said office and to do and comply with all the things in this our letter or appertaining to it, and for their accomplishment and execution give all the favor and help that is needful for all that is herein and for each part of it. And that the above may come to the knowledge of all and that none may pretend ignorance, we order that this our letter shall be read before the public notary in the markets and open spaces and other accustomed places in the city of Seville, and in the city of Cadiz, and in all the other cities, towns, and villages of these kingdoms and lordships. And if hereafter any person or persons act against it, the said justices shall execute upon them the penalties contained in this letter, so that the above shall be observed and shall take effect without fail. And if anyone of the others does not comply, he shall be subject to a fine of ten thousand maravedis for our chamber. Furthermore, we order the man to whom this letter shall be shown to appear before us in our court, wherever we may be, for fifteen following days under the said penalty, for which we order whatever public notary may be called for this, shall give testimony signed with his seal, that we may know that our order has been executed.

Given in the city of Valladolid, the 6th of August, in the year of the birth of the Lord Jesus Christ, 1508. I, the King.

I, Lope Cunchillos, Secretary to the Queen our Lady, caused this to be written by order of the King her father.

Witnessed: The Bishop of Palencia; Licentiate Ximénes.

By the terms of the Letters Patent, Amerigo was commanded to stay at home and devote himself to the difficult but essential task of carrying out his duties as Pilot Major. All pilots of Spain were by the same mandate ordered to give heed to Amerigo's instructions, under penalty of nonemployment. "All captains of ships, master mariners, pilots, mates" were ordered to "consent and allow" Amerigo to hold the office of Pilot Major and to comply with his efforts to execute the duties thereof, and the king's edict was so publicized that none could pretend ignorance of it. It was to be an experiment in education by compulsion.

Thus Amerigo was fortified to continue his struggle against the resistance of the pilots, a resistance nonetheless real now that it no longer dared be open. In his favor was his great reputation as the man who had diagramed the stars of the Southern Hemisphere and by the discovery of a continent had effected a revolution in cosmography. He was being looked upon as the master geographer of his time and was now a sort of navigator statesman. His position as an authority in astronomy was no doubt enhanced by the fact that his nephew Bartolomeo Vespucci had two years before become professor of astrology (astronomy) at the University of Padua, and in the year of Amerigo's appointment as Pilot Major, had published at Venice a work entitled *Lodi del trivio e del quadrivio e dell' astrologia*. It helped Amerigo that there was such scholarship in the family and that Professor Bartolomeo Vespucci was spoken of as an "expert in astronomy, and most excellent in the science of mathematics." Amerigo himself was now called "Astronomer to the King of Spain."

But in spite of his great reputation he could not find willing ears among the pilots of Spain. They would not be taught. It was one thing to be appointed Pilot Major, and another to carry out single-handed so tremendous a task, so far-reaching a reform as universal adoption of his method of determining longitude by lunar distances. He was one man against an entire profession. Even with the backing of King Ferdinand and the formidable Letters Patent he could not win.

A few men, of course, were teachable, so that through them his method of lunar distances was handed on. Some of the Portuguese had learned it from him when he was in Lisbon. Because of his naming of Cananor and thus practically establishing the location of the Line of Demarcation, Portugal had a constant reminder of his accuracy in longitude, the more impressive, the more they checked on it. Six years after his appointment as Pilot Major, in 1514, a man named Werner wrote in an edition of Ptolemy's *Geographia* a description of the method which reads like an echo of what Amerigo's procedure and teaching must have been:

> The geographer should betake himself to one of the given places and there he should observe the distance between the moon and one of the planets, which distance, indeed, if we compute it in terms of the correct motion of the moon per hour, shows how much time there would be up to the conjunction of the moon with this planet, or how much time had elapsed since the conjunction. Afterward the geographer should calculate this same conjunction in relation to midday at the other place where he was not present, by means of the tables which were verified for that place while he was away. Finally, by comparing these two times in relation to midday at these places he will find the longitudinal distance between these two places.[1]

In 1517 the Portuguese astronomer Ruy Faleiro, giving instructions in Spain to Magellan, mentioned in his *Regimento* as methods of determining longitude: (1) the declination of the moon, (2) variation of the needle, and (3) the conjunction of the moon with the planets. The first was of no avail at that time for lack of sufficiently accurate tables; the second was illusory and impossible; and the only practicable one was the third, the one in which Amerigo had pioneered. But the general refusal among the Spanish pilots to have anything to do with science was maddening. Faleiro actually went insane in Spain when his utterances there met with nonacceptance. Amerigo, of firmer mind, must often have felt heartbroken by the reception most men accorded his teaching, for what he had to give was of utmost importance, yet the majority were blind to it. Demonstrations, explanations, attempts to persuade—all were futile. His life was no doubt shortened by the hopeless struggle.

A dozen years after his appointment as Pilot Major the state of affairs was described in Antonio Pigafetta's *Treatise on Navigation:* "At the present time the pilots content themselves with knowing the latitude, and are so proud they will not hear speak of longitude." The extent of this opposition is substantiated by the sixteenth-century Portuguese statement: "There be some that are very inquisitive to have a way to get the longitude, but that is too tedious for seamen, since it requireth the deep knowledge of astronomy." It took generations to educate the old sea dogs.

Another phase of his work as Pilot Major tended to sustain his faith in his usefulness. The terms of his appointment made him custodian, with the officers of the *Casa de Contratación* in Seville, of the royal chart. It was Amerigo's duty to keep this general marine chart up to date, adding to it and correcting it as information of new discoveries was brought to him and supervising the copying from it of all charts to be used by mariners in transoceanic navigation. For example, one of the first things he must have added to the royal chart was the completion of the island contour of Cuba, which Ocampo had circumnavigated in 1508, thus ending the old argument which had so often angered Columbus. He also must have entered upon the royal chart the results of the voyage of Pinzón and Solís after their return in November, 1509. These were: their exploration from Cape Caxinas to the Gulf of Amatique and then north to Cape Catoche, thus completing the last unknown section of the Caribbean Sea, and their investigation of the west coast of the "half island" of Yucatan, the beginning of discoveries in the Gulf of Mexico. It was his duty also to keep a record of such facts as that Sebastian Cabot had attempted a northwest passage at fifty-eight or sixty degrees north, and obviously would not have faced the difficulties of an attempt at that latitude had he not felt certain there was no strait anywhere between sixty degrees north and his farthest south "at the latitude of Gibraltar."

Perhaps the most congenial part of Amerigo's official duties was the making of maps, for which work he trained his nephew Giovanni to assist him. Since he did his cartographical work in his official capacity and with the knowledge that had been entrusted to him by the government, he did not sign his maps, and thus in later times men had no maps which could be identified as by his hand. Furthermore, cartographical work quickly fades from men's minds when superseded, and maps in active use seldom survive the generation in which they are produced unless they are in bound volumes—maps for the use of mariners least of all. While there can be no certainty, it is believed that he made the valuable suggestion that if the surface of the earth could be divided into theoretical squares, a map showing such squares by means of lines representing longitude and latitude would be very useful.

The Portuguese government, as well as the Spanish, appreciated his cartographical work. Herrera says that in 1511 the Portuguese, "desiring to sail through the ocean belonging to the crown of Castile, with much importunity begged maps from Américo Vespucio." This, of course, was presumptuous on their part. Their own government did not permit maps to leave Portugal and forbade their export under pain of death. They must have known that Amerigo would not be permitted to give them maps belonging to the government of Spain. The *Casa de Contratación* took care to see that all official charts were guarded from the eyes of Portuguese spies.

There was in existence in Spain, however, at least one Portuguese map which showed the continent Amerigo had discovered and which was partly the work of his hand. When Peter Martyr, member of the Council of the Indies and a scholar pledged to careful research, sought for proof of the reported great size of the new continent, he went to the home of Bishop Fonseca, who was officially in charge of all explorations and was hence the best authority in Spain on discoveries in the Western Hemisphere; and Bishop Fonseca showed him, for proof, the work of Amerigo. Peter Martyr tells of his investigation in his "Second Decade" addressed to Pope Leo X:

> This continent extends into the sea exactly like Italy, but is dissimilar in that it is not the shape of a human leg. Moreover, why shall we compare a pigmy with a giant? That part of the continent beginning at this eastern point lying toward Atlas, which the Spaniards have explored, is at least eight times larger than Italy; and its western coast has not yet been discovered. Your Holiness may wish to know upon what my estimate of *eight times* is based. From the outset, when I resolved to obey your commands and to write a report of these events, in Latin (though myself no Latinist), I adopted precautions to avoid stating anything which was not fully investigated.
>
> I addressed myself to the Bishop of Burgos, whom I have already mentioned and to whom all navigators report. Seated in his room, we examined numerous reports of those expeditions, and we likewise studied the terrestrial globe on which the discoveries are indicated and also many parchments, called by the explorers, "navigators' charts." One of these maps had been drawn by the Portuguese, and it is claimed that Americus Vespucius, of Florence, assisted in its composition. He is very skilled in this art and has himself gone many degrees beyond the equinoctial line, sailing in the service and at the expense of the Portuguese. According to this chart, we found the continent was larger than the caciques of Urabá told our compatriots.

In 1511 the Portuguese had no right to expect that the Spanish would give them permission to sail "through the ocean belonging to the crown of Castile." That ocean was the Spanish Main, the Caribbean. The Portuguese sought cartographical aid from Vespucci because they believed that to the west of the Caribbean they might find a strait leading into the other ocean beyond the New World. Their application to Amerigo for maps was evidence that they had accepted his conception of the existence of that other ocean (the Pacific), as a necessary corollary to his conception of a new continent and a Western Hemisphere. This was two years before that ocean's reputed "discoverer," Balboa, upon being assured by native Indians of its nearness to the Caribbean, led an expedition across the Isthmus of Darien toward that ocean and became the first European to set eyes upon it.

The Portuguese were unrealistic in their expectations. Nor could they much longer prevent the Spanish from exploring in the southwest for some possible passage into the other ocean. The time soon came when Amerigo's idea of seeking a strait at the southern end of the New World bore fruit in the voyages begun by Solís in 1515 and by Magellan in 1519.

Another phase of Amerigo's work for the Spanish government grew out of his long experience in trade. He was consulted by the Cardinal Ximénes, the Inquisitor-General, on the question of taxation of commerce with the New World. Cardinal Ximénes, who had been Provisional Regent of Castile after the death of Queen Isabella, was in 1508 the most powerful man in Spain next to the king. In answer to the Cardinal's question whether goods shipped to the Spanish islands in the New World should be handled exclusively by an individual monopoly paying profit to the Crown, or whether, as Amerigo said he understood was the Cardinal's opinion, there should be unrestricted trade, Amerigo replied in a letter dated December 9,[2] that the trade with the West Indies was too complex and of too varied a nature to be controlled by a monopoly, since the Spanish colonists would not naturally trade only with Spain, but would buy from other countries and from the Canaries and the Portuguese islands. But, he went on to say, the Crown would reap a profit conveniently by either of two ways: to lay an import tax on all goods entering the West Indies, while permitting a natural flow of trade, or to commission various merchants through whose hands all goods must pass, they to share profits with the Crown, with due provision for securing honest records of all transactions through a system of supervision by royal treasury agents. He refrained from indicating any preference for either of the methods.

Trade with the New World brought up many fascinating problems in which Amerigo must have taken a keen interest. What did the New World have which the Old World lacked? What in the form of vegetation and animal life and manufactured goods should the Old World contribute to the New? He had been handling foodstuffs and materials for many years, and he gave much thought to determining what articles of "usefulness to human living" should be exchanged with the countries beyond the ocean. He was a specialist in his knowledge of the raw materials and manufactured goods of Europe. He had made note on his voyages of the species of vegetables and fruits and various materials used by the natives of the New World. No man of his day was better prepared to make an intelligent selection of articles in one hemisphere which would be of maximum benefit in the other.

The New World gave to Europe corn, chocolate, coffee, tomatoes, "Irish" potatoes, and lima beans; many kinds of fruit, such as cassava, guava, papaya, and avocado; alpaca wool; mahogany and many other valuable woods; the turkey, quinine, tobacco, and rubber. Fully half of all the materials that later came to be used in manufacture were contributed to mankind by the natives of the Western Hemisphere.

The Old World's agricultural gifts to the New World necessarily had less to do with changing the course of civilization, but they were numerous and important. As listed by Herbert I. Priestley in his *History of American Life*, they were wheat, barley, rye, some beans, chick-peas, lentils, almonds, mulberries, cherries, walnuts, chestnuts, medlars, tulip trees, linen, flax, indigo, alfalfa, canary seed, quinces, apples, apricots, most of the pitted fruits (not plums), oranges, limes, lemons, citron trees, cedars, pears, rosemary, willows, broom, roses, lilies, old-fashioned flowers, sugar cane, bananas (some varieties), tamarinds, mangoes, grapefruit. Arabian horses from Andalusia and various kinds of seeds were sent to the New World in 1509. The *Casa de Contratación* successfully sent almonds, figs, cherries, pomegranates, and quinces, kept on the decks in half barrels filled with earth. Amerigo may have shared in planning the sending of rice, which was first carried over in 1512.

During the three and a half years that remained to him after his appointment as Pilot Major he continued to suffer from the ravages of malaria, for in his day that disease was incurable. It progressively enfeebled his efforts to teach navigation to the unwilling pilots and eventually forced him to realize that he himself could never hope to do any more exploring. When he felt himself failing, did his thoughts turn to the country of his birth? We do not know whether he made a trip to Florence late in his life, but it would appear that he did if he, not his grandfather, was the "Amerigo Vespucci" of the portrait by Leonardo da Vinci mentioned in Giorgio Vasari's *Lives of the Painters*.[3] Vasari wrote:

> Leonardo was so much pleased when he encountered faces of extraordinary character, or heads, beards or hair of unusual appearance, that he would follow any such, more than commonly attractive, through the whole day, until the figure of the person would become so well

impressed on his mind that, having returned home, he would draw him as readily as though he stood before him. Of heads thus obtained there exist many, both masculine and feminine, and I have myself several of them drawn with a pen by his own hand, in the book of drawings so frequently cited. Among these is the head of Amerigo Vespucci, which is a very beautiful one of an old man, done with charcoal, as also that of the Gypsy Captain Scaramuccia.

Leonardo's charcoal drawing of Amerigo Vespucci is today unidentified, and it may have been lost. If it was a portrait of Amerigo's grandfather, it was done when Leonardo was not yet twenty; if it was a portrait of the Pilot Major, it could have been drawn during any of Amerigo's later years, for Leonardo had returned to Florence in 1500. In any case, artists who pictured Amerigo years after his death all gave his features the same characteristics, following one original conception, and this may have been Leonardo's. All the artists pictured him with a typical Florentine countenance, with prominent nose and a forehead that slanted somewhat in line with it; with brilliant eyes and well-formed, handsome lips and chin. The deep-lined cheek and the thinning hair accentuated the air of intellectual ardor, the stamp of genius that marked the face.

During his last years Spain witnessed the departure to the New World in 1509 of an expedition headed by Hojeda and Nicuesa, who carried seeds to the mainland. Amerigo was cognizant of the sailing of Don Diego Columbus, son of the admiral, who, partly because he was anxious to look after his inherited property in Española, took ship in May, 1509, with his wife, his uncles Diego and Bartholomew, and his younger half-brother, Ferdinand. King Ferdinand had married Don Diego to Doña Maria de Toledo, who was closely related to himself, to keep the claims of Columbus within the royal family.

News which touched Amerigo deeply was the fate of Juan de la Cosa, who had sailed on his thirteenth crossing of the Atlantic, and who was killed in a fight with Indians in Venezuela on February 28, 1510. His body was found, swollen and, like a hedgehog's, with many poisoned arrows in it. Funeral rites were held for him in Spain. Thus was lost a man with whom Amerigo had been much associated, a man who was a splendid navigator, skillful, open-minded, and a gentleman. Years earlier, notwithstanding resentment against one who insisted that Cuba was an island, Columbus had called Juan de la Cosa a "clever man," "a master in the art of navigation." Herrera called him "the best pilot that existed for those seas; a man of great courage and merit."

The loss of Juan de la Cosa preceded Amerigo's death by just two years. Time was not given to the Pilot Major to see the realization of his dream of finding a strait through the New World to the farther ocean and to India. He was not to enjoy the longevity usual in his family. With his strong constitution undermined by the recurrent malaria, broken at last in health, he died in Seville on February 22, 1512, at the age of fifty-eight.[4]

The paucity of his estate gives testimony to his probity. He died poor, although he had managed the commercial affairs of two great houses, as well as much of the naval equipment of Spain. His widow was accorded a pension of 10,000 maravedis as "repayment and reward for the services which her husband has rendered to us," and twelve years later this pension was continued to her sister Catalina. The king named Giovanni, his nephew, pilot of His Highness, and the young man was given the exclusive right in Spain to construct and give out copies of maps.[5] Juan Díaz de Solís and after him Sebastian Cabot were Amerigo's successors in the office of Pilot Major.

Amerigo Vespucci was the first European, according to incontrovertible record, to have reached the shore of Brazil, and he was the first to explore the whole coastline of Brazil. He was also the first on the coasts of Colombia, Uruguay, and Argentina. All four countries have the same reason for honoring Vespucci that Cuba, Haiti, Puerto Rico, and the Dominican Republic have for honoring Columbus. He named one of the countries of South America, "Venezuela" (Little Venice). He discovered three of the world's greatest rivers: the Amazon, the Pará, the Plata. He explored more miles of previously unknown coastline than any other explorer in the world's history—more than six thousand miles of coastline, conservatively estimated. He was the first observer to record the existence of the equatorial current. He was the first explorer to go south of the equator on the western side of the Atlantic. He was the first to go south of the latitude by which the Portuguese rounded the Cape of Good Hope; that is, he was the first man in history to sail through the fifteen degrees of latitude from thirty-five degrees south to fifty degrees south.

He became, as Ober has said, "more proficient in astronomy and cosmography than any other person of his age and time." He first applied astronomy to the determination of longitude, and learned to apply it with increasing skill after his initial error. By devising his method of determining longitude he proved himself one of the great original thinkers of the world. We who possess elaborate and accurate instruments sometimes forget the great exercise of genius responsible for devising a primitive method which requires only knowledge and a simple tool.

Vespucci was the discoverer of the fact that the great continent which he explored was not part of Asia, as men thought, but a new continent.[6] He made a remarkable guess as to the shape of South America. The Gulf of Mexico was not so well mapped until 1527, and North America not for another generation later, as South America was in the time of Vespucci. No other area as large has been discovered by any one man, an achievement unequaled in the history of exploration. Those who live in the Americas find it no extravagance to say with Pietro Canovai, "One cannot raise one's eyes to the heavens without thinking of Galileo, or lower one's eyes to the ground without thinking of Vespucci."

As Pilot Major of Spain he planned and inspired a series of expeditions that sought for a strait in unexplored latitudes, and he left as a heritage to Spain and to Magellan the dream of finding a passage at the southern end of America.

In the mind of Vespucci, the geographical disposition of land and water in general outline of approximately one-half the surface of the globe first took reasonably correct form. No more important thinking was ever done in the field of cosmography. His work in pushing back the veil from the unknown was second to no man's, not even to that of Columbus. He effected a veritable revolution in geography.

Magellan, it may be noted, served no new idea; for several men before him had sought a western route to Asia. Bartolomeu Dias and Vasco da Gama served no new idea; for the Portuguese had been attempting for many years what these men achieved. And Columbus? In the light of the teachings of the ancients, and the letters of Toscanelli which encouraged Columbus to attempt a crossing of the western ocean, it is fair to say that Columbus served an old idea which other men had before him. The best statement of what he did is in his own words: "I gave the keys of those mighty barriers of ocean which were closed with such mighty chains." In showing that the Atlantic could be crossed, he did not contribute any new idea, but he gave the world a deed, gloriously accomplished. Thereafter, because he was deductive and not inductive, he forced the facts and ignored the logical consequences of his own observations.

Vespucci, whose accomplishments were themselves of no second order, contributed the thought which alone gave significance to the deed of Columbus. The achievement of Columbus meant to Europe nothing more than the opening of another trade route to India, until Vespucci discovered that the way to India was blocked by a new continent and thus gave the world something of vaster importance. The idea of Columbus that he had found a western route to Asia faded like steam, but Amerigo's idea proved permanent. With entire justification there was placed in 1719 upon the ancient mansion of the Vespucci in which Amerigo was born, a tablet bearing the inscription:

To Amerigo Vespucci, a noble Florentine,
Who by the discovery of America
Rendered his own and his Country's name illustrious;
The Amplifier of the World.

Amerigo Vespucci and Christopher Columbus were both given credit for what the other accomplished. This was not fair to either. When it became known that a popular narrative purporting to have been written by Vespucci had wrongly given Vespucci credit for what Columbus had done, it was believed that Vespucci's renown as the discoverer of the New World was somehow stolen from Columbus. Literally, the contrary was the fact, for Vespucci gave meaning to 1492—the foremost meaning which 1492 has acquired. After this meaning had been revealed, after Vespucci had revealed what actually lay beyond the Atlantic, Columbus began to receive credit for what Vespucci had done. The afterfame of Columbus took its luster in large measure from the discovery of Vespucci, and thus Columbus won posthumous glory. Only recently Columbus himself has been discovered.

Amerigo's name has been honored above those of all other explorers. We now know that he deserved the honor. Unquestionably, it was he who uncovered the existence of the new continent. In this sense he was indeed the discoverer of America, the discoverer of the Western Hemisphere, "the Amplifier of the World."

Appendix A

CHRONOLOGY OF VOYAGES OF EXPLORATION, 1486–1522

The date of commencing a voyage or the date when new land was sighted is usually less important than the date when the new geographical knowledge was brought to Europe and made available to other explorers.

Bartolomeu Dias sailed in 1486; discovered the Cape of Good Hope in 1487; returned to Lisbon in 1488.

Columbus (first voyage) sailed August 3, 1492; sighted land October 12, 1492; discovered islands in the West Indies, Cuba, Haiti; arrived in Lisbon March 4, 1493.

Columbus (second voyage) sailed September 25, 1493; discovered additional islands, including Jamaica; sent various reports home; returned June 11, 1496.

John Cabot sailed early May, 1497; reached land (Cape Breton Island?) June 24, 1497; returned to England about July 30, 1497.

Columbus (third voyage) sailed May 30, 1498; sighted Trinidad July 31; touched coast of South America August 2, 1498; report sent home autumn 1498. Columbus was brought home in irons November, 1500.

John and Sebastian Cabot sailed early May, 1498; explored coast of North America, Labrador to Maryland ("latitude of Gibraltar") from end of July to autumn, 1498; returned to England late autumn, 1498.

Vasco da Gama sailed from Lisbon July 8, 1497; reached India; news brought to Lisbon July 10, 1499; Da Gama returned August 29, 1499.

Amerigo Vespucci (Spanish voyage) sailed at same time as Hojeda from Cadiz May 18, 1499; landfall late in June, 1499, on coast of Brazil at about four degrees N.; explored three thousand miles of northeastern and northern coast of continent; returned to Cadiz in middle of June, 1500. Hojeda who followed the coastline for about one-fourth of the distance Vespucci explored, returned in April, 1500.

Peralonso Niño and Cristóbal Guerra sailed June, 1499; accomplished very little more than the third voyage of Columbus; returned April, 1500.

Vicente Yañez Pinzón sailed November 18, 1499; landfall at ten degrees S. on coast of Brazil January 20, 1500, and sailed northward to Brazilian elbow; returned July, 1500.

Diego de Lepe sailed December 18, 1499; landfall at four degrees S. on coast of Brazil February 14, 1500, and sailed northward; returned June, 1500.

Rodrigo de Bastidas explored the Gulf of Darien in 1500.

Pedro Alvares Cabral sailed from Lisbon March 9, 1500; landfall April 24, 1500, on coast of Brazil at eighteen degrees S. and sailed northward to 16° 17′ S. News reached Lisbon end of May, 1500; Spain was informed by royal letter of July 29, 1501. Cabral returned in summer of 1501.

Amerigo Vespucci (Portuguese voyage) sailed from Lisbon May 13, 1501; sighted coast of Brazil on or before August 15 at about five degrees S. and explored coast to fifty degrees S.; returned to Lisbon in June, 1502.

Columbus (fourth voyage) sailed May 11, 1502; explored coast of Honduras, Veragua, and Isthmus; returned November 7, 1504.

Juan de la Cosa, in 1501, to Darien and Urabá; made other voyages in 1505, 1507, and 1509, as much for commercial purposes as for exploration.

Vicente Yañez Pinzón and Juan Díaz de Solís sailed July 29, 1508; explored Honduras, Yucatan; returned November 14, 1509.

Sebastian de Ocampo circumnavigated Cuba, 1508.

Juan Díaz de Solís sailed in 1515; explored River Plata and was killed there. News reached Spain in 1516.

Ferdinand Magellan sailed in 1519; discovered Strait of Magellan in October, 1520. Remnant of his expedition after his death completed circumnavigation of globe September 6, 1522.

Appendix B

LINEAR MEASUREMENTS OF SIGNIFICANCE IN THE HISTORY OF EXPLORATION

League: from 2.42 to 4.6 English miles.

Roman mile: 4,860 feet; 1,620 English yards. This is the measure given by Webster's and Funk & Wagnall's dictionaries. The Century dictionary gives 1,617 yards, and the *American Encyclopaedia* gives 1,614 yards for the ancient Roman mile, and 1,628 yards for the modern Roman mile. "The Roman mile consisted of 5,000 Roman feet. The Roman foot changed through the centuries, and at no time was it precisely defined. . . . Most authorities agree that the Roman foot was within the limits 11.64 to 11.67 U.S. or British inches, but there may be considerable evidence for values somewhat outside these two limits. The values 11.64 and 11.67 inches for the Roman foot give values 1,617 and 1,621 yards, respectively, for the Roman mile. . . . We have no information readily available as to when the changes were made in the Roman mile between the ancient and the modern period, and we do not know the value for its length at the time of Columbus."—Statement received by the author from the National Bureau of Standards.

Length in English miles of one Roman mile: .92045.

Geographical or nautical mile: length of one minute of longitude on the equator, 6,087.15 feet; or, mean length of a minute of longitude, 6,082 feet. U.S. Coast Survey nautical mile, 6,080.27 feet. Admiralty knot, 6,080 feet.

One degree on the equator: 69.172 English miles.

SIZE OF A DEGREE

Estimated by	*Roman Miles*
Modern science	75 15/100
Eratosthenes (276–195 B.C.)	87½
Ptolemy (2d century)	62½
Alfragano (c. 820)	77 11/12
Toscanelli (1397–1482)	75⅗
Regiomontano (1436–1476)	80
Columbus	56⅔
Vespucci (until 1500)	66⅔
—— (revised estimate, 1501)	75

CIRCUMFERENCE OF EARTH AT EQUATOR

Estimated by	*Roman Miles*	*English Miles*
Modern science	27,054	24,902
Eratosthenes	31,500	28,919
Ptolemy	22,500	20,710
Alfragano	28,050	25,819
Toscanelli	27,216 ?	25,050 ?
Regiomontano	28,800	26,509
Columbus	20,400	18,777
Vespucci (on Spanish voyage)	24,000	22,091
—— (on Portuguese voyage)	27,000	24,852

According to Uzielli, *La vita e i tempi di Paolo dal Pozzo Toscanelli,* Toscanelli was the first to shake off the yoke of the classical measure of distance. Uzielli argues that because the Florentine mile was the mile with which Toscanelli was most familiar, it was the one he ordinarily used and that in this he was a model for Regiomontano, who consequently believed that the measurements of Toscanelli were in terms of the Florentine mile. On Toscanelli's map described in his letter to Fernando Martinez, there were twenty-six spaces of two hundred and fifty Roman miles each between Lisbon and Quinsay in China; this distance, Toscanelli said, was almost a third of the earth's circumference. Toscanelli undoubtedly intended each space to represent four degrees of sixty-two and a half Roman miles each, or a total of a hundred and four degrees, which was "almost a third." Uzielli argues that Toscanelli used the Ptolemaic measurement of sixty-two and a half miles in his letter because he was dealing with distance at the latitude of Lisbon and wished to give it in terms familiar to his Portuguese friend. Sixty-two and a half Roman miles at the latitude of Lisbon were equivalent to seventy-five and three-fifths Roman miles of longitudinal distance at the equator. Giving Toscanelli the benefit of this favorable interpretation, we may believe, if we will, that his estimate of the earth's circumference was in error by only one hundred and forty-eight English miles.

Although Eratosthenes was the parent of scientific geography, his terrestrial measurement was grossly inaccurate, according to E. H. Bunbury, in his *History of Ancient Geography*. Because his observation of latitude was approximately correct, it has been assumed that Eratosthenes *must* have known the true length of a degree, "but he in fact followed the converse method of starting from what he believed to be a well-ascertained terrestrial measurement"; that is, of the distance between two places. He was right in theory, but very wrong in his actual estimate of the earth's circumference as two hundred and fifty thousand stadia. He added two thousand stadia to this estimate in order to arrive at a number evenly divisible by the number of degrees in a circle. Estimates of the Greek measure of length known as the "stadium" vary from six hundred and six feet, nine inches, to six hundred and thirty feet, eight inches. The supposed close approximation to accuracy of Eratosthenes in estimating the earth's circumference is an erroneous assumption with no better foundation than the desire to believe that Eratosthenes was close to the truth. It is a conclusion, as Bunbury says, "attained by a series of arbitrary changes and alterations of numbers made with the express purpose of bringing about a correct result." The most favorable computation thus made has unjustifiably credited Eratosthenes with an estimate of the earth's circumference of twenty-four thousand seven hundred and sixty-three English miles.

LONGITUDES EAST OF CADIZ ACCORDING TO PTOLEMY

From the *Cosmographia*, editions of 1477 and 1482. Since the exact location of Ptolemy's prime meridian is uncertain, longitudes are given as east of Cadiz. Cadiz, according to Ptolemy, was five and one-sixth degrees east of the prime meridian, but for convenience it is here considered as five degrees east of it. The actual longitude of Cadiz is 6° 16′ W. (of Greenwich).

Place	*Ptolemaic Estimate*	*Actual Longitude*
Ferrara	29	About 18
Alexandria	55½	About 36
Taprobana Insula (Ceylon?)	119	About 86
Caligut (Calicut)	124	About 82
India intra Gangem	127	The mouth of the Ganges is about 97 degrees east of Cadiz.
India extra Gangem	147	
Sinarum regio	167	. . .
Catigara sinaru statio (1477)	172	Sunda Strait is about 111 and Bali Strait about 120 degrees east of Cadiz.
Catigara (1482)	175	
Seylam (Ceylon)	175	About 86
Java Minor (Java?)	201	About 109
Mangi regio (China)	215	. . .
Java Major (?)	220	. . .
Zipangri (Japan)	260	From about 137 to 148

NOTES

Chapter One

1. Whatever may have been the superstitions of the illiterate in Europe in the fifteenth century, the beliefs which the learned of the time entertained are a matter of record—in the published geographies, in the contemporary maps, in the accounts of travel which were most popular, and in the classical authors who were held in highest repute. "The Voyages and Travels of Sir John Maundeville," a French manuscript which first appeared in 1356, mentions a man who traveled eastward from Europe until he reached an island where he heard men speak his own language; thence he returned westward to Europe and went into Norway and there recognized that same island.

Chapter Two

1. In the tax list of 1457 it is recorded that Amerigo's father paid 200 florins each for himself and wife and five children. The gold florin weighed 54 grains, so that 106 florins weighed one pound (Troy). Amerigo's father thus paid taxes amounting to more than $7,000 worth of gold. Considering the purchasing power of the florin, it is apparent that he was a rich man in 1457.

2. March 9 is the only day in the year ever named as Amerigo's birthday. It is so given in a record in the Florentine state archives. In the Florentine calendar each year began, not on January 1, but nearly three months later, on March 25. Because of this overlapping, a date before March 25 in the Florentine reckoning, while close to the end of the Florentine year, was in the first three months of the next year of our calendar.

There has been error with respect to the year of Amerigo's birth, because until the end of the nineteenth century certain statements in old records were generally accepted as correct. These records in documents still existing in the archives were of two kinds: (1) records to establish the year in which a citizen would be old enough according to law to take a public office, and (2) declarations for tax purposes. In one record "d'Approazione d' età" (acceptance of age) of the Uffizio delle Tratte (Libro 2° Eta n. 27, numero antico 33, f. 116 r°), is the statement:

"Amerigo di ser Nastagio di ser Amerigo Vespucci a dì VIIII di Marzo MCCCCLI" (Amerigo son of Signore Nastagio son of Signore Amerigo Vespucci on the 9th of March, 1451). This date would seem to be amply supported by the declaration for tax purposes of 1480, in which Amerigo's age was given as 29. But the "MCCCCLI" may have been an error of an amanuensis, since Amerigo's eldest brother, Antonio, was born in 1451; and the date of birth deducible from the declaration in 1480 is contradicted by every other similar declaration made in other years. Acceptance of the year 1451 was furthered, I believe, by misconstruing what was not at all a record of birth, but a notarized statement concerning a visit to the Paradiso Monastery in which occur the words: "ser Amerigo di Stagio Vespucci il di 28 Marzio 1451." In all probability the son and father here named were our hero's grandfather Amerigo and great-grandfather Anastasio, who was called Stagio ("detto Stagio"). Our Amerigo's father was called "Nastagio" or "Anastasio," but not "Stagio."

Evidence that the true date was 1454 (March, 1453, Florentine calendar) is furnished by the archives of S. Maria del Fiore in Florence, in which the Register of Baptisms (*Registro dei battezzati di S. Giovanni Battista di Firenze*) from November 14, 1450, to the year 1460 contains on sheet No. 92, under date of Monday, March 18, 1453, the following entry: "Amerigo et Matteo di ser Nastagio di ser Amerigo p. S. Lu. Dogns.ti" (Amerigo and Matteo of Signore Nastagio son of Signore Amerigo, of the people of Santa Lucia d'Ognissanti). A hand drawn in the margin indicates the entry, and there is a circle attached, in which is written: "Truovatore dell' Indie nuove" (Discoverer of the new Indies). The "Matthew" (Matteo) was Amerigo's saint's name. A facsimile of the full page is given by Enrico Masini in *Atti dell VIII Congresso Geografica Italiana*, II (1921), 278. At the top of the page under date "Saturday, March 16, 1453" are six baptismal entries; eight under "Sunday the 17th"; and six under "Monday the 18th," the fifth of which is Amerigo's. Entries for "Tuesday the 19th" and "Wednesday the 20th" follow on the page. This is a record of date in which there cannot be any conceivable error of an amanuensis.

The baptismal date, March 18, fits perfectly with the accepted day of birth, March 9, since it was the custom to baptize infants within a very few days after birth.

The baptismal record is corroborated by a declaration for tax purposes *in the handwriting of Amerigo's father*, who in 1457 described Amerigo as four years of age. This declaration, which is the nearest in point of time to Amerigo's birth, is more reliable than records in 1470, 1480, and 1498 which contradict it and each other. The combined evidence of the baptismal register and the father's statement I take to be conclusive.

In the declaration of 1457 the age of Amerigo's mother is given as twenty-two, of his eldest brother, Antonio, as six, of Girolamo as five, of Bernardo as three, and of his sister Agnoletta as one. If the age of Amerigo as given in this record is not accepted, then the ages of both elder brothers and of the mother cannot be accepted. If Amerigo, the third son, was born in 1451, then his mother would have had to be older, and so would Antonio and Girolamo. The baptismal record should be searched for the dates of baptism of the two elder brothers, for their bearing upon the year of Amerigo's birth.

3. Could Amerigo's father, the donor of the painting by Ghirlandajo, have engaged any better artist? Andrea del Verrocchio, who three years before had captivated every Florentine with his "David" in the Bargello, was in 1472 at work on the sculpture for the tomb of Giovanni and Piero de' Medici in the sacristy of San Lorenzo. Among Verrocchio's pupils, the talented Lorenzo di Credi was a mere boy, too young to be entrusted with so important a commission as the Vespucci family portrait. The twenty-two-year-old Pietro Perugino was devoted to depicting idealized saints rather than real people. The twenty-year-old Leonardo da Vinci was available, but he was an unknown quantity, having enrolled only a few weeks before with the painters' guild in Florence. The logical man for the fresco in the Ognissanti chapel was Sandro Filipepi, called after his father's nickname, Botticelli. He was born around the corner, in the Via Nuova, and was not without honor in his own district, having finished his apprenticeship under Fra Filippo Lippi and having been building a reputation for four years; but he could not accept the commission to paint the Vespucci family, since the Medici had already become his patrons and were keeping him busy.

It was easy for anyone familiar with the Vespucci family to identify various members of it in Ghirlandajo's fresco. At the extreme sides were the donors of the picture, Amerigo's parents, Ser Nastagio Vespucci and Lisabetta Mini. The father was then forty-six, and the mother not far from the same age. The white-haired grandfather, whose face was turned from the spectator almost as completely as was the grandmother's, had died at the age of seventy-four, in the same year when the fresco was made. He was kneeling near the middle of the group close to his namesake, young Amerigo. All these older persons were dressed in black, the favorite color of men and women of maturity. Forming the background and facing the spectator were the five grandchildren. From left to right they are: Antonio, the eldest, born in 1451, Girolamo, in 1452, and Amerigo; and on the other side of the picture, Bernardo, born in 1455, and Agnoletta, about 1456.

Anyone who did not know the family would have asked about the portrait of the woman with downcast eyes. Was she the widow of Amerigo's deceased uncle Jacopo? And whose was the portrait of the young woman with the attractive coiffeur? Was she La Belle Simonetta, the wife of Amerigo's cousin Marco? Simonetta Cattaneo was a tall blonde, daughter of a leading Genoese family with Teutonic forebears. She and her husband and Giuliano de' Medici, brother of Lorenzo the Magnificent, were of the same age, one year older than Amerigo. Lorenzo gave a Vespuccio-Cattaneo nuptial feast at Careggi; from the moment she was brought home by Marco, all Florence fêted her and the poets sang her praises. She was a new vision of loveliness to the artists. Giuliano was deeply in love with her, but she held him to a platonic adoration. Lorenzo wrote poems on her beauty and character; Giuliano gave a pageant (the Giostra, January 28, 1475) in her honor; after her death by consumption in April, 1476, Poliziano wrote *Stanze* in memory of Giuliano's passion for her. Botticelli was inspired by her beauty when he painted his Venus (Birth of Venus), and the tall figures of his Primavera, and Pallas and the Centaur, and so forth. Primavera was painted for the villa at Castello belonging to Lorenzo di Pier Francesco, Amerigo's patron. Simonetta was buried in the Vespucci chapel, and Botticelli was later buried just outside. Simonetta Vespucci was unquestionably a link between the young men in the Medici and Vespucci families. It is likely that Marco and Amerigo were intimates and students together under Amerigo's uncle, and also likely that Amerigo was intimately acquainted with Giuliano de' Medici.

The Ghirlandajo fresco in the chapel in the Ognissanti church was whitewashed in 1616, and it was not uncovered until 1892.

4. Amerigo's notebook contained the following: "Arise betimes in the morning and sleep not so much, young man, who until now hath excessively played the fool, dancing and frolicking! Do not loll around or remain longer in idleness, but tire thyself out a little before old age comes upon thee and bodily vigor fails, and thou movest unhappy and ill content. For if thou endeavorest a little in virtue, before death comes or extreme old age, believe me when I say that thou wilt die happy, and thereafter repose in eternity, in the glory of the saints, where there is no infirmity, or old age, or deficiency." On the last page of his notebook Amerigo wrote: "Let us not wish to be chatterers or speakers of many words, and let us shun the company of sarcastic men and those greedy to rob their fellows, and also the deceivers of their friends and relatives; and if in our establishment there are 20 or 25 persons, we will not boast that there are 40 or 50, but in the shortest way let us take pains to comprehend many things praiseworthy and eternal, and by so doing begin to warm the mind with the love of virtue." Manuscript #2649, Riccardiana.

5. In the survey for tax purposes, "portata al catasto," of 1480, the occupation of Amerigo's brother Antonio is given as "notary." Girolamo is described as "connected with the woolen industry [or cloth-making business], but now out of work," and Bernardo as "attending to the woolen business, but without any income."

6. Catigara (variant spellings: Cattigara, Cattegara, Kattigara, Cattigra, Kattigra, Kattegra) was probably not the actual name of some Far Eastern seaport, nor was it a corruption of an actual name. It was a European name for such a seaport, to be understood in light of its derivation, which appears to have been from "Cathay" (derived from "Khitai," the name for northern China, at times used as a name for all China), plus the Greek ἀχορά (*agora*, meaning market place or emporium). An equivalent for Catigara would be "Portus Sinarum" or "Port of China" or "Chinese Mart." There have been various theories as to its location. M. Gosselin believed it was not far from the present Martaban in the Gulf of Tongking. Others believed it was a port on the coast of Cochin China, or on the coast of China in Fukien Province, along the Formosa Strait near Foochow. From its position on Ptolemy's maps it would seem to have been a place on the western coast of Sumatra. It was probably a trading port at which goods from China were transferred from Chinese junks to Malayan or Arabian ships. Its latitude as given by Ptolemy, eight and a half degrees south, seems to point either to the vicinity of Sunda Strait, between Sumatra and Java, which is at about seven and a half degrees south, or to Bali Strait, which is at eight and a half degrees south. All attempts to identify Catigara are pure conjecture, of course, and its longitude, given by Ptolemy as fifty-two degrees east of Cape Kory (Comorin, the southern tip of India), was undoubtedly very much exaggerated. But from early times mariners knew their approximate latitude, and since Ptolemy placed Catigara at eight and a half degrees south, I contribute as my guess that it was on the western coast of Sumatra near Sundra Strait, or on the southern coast of Java near Bali Strait.

7. Cosimo de' Medici transferred the Monastery of San Marco to the Dominicans. He founded the Medicean Library in 1444, having a private library at his palace in the Via Larga, and also developing one at the monastery, for which he had copies of books made. Cosimo's library was added to by his son Piero, but it owed most to his grandson, Lorenzo the Magnificent, who from 1469 employed agents to obtain more than one thousand precious manuscripts. The Medicean Library was later sold to the Dominicans.

8. The first printed edition of the *Cosmographia* of Claudius Ptolemaeus was that of 1475, published at Vicenza. This was a text without maps. The second printed edition (Bologna, 1477) was one to be particularly prized, for it contained twenty-six maps of Europe and the known parts of Asia and Africa, printed from copper plate by Taddeo Crivelli and hand-colored. In this edition there was an error in date made by the printer, Dominicus de Lapis, who had set the type for MCCCCLXII instead of MCCCCLXXVII. The third edition (Rome, 1478) was also a treasure to a booklover, for its twenty-seven maps,

though uncolored, were examples of very superior copper engraving. A fourth edition was brought out soon afterward in Florence.

9. Toscanelli's character was no less remarkable than his mind; for in a world of violence and cruelty and in a city that knew the bitter conflicts of commercial rivalry, he had never been heard to speak ill of anyone. He had dissociated himself from the clique of selfish intellectuals in Florence, of whom he wrote: "Among them is a craze, or greed for glory, not the true sort, but only ephemeral and apparent, and in order to attain it they have no regard for the reputation of others." He himself did not seek anything but the satisfaction of serving others and of giving the world the results of his scientific work. This generosity of spirit was infectious, so that no young man who became acquainted with him could fail to be moved with a desire to emulate him.

Toscanelli was of tremendous mental stature. He was the central figure of the Renaissance, the dominant link between old knowledge and new enterprise. More than any other man preceding Leonardo, he exemplified in his scientific researches the Florentine spirit of inquiry. Judged by the caliber and accomplishment of the men he inspired, his importance as a teacher was unique. He was one of the most influential personalities in all history, belonging to what Heine called "the apostolic succession of great souls." Who else ever shaped the careers of four such men as Prince Henry the Navigator, Christopher Columbus, Leonardo da Vinci, and Amerigo Vespucci?

He owned a planisphere, which he had hanging on a wall in his house, the map of the world made by Castellani. This map had very much interested the Portuguese ambassadors, who had in turn transmitted some of Toscanelli's ideas to their master, Prince Henry the Navigator.

He had maintained contacts with the Portuguese for many years. It was a suggestion of Toscanelli's made to the ambassadors of Portugal which had given Prince Henry the idea of seeking a route to the Indies by sailing around Africa. And so Prince Henry had begun to send ships down the west coast of Africa, and first they rounded Cape Bojador, and then Cape Blanco, and then Cape Verde. And after Prince Henry died the Portuguese continued his work, and in 1475 they passed the equator. Toscanelli was too old to live to see whether they would succeed in sailing around Africa, but he had faith that it could be done.

For some time, however, he had had a new and better idea. Now, when anyone asked him whether one could reach India by any other route than those monopolized by the Moslems, he had ready an answer that fired the imagination. For he had thought to himself that since the earth is a sphere, it should be possible to reach the Indies by a route to the westward as well as to the eastward. Men in all the past had been thinking of Asia as lying to the east. Why not make an about-face, and think of it as west?

The idea was by no means original. At the beginning of the Christian era Strabo had said that India could be reached by sailing about seventy thousand stadia (more than eight thousand English miles) toward the west. Seneca, the tutor of the Emperor Nero, who deserved a better pupil, in his tragedy *Medea* gave the mystical prophecy: "The future years, after centuries, when the mystery of the ocean is uncovered and an unknown land appears, and the navigator discovers new regions, and Thule [Iceland?] is no longer the land farthest away." Cornelius Nepos related a story told by Quintus Metullus Celer, proconsul in Gaul, that the King of the Suevi presented to Celer several Indians who had been carried by storms from the waters of India and had passed over the ocean to the shores of Germany. Nor were definite and seemingly conclusive indications lacking that Asia was much nearer across the western ocean than it was by eastward journey. The pope had appointed a bishop for Markland and Vinland as well as for Greenland; and if Markland was not on the mainland to the west, Vinland, at least, was. The tales of the Norsemen were more than rumors. Being a dealer in skins, Toscanelli had heard it said that as early as the thirteenth century the hides of animals of the general form of cattle, but much larger than medieval European cattle, had been brought from beyond Greenland over the ocean and had been traded in Italy. There was a strong probability that Italian adventurers had even attempted to cross the western ocean.

Lancellotto Malocelli, of Genoa, late in the thirteenth century sighted the Canary Islands. He had probably hoped to reach Asia by sailing around Africa. Two Genoese, Ugolino and Vadimo Vivaldi, sailed in the month of May, 1291, with two ships from the port of Genoa through Gibraltar toward the west ("directione di Ponente") to attain "through the ocean the Indies." A certain Thedisio d'Oria went with them. Their expedition was a commercial undertaking, with well-chosen, able-bodied men. According to Moorish records one ship was wrecked on the west African coast; the other sailed on. The Vivaldi brothers did not continue to follow the African coast, which was well known to the Genoese as far at least as Guinea, but when almost opposite the Canaries, they turned westward to attempt the ocean. Thereafter—no one knew.—Sources: Magnaghi, "Precursori di Colombo?" and Major, *The Life of Prince Henry of Portugal.*

The Dane, Claudius Clavus Swart, claimed to have voyaged to Greenland, which he included in his map of about 1430. In the North were rumors of other lands far west of Ireland. Toscanelli brought hints like these to a focus upon the minds of his contemporaries and thus changed the direction of the thinking of mankind.

10. The essential features of Toscanelli's map were preserved by Martin Behaim, who used them in his famous terrestrial globe of 1492. What Amerigo would have noticed about them was the contour of the coast of Asia, the corner of India jutting out to the eastward at approximately six degrees south, and the apparent southern end of India at fif-

teen degrees south. He would have felt disappointment at not seeing the name "Catigara," either at the latitude given it on the map of Ptolemy or anywhere else; but, he would have reminded himself, Catigara was on the other side of the southern tip of Asia, facing the west.

The twenty-six spaces of two hundred and fifty Roman miles each on Toscanelli's map represented one hundred and four degrees. That left two hundred and fifty-six degrees for the distance going eastward from Lisbon to the farthest end of Asia. But that was forty-five degrees greater than Ptolemy's estimate. Could it be that Ptolemy had so greatly underestimated the eastward extension of Asia? Messer Paolo, who had studied the making of maps for so many years, no doubt thought he had good reason for disagreeing with Ptolemy, and this very disagreement may have appeared to some as evidence of his carefulness as a scholar.

No one at that time knew that the actual distance eastward from Lisbon to the end of Asia was only about a hundred and thirty-five degrees and that Ptolemy's estimate of about two hundred and ten degrees was not an underestimate but a tremendous exaggeration. Toscanelli's additional forty-five degrees was hopelessly misleading. His map brought the exaggeration in the east-west extension of Asia to nearly one hundred and twenty degrees, with an equivalent underestimation of the distance westward from Portugal to China. It conveniently eliminated one-third of the circumference of the earth. In spite of this error, however, Toscanelli's idea of a westward voyage was fundamentally sound, even if it were to lead to surprises which would utterly confuse Christopher Columbus and would challenge Amerigo Vespucci to find true explanations. "Young man, look to the West!" was Toscanelli's clarion call to the two most outstanding geographical discoverers of all time.

The theory has been advanced that Columbus may have forged Toscanelli's letters to himself; or as Salvador de Madariaga says, Columbus when in Lisbon may have made a copy of Toscanelli's letter to Fernando Martinez and may have forged the accompanying notes. The charge cannot be proved. Whether Columbus did or did not have a direct correspondence with Toscanelli, Toscanelli's idea affected him, and nonetheless deeply if he thought enough of it to steal it. In reference to Behaim's globe, which used the features of Toscanelli's map, Las Casas later declared to Columbus: "I am persuaded that your whole voyage leans upon that map." After all, Toscanelli's map seemed very convincing. Could anyone who examined it possibly have dreamed that the islands "Antilia" and "St. Brandon" were imaginary? Were there not as many true stories told about them as about Java and Cipangu? How could anyone who knew the painstaking accuracy with which Toscanelli had recorded his observations of comets suspect the old man of having lacked definite knowledge and of having drawn his fascinating map from hearsay and imagination?

11. Page 22 in Antonina Vallentin's *Leonardo da Vinci*, New York, 1938.

12. In the survey for tax purposes, of 1480, Amerigo is described as being in France with Guidantonio Vespucci, ambassador ("e in Francia chon messer Guidantonio imbascatore").

13. The map owned by Amerigo Vespucci bears the maker's name and the date: "Gabriell de Valsqua la feta en Matorcoa lany MCCCCXXXVIIII" (Gabriel de Valsqua made this in Majorca in the year 1439). Valsqua's name has been variously given as Velasca, Valseca, Vallesecha. On the margin is written: "Questa amplia pelledi de geografia fue pagata de Amerigho Vespucci CXXX ducati di oro di marco" (This full skin map was bought by Amerigo Vespucci for 130 gold ducats). The map is surprisingly accurate in general contours. However, it does show Italy half its width too far west in relation to Gibraltar. In this map, then, the distance from Ferrara to Cadiz is less than correct, the more since Cadiz is a little too far east in relation to Gibraltar. The fact is of interest in connection with Vespucci's determination of longitude during his first voyage.

In 1838 the map belonged to the private library of Count Montenegro, at Palma. During a visit from George Sand the map was unrolled and laid out on a table for her inspection. The attendant placed upon one corner of the parchment a full and open inkwell which proved to be of insufficient weight, for the parchment rolled up with the inkwell inside. Great damage was done. The disfigurement, however, was skillfully removed, and the ink-stained portions of the map were restored. (See George Sand: *Un hiver a Majorque*, Paris, 1869, p. 63.) In 1892 the owner of the map, the Count de Montoro (Montenegro) was offered $100,000 security and a steamboat by the City of Chicago to fetch it to the exhibition. In the twentieth century the owner offered to sell it to the Library of Congress for one hundred thousand dollars. The map has been reproduced by the Hydrographic Commission of Spain, 125 copies, with a monograph by Gómez Ímaz.

14. Lorenzo's letter to Vespucci is given by Rambaldi, Cap. I.

15. Amerigo's nephew Giovanni may have grown up in Florence and as a young man joined his famous uncle in Spain. It has been stated by several writers, upon what authority I have been unable to ascertain, that he accompanied Amerigo to Spain in 1491.

Chapter Three

1. The source of information regarding life on shipboard is given by Jayne in *Vasco da Gama and His Successors* as the *Consolat del Mar*, the first extant edition of which was published at Barcelona in 1494.

2. The statement that the Indies (islands of the West Indies) which Columbus had discovered "are only twice as far beyond the Azores as the Azores are from Cadiz" is in error by only 50 statute miles. The distance from Cadiz to Flores in the Azores is about 1,350 miles, and from Flores to the island of Española is about 2,750 miles.

3. Maravedis and castellanos were about the same in value, equalling one-sixteenth of an ounce of gold, or about sixteen shillings. Debased maravedis were worth from about one silver franc (20 cents) to less than an English penny. It is impossible to determine with any exactness or even close approximation what the purchasing power was of the various sums Vespucci was given to expend in fitting out expeditions, or which he received as salary.

Chapter Four

1. Hojeda and Juan de la Cosa, with three pilots, a surgeon, an apothecary, and twenty-six men of their crew and with Fernando de Guevara in command of their companion ship, sailed from the northern coast of South America before the end of August and arrived at the port of Yaquimo on the southern coast of Española on September 5. This is the statement of Navarrete, quoted by Markham in the "Voyage of Hojeda" pp. 33, 34, Hakluyt Society Publication No. 90: "On the 30th of August they turned on their homeward voyage for Española or Santo Domingo, and entered the port of Yaquimo on the 5th of September, 1499, with the intention of loading with brazil wood, according to what Don Fernando Columbus says. . . . Hojeda removed his ships to Surana, in February, 1500." The evidence is conclusive that Vespucci's two ships did not return to Spain in consort with those of Hojeda, for Nicolas Perez said that the pearl-collecting expedition of Cristóbal Guerra and Peralonso Niño, with a hundred and fifty marks in weight of pearls, returned to Castile sixty-one days after February 6, 1500, or on April 6, and that "within a few days" Hojeda's squadron (with Juan de la Cosa) also returned, and that there in Castile both fleets met and related to each other the events of their voyages. Vespucci did not return to Cadiz until the middle of June.

2. Masini gives the following: "When Giovanni da Empoli appeared in the Palazzo Vecchio before the Gonfaloniere Pietro Soderini, the *signoria*, and many prominent citizens, and recounted the story of his voyage to Malabar, begun at Lisbon the 6th of April, 1503, for the House of Gualtierotti and Frescobaldi, he told how after 28 days of navigation he reached the Island of Ascension, and subsequently, as he affirmed, the Land of Vera Croce or 'Bresil,' so called, which was previously discovered by Amerigo Vespucci."

3. Alberto Magnaghi in his *Amerigo Vespucci, studio critico*, p. 164 says of two place names on Juan de la Cosa's map that the dates of these "*S. Ambrosio* (April 4) and *S. Elmo* (S. Erasmo, June 3)" do not accord with the time of the voyage of Vespucci and that these names could not have been given by Pinzón or De Lepe. Since the names are there where only Vespucci had been, I find no other explanation than that Vespucci used them without reference to dates in the church calendar. I have been unable to ascertain the meaning of "El Macareo" on La Cosa's map just north of the estuary of the Amazon.

Most of the place names on my map of Vespucci's Spanish voyage are from Juan de la Cosa's map. "Las Gaias," "Costa de Gente Brava," and all the names on the land side of the coast, except "Lago" and "Aldea Quemada," are from the maps of Cantino, 1502, Canerio, 1502, Waldseemüller, 1507, and the Ptolemy map by Ruysch, 1508. "Lago" is from La Cosa, and "Aldea Quemada" from the Carta di Weimar, of Ribero.

4. Determination of latitude by the early navigators was very nearly accurate. Positive evidence of the skill and carefulness of navigators in their use of the astrolabe and quadrant, even in mid-ocean, is to be found in the uniform accuracy with which they made their landfalls in the Azores or in Europe at or near the islands or ports to which they chose to return. Vespucci's error in latitude near the equator when "the Guards . . . were scarcely visible" is no measure of his usual estimates.

5. Judging by the illustrations of Vespucci's two ships drawn on Juan de la Cosa's map of 1500, his caravels had three masts: the tall mainmast, a foremast, and a short mast at the stern at the peak of the high poopdeck. A square sail hung from mainmast and foremast, and a lateen sail from the sternmast, or mizzen. Forward was a high-pointed bowsprit that carried a spritsail in a following wind. The mainmast of one ship was topped with a circular platform from which the men could sight a consort five or even six leagues away. Contrary to what landsmen suppose, mariners in the days of Columbus and Vespucci preferred small ships, because large ships were more likely to bend or break in the middle, or hog, as it was called, and were more unmanageable in rough weather.

6. The record of 81 and 60 on Juan de la Cosa's map of the run in leagues of Amerigo Vespucci's ships on August 2 and 3 would seem excessive, if not impossible, were it not firmly substantiated by recent observations of the speed of the current taken on a ship on the same course.—On the "Pilot Chart of the Central American Waters" for March, 1926, furnished by the Hydrographic Office of the Navy Department, U.S.A., we read: "Second Officer A. R. Payne of the American steamer *Elkhorn*, Captain Smukler, reports that on November 16 and 17, 1924, from lat. 2° 00′ N., long. 46° 15′ W., to lat. 3° 05′ N.,

long. 48° 00′ W., the current was setting northwest at 2.9 knots; thence to lat. 6° 03′ N., long. 52° 04′ W., it was northwest, 3.5 knots." Eighty-one leagues at 4 Roman miles a league was about 290 English miles. The current accounted for about 90 of these miles, so that the sailing speed of the ships was about 7.5 knots. It is generally agreed that ships of that period had a maximum speed under favorable conditions of 8 knots.

7. An astrolabe was a rather awkward device for determining the altitude, or angular distance from the horizon, of a star or other celestial object. It consisted of a swinging weight to show the vertical, and a circle or part of a circle marked at degree intervals, with a movable pointer arm to catch the angle of an observation. It required three men to use it: one to hold the pendulum suspended, another to manage the pointer arm, and a third to read the angle at the proper instant. Even a small astrolabe could be worked satisfactorily on land or on the steady deck of a ship in quiet inland waters, but it was mischief to manipulate any astrolabe on a rolling ship, and it there necessitated the averaging of many readings to cancel out errors. The larger an astrolabe, the more accurately readings could be taken, theoretically; but since metal was too heavy for a large one, and in that case wood had to be used, and since wood when wet or exposed to damp air during a long voyage was subject to warping, an astrolabe could not be considered anything like a precision instrument except under fairly ideal conditions.

8. The earliest record of an observation of an eclipse in Mexico was in 1537–1538, when the Spaniards established the longitude of Mexico City as west of Toledo about one hundred degrees. By an eclipse in 1544 they found it to be one hundred and three degrees, and this was the official figure for many years. Since the actual longitude of Mexico City is ninety-five degrees west of Toledo, it is obvious that the method of timing eclipses was not in the right direction, but led from bad to worse.

9. Gerard of Cremona, in the twelfth century, wrote *Theoretica planetarum*, which was a summary of the *Almagest*. In it he described a method of determining longitude by noting the distance of the moon from a fixed point in the heavens. It is possible that this may have helped Amerigo Vespucci to conceive of the method which he originated.

10. Previous to Vespucci's work in endeavoring to determine longitude, only about half a dozen points of longitude on the earth's surface had been determined with anything like accuracy. These had been chiefly the work of Arabs, who were more concerned than Christians with geographical positions, because they wished all their mosques in every land to be built to face Mecca.

11. Computations of the correct times for conjunctions in the year 1499 at Ferrara and at Vespucci's positions were made by Melvin V.

Landon at the University of Maine. Mr. Landon used the tables prepared by P. V. Neugebauer, *Tafeln zur astronomische Chronologie*, 3 vols., 1912, 1914, 1925, and also "Genaherte Tafeln für Sonne und Planeten," in *Astronomische Nachrichten*, No. 5937, Vol. CCXLVIII, March, 1933. Mr. Landon claims that his findings are in general correct to within thirty minutes. To quote Mr. Landon: "Most calculations fall well within these limits. The conjunction for August 23, 1499, is probably correct to within a few minutes." For the conjunction of the moon with Jupiter on September 15, 1499, Mr. Landon gives the most probable time as 10:45 A.M. for the meridian of Greenwich, within a limit of error of half an hour.

12. Whether Vespucci would have subtracted close to the correct number of minutes for parallax, we cannot say, but he doubtless understood parallax. Ptolemy, in his *Almagest*, dealt with parallax in determining the distance of the moon from the earth, which he gave as 59 times the earth's radius, and which he therefore thought to be about 195,000 English miles, instead of the actual 238,800 miles.

13. Cook, *A Voyage to the Pacific Ocean*, p. 322.

14. The use of a modification of Vespucci's method subsequent to the invention of the chronometer is further evidenced by the following statement from *A Voyage to the Pacific Ocean* by Captain James Cook, pp. lxiii, lxiv: "There were few, even of the petty officers, who could not observe the distance of the moon from the sun, or a star, the most delicate of all observations, with sufficient accuracy. . . . Nor is there, perhaps, a person who ranks as an officer, and has been concerned in them, who would not, whatever his real skill may be, feel ashamed to have it thought that he did not know how to observe for, and compute the time at sea; though, but a short while before these voyages were set on foot, such a thing was scarcely ever heard of amongst seamen; and even first rate astronomers doubted the possibility of doing it with sufficient exactness. . . . Liberal rewards were given to mathematicians for perfecting the lunar tables."

15. In the *Journal of the First Voyage of Columbus*, in the entry for January 13, 1493, we read that Columbus, who had anchored in Samana Bay, Española, "was anxious to leave it in order to go to another better harbor, since that was somewhat exposed and because he wished to see in what harbor he might await the conjunction of the moon with the sun, which he expected on the seventeenth, and the moon in opposition with Jupiter and in conjunction with Mercury, and the sun in opposition to Jupiter, which is the cause of great winds." There is nothing in this passage to make us believe that Columbus several years before Vespucci had caught the idea of observing conjunctions of the moon with the planets as a means of determining his position. Columbus was inter-

ested in the approaching eclipse ("conjunction of the moon with the sun") and in the opposition of the moon with Jupiter and the conjunction with Mercury, and the opposition of the sun to Jupiter because he believed in the age-old superstition that these various phenomena were responsible for the weather, causing wet and dry spells and all manner of storms; and in consequence as a cautious mariner, he sailed out of Samana Bay, which was exposed to winds from the east, on the sixteenth of January, the day before the conjunction. These old superstitions still linger in the popular notion that the full moon tends to bring fair weather.

16. Columbus referred to the West Indian slave trade, which he had himself instituted, when he wrote: "I believe that sea folk will soon take the bait, for these masters and sailors are sailing back all wealthy and intent on returning to carry away slaves at 1,500 maravedis apiece."

17. The Spanish Kings disapproved of the scheme of Columbus for making slaves of the Indians, and on June 20, 1500, ordered Pedro de Torres to set at liberty the Indians which had been sold by order of the Admiral. This order came a few days after Amerigo Vespucci and his crew had "shared" and sold their 200 slaves in Cadiz.

Chapter Five

1. It was more than seven hundred miles to the Fortunate Isles, or Canaries, and the passage took upwards of seven days. The route followed the African coast until opposite Fuerte Ventura Island, and there the ships steered south of west and fetched a course to the south of Gran Canaria, an island named from the large dogs that overran it in early times. When they sighted the volcanic peak of Teide which stood up for twelve thousand feet on Tenerife, the pilots steered by this guide to clear the south of Tenerife, and so came to the island of Gomera.—The valleys of Gomera were well wooded and abounding in streams of pure water. The climate there was gentle, with refreshing moisture from the winds of the western ocean. Life was so pleasant in the Canaries that the ancients had looked upon those islands as the Elysian Fields. A break in the cliffs of Gomera formed the little port of San Sebastian. There the caravels had to ride at anchor in the open, while the small boats carried the empty casks ashore to be filled, and brought them out through the surf. It was slow work also to cut wood and get it aboard so that there would be fuel for cooking and for the fires at night which would give comfort to the men on deck.—The caravels set sail from Gomera about the third of June.

2. In Vespucci's mind, the Cape of Catigara was a considerable distance east of the Ganges. He probably thought it to be not far from the

longitude of Zipangu (Japan), wherever that might be. As to latitude, he thought his farthest south was within two or three degrees of the cape.

3. The estuary of the Amazon is a hundred and fifty miles wide. The principal channel in the estuary, the most northerly, is sixteen miles wide, between Ponta Pedreira and Ponta Canaes, about sixty miles inland from the continental coastline. The Pará is forty miles wide at its mouth, and thirty miles wide opposite the city of Pará. It narrows to a width of twelve miles at the mouth of the Tocantins, about one hundred and thirty-eight miles inland from the continental coastline. One of the rivers Vespucci discovered was the Amazon, and the other the Pará. The evidence of place names seems to indicate that the river which he ascended was the Amazon. He could not have determined accurately the direction of flow of these rivers until he had sailed in through each delta for more than a hundred miles from the coastline. He ascended more than seventy miles above one of these points. Whichever of the rivers it was that he ascended, he undoubtedly entered the delta of the Amazon and was the first of all Europeans to do so.

4. The low coastal region offered no protection. Fortunately, it was between the time of full moon and new moon, for at the spring tides a dangerous bore races up the estuary of the Amazon, a wall of water ten to fifteen feet high, advancing in places at a speed of forty-five miles an hour.

5. Paul Russell Cutright, in *The Great Naturalists Explore South America*, New York, 1940, p. 195, writes: "The average person is accustomed to birds with extremely long legs, vermiform necks, and bills of varying shapes and dimensions, but is never quite prepared for the first look at a toucan with its perfectly enormous bananalike beak. This mandibular structure is so large, so out of proportion to the rest of the body, that at first glance nothing is visible but beak. It projects from the head like the snout on a proboscis monkey and adorns each of the seventy existing species. The only bird comparable to the toucan in its beak is the hornbill of the old world. The latter, however, is confined to the eastern hemisphere while the toucan is found only in tropical America. . . . Although the size of the beak exposes the toucan to considerable ridicule, the remarkable coloration makes partial amends. The predominant colors in the various forms are red, blue, yellow, orange, and black; and none of these is subdued." Quotation by permission of the Macmillan Company, publishers.

6. Columbus, the romanticist, thought that *the* Terrestrial Paradise was situated not far southeast of the Gulf of Paria; Vespucci, the realist, thought himself in *a* terrestrial paradise—quite a different thing.

7. In 1499 Polaris was approximately three and a half degrees from the North Pole. The "Guards" are the two bright stars which mark the

edge of the Little Dipper farthest from Polaris. In late July, when Vespucci was at his farthest south on this voyage, at about three and a half degrees south of the equator, Polaris at 7 P.M. was three degrees below the pole, hence about six and a half degrees below the horizon. Kochab, the brighter of the Guards, the one at the top of the dipper, was then about ten degrees above the horizon, and before midnight had gone below the horizon.

8. The almanac by Johann Müller, called Regiomontano, of Königsberg, contained *Ephemerides astronomicae* for 1475–1506, and had been first published in Nürnberg in 1474. It was reprinted in 1484, 1488, and 1492. Amerigo used a copy of one of the earlier editions, for the 1492 edition by error omitted the conjunction of August 23, 1499. Regiomontano was the first of the moderns to exhibit trigonometry as a science, and is credited with being the inventor of the tangent. He deferred to Toscanelli as master and arbiter. He died in 1475 at Rome at the age of forty. His tables superseded all others, because of their comparative accuracy. The *Alfonsine Tables,* which previous to Regiomontano's almanac had been accepted throughout Europe, were prepared in 1252 by Christian, Jewish, and Moorish astronomers under the patronage of Alfonso X of Leon and Castile. They were first printed in 1483. They differed only slightly from Regiomontano in the longitudinal distances between Italian and Spanish cities.

9. The sixteen and two-thirds leagues to a degree meant along the equator. On his Spanish voyage, for convenience and for the reason he stated, he gave four miles to a league. He thought in terms of Roman miles. The league varied from 2.42 to 4.6 English statute miles. One measurement of the Spanish league was 2.66 miles. The common sea league was 3.84 miles. He was in error as to the circumference of the earth according to Ptolemy and Alfragano. He confused Alfragano with Abulfeda, a confusion which the Arabs themselves made. It was Abulfeda who gave sixty-six and two-thirds miles to a degree. The size of degrees according to various cosmographers may be found in a table of linear measurements in the Appendix.

10. The statement does not imply a lack of familiarity with the voyages of the Portuguese. The unhappy experiences of those Portuguese who had gone to live in the Torrid Zone in Africa were well known. It was said, with exaggeration, that half the inhabitants of Portugal died in Guinea. Most of those who attempted to dwell in the tropics speedily succumbed to fever and disease. What Vespucci meant by "live" was not merely to survive while on a ship in the Torrid Zone, but to live on land with continued good health.

11. In this sentence Vespucci reveals his awareness of the spirit of the Inquisition, and his repugnance toward it. He reveals also his awareness of the mentality of men like John Michael Albert, a physician in Ber-

gamo (1460–1490), who wrote even after the equator had been passed by the Portuguese that the Torrid Zone is "arid, sterile, and uninhabited"; or of men like Alessandro Achillini, who in 1505 wrote a treatise in which he said of the Torrid Zone, "It is unprofitable to ask whether fruits grow there or whether the air there is more temperate, or whether the animals living there have temperate constitutions," for these, said he, are "matters which natural experience does not reveal."

12. It is interesting that Columbus was the first European on the coast of Venezuela (at the Gulf of Paria), which country was named by Vespucci; while Vespucci was the first European on the coast of Colombia (at Cape de la Vela), which country was named in honor of Columbus.

13. On October 18, 1498, Columbus sent five ships to Spain with six hundred slaves. Vespucci's two hundred and thirty-two slaves on two caravels shows that his ships had the same average capacity.

14. These malarial attacks began some weeks after his landing at Cadiz, for that landing was "a month ago" at the date of this letter written in Seville. From the cycle of quartan agues, we know that the first attack occurred from four to seven days previous to July 18 and that the infection was received after his arrival in Spain.

15. Vespucci was globe-minded. A spherical map was more important than one on a plane surface. It is a pity that the maps he sent to Lorenzo have not survived the centuries.

16. The Portuguese and the Spanish withheld from each other all marine news except what was to their obvious advantage to divulge. The Portuguese announced at once the essential fact of Da Gama's success, but they gave out no more details than were necessary. Vespucci had not been informed correctly as to the date of Da Gama's voyage. The ships had been sent, not two, but three years before, in 1497, and the first word of Da Gama's success had been brought to Lisbon on July 10, 1499, eleven months previous to Vespucci's return. Da Gama himself returned home late in the summer of 1499.

Chapter Six

1. Two months after the signing of the Treaty of Tordesillas, the mathematician Jayme Ferrer had been called in by Ferdinand and Isabella. Ferrer had used the measure sixteen and two-thirds leagues to a degree and had decided, in consequence, that three hundred and seventy leagues were in round numbers twenty-three degrees (actually 22° 12′) on the equator. While Columbus would have none of this, refusing as he said, to be "carried astray by the new calculations," Vespucci held to the measure Ferrer used.

2. The agreement between Spain and Portugal for determining and marking the Line of Demarcation established by the Treaty of Tordesillas, was in the form of an exchange of notes in May, 1495. See Morison, *Portuguese Voyages to America in the Fifteenth Century*, p. 89.

Chapter Seven

1. Place names on my map of Vespucci's Portuguese voyage have been compiled from the map of Canerio (1502), the Carta di Autore Italiano (1502), the maps of Waldseemüller (1507) and Ruysch (1508), the map of 1523 in the Biblioteca Reale di Torino, the list of names on the map of 1527–1546 in Nordenskiöld's *Periplus*, the list of Vespuccian data in Chapter X of *The Discovery of North America by* Henry Harrisse, and from the scholarly conclusions of Alberto Magnaghi in his *Amerigo Vespucci, studio critico*. I believe all the names on my map to be of Vespuccian origin except Porto Seguro, which was named by Cabral. Though considerable divergence prevailed among the calendars in use at the close of the Middle Ages, the dates of most saints' names are beyond dispute. The use of these names by the early explorers furnishes a reliable means of dating discoveries. Thus when we find on the earliest maps of the coast of Brazil a time sequence in the dates of saints' names from S. Rocco, August 16, to San Vincenzo, January 22, we recognize Vespuccian data, for Vespucci's voyage in 1501 and 1502 is the only voyage known, previous to the making of those maps, which came at the right season of the year to accord with these dates. Vicente Yañez Pinzón could not have given those place names, for he made his landfall at what he called "Cabo de Consolación" at ten degrees south on January 20, 1500, and sailed north and west. Diego de Lepe could not have given them, for he landed at four degrees south on February 14, 1500, and sailed north and west. Pedro Alvares Cabral could not have given them, for he made his landfall on April 24, 1500, at about eighteen degrees south, and sailed north to Porto Seguro, and then to what he called Monte Pascoal, where he erected a cross at about 16° 20′ S. (the modern Santa Cruz), and thence departed from the coast by the third of May. Gonzalo Coelho voyaged (1503–1504) only to eighteen degrees south. Juan Díaz de Solís, who went as far as the River Plata (where he was killed), did not begin his voyage until 1515. Magellan started four years later.

Monte de Sam Vicenso, January 22, which appears at six or seven degrees south on the Canerio and other early maps, was probably named by Pinzón. It appears that he gave the name "Cabo Sancta Croxe" to what Vespucci called Cape S. Augustine, and I believe he named "S. Maria de Gracia" and "S. Maria de Rabida," which appear near Capes S. Rocco and S. Augustine on the Canerio and Waldseemüller maps.

2. Alberto Magnaghi makes an effort to find the origin of the name "Cananor," with a conclusion not at all satisfying to himself. He feels that "Cananea" would present less difficulty than "Cananor," which to him has no meaning. But he faces his problem squarely and shows that the earliest maps had it "Cananor" not "Cananea." Varnhagen could do nothing better than to offer the suggestion that Cananor might be an American Indian name.

3. During his voyage Vespucci may have had the name "Cananor" in a corrupted form given him by Guaspare, in the form of one of the names mentioned in his letter to Lorenzo, a form such as "Calnut" or "Conimat" or "Cuninam"; but in that case he got the spelling corrected upon his return to Lisbon. "Calemur," for instance, was a very common misspelling for "Cananor"; and "Chananon" was the spelling in a narrative of Cabral's voyage by a member of that expedition.

4. P. Cazal is authority for the statement that in 1817 there existed a *padrão* of European marble on a cliff near the bar at the entrance to Cananor, now Cananea.

5. Had the Strait of Magellan been discovered by anyone before Magellan? Magellan declared that he had seen a map which showed the existence of the strait. A cosmographer, in a work published at the time of Schöner's 1515 globe, spoke of Basilae Regio as being not far from the Cape of Good Hope; and said that the Portuguese had explored it and had discovered a strait from east to west which resembled Gibraltar and that Mallaqua was believed to be not far distant therefrom. This strait which "resembled Gibraltar" was imaginary. It lay between an imagined southern end of South America and the coast of Australis, that antarctic continent of ancient geography. The shores of these two continents were supposed to approach each other somewhat as the shores of Spain and North Africa do.—There is no evidence that any expedition previous to Magellan's went beyond Vespucci's farthest south to the latitude (about fifty-two and a half south) of the entrance to the strait. There is, in other words, no evidence to substantiate the statement of Valentine Ferdinand, a German trader who in 1503 lived in Lisbon, and who, writing of the discovery of the land of Santa Cruz, said, "Indeed, when the two following years had elapsed, the other fleet of this Christian king appointed for the purpose, explored the shore of this land for seven hundred and sixty leagues or thereabouts and finally went so far towards the south that the Antarctic Pole was elevated 53 degrees. Finding extreme cold they returned home across the ocean." The "53" may very well be a copyist's error for "50." The Jagellonicus Globe of 1510 (Jagellonicus University Library in Cracow), which is marked with parallels of latitude for every ten degrees, gave South America its true extension to the actual latitude of the open water beyond Cape Horn, or a little more than fifty-six degrees south. This was,

however, without showing a strait, and a careful study of the Jagellonicus Globe (which has no Australis) suggests that the coastline drawn from fifty degrees south in a generous sweep to fifty-six degrees south, and thence northwest on the Pacific Ocean side of the continent up to Yucatan, was imaginary, and was accurate in its terminal latitude solely by accident.

The New York Public Library says of the Lenox Globe, which it owns, that this globe "has no date or signature, but the character of its cartography suggests the period around 1510." Fite and Freeman, in *A Book of Old Maps*, say that "the most probable date is 1503 to 1507." The Lenox Globe, like the Jagellonicus, places clear water south of South America. At the New York Public Library I was very kindly given permission to measure the latitude of the southern end of the continent on the Lenox Globe, and I found it to be slightly more than fifty-five degrees south. The correct latitude of Cape Horn is 55° 59′ S. I believe, however, that in this particular, the near accuracy of the Lenox Globe, like that of the Jagellonicus Globe, is accidental.

Chapter Eight

1. Vespucci's account of his meeting with three (a third arrived later) ships of Cabral's expedition at Cape Verde is corroborated by a letter written in July, 1501, from Lisbon by Matteo Cretico. According to Cretico, a Portuguese pilot reported that these ships returning from India had met the fleet of Vespucci: "Arrived at Cape Verde and Bexamche (Beseneghe), they met with three ships that our king of Portugal sent to discover the new land which they had found when they were going to Calicut."

2. There were fourteen ships. Vespucci's informants forgot to tell him of the ship that Cabral sent from the land of Santa Cruz to Lisbon with the report of the discovery.

3. Professor Samuel Eliot Morison says in *Portuguese Voyages to America in the Fifteenth Century*, p. 110: "Southwest was a manifest mistake for southeast, as Cabral could not have made the course he did with a S.W. wind, nor do the trades blow in that direction." However, the Italian text "per il vento" means "on the wind"; that is, not with a following or fair wind, but by traverse sailing with wind before the beam, as Portuguese ships were capable of doing. If Cabral's ships sailed from the Cape Verde Islands to Sierra Leone, they would have met wind in the direction stated at Sierra Leone and from Cape Palmas to Cape Lopez just south of the equator on the African coast. They probably turned westward from south of Cape Palmas or from near Cape Lopez. The total distance they sailed, as given by Vespucci in the fol-

lowing sentence, was too great for a direct route from the Cape Verde Islands to their landfall in Brazil, but it fits well enough with the circuitous route.

4. "Four and a half miles" is Vespucci's individual estimate, for the Portuguese held to a different measure. When the *Anunciada*, one of the very ships Vespucci had just met, returned to Lisbon, the owner of its cargo, Bartolomeo Marchioni, writing to Florence, June 27, 1501, commented on the number of leagues it had voyaged and said, "each league being three and a half of our miles." "A league being four and a half miles" is one of the most important statements in any of Vespucci's letters, for this revised estimate of the length of a league, since he does not report any change in his estimate of the number of leagues (sixteen and two-thirds) in a degree, points to an almost perfect estimate of the earth's circumference. Note that $4\frac{1}{2} \times 16\frac{2}{3} \times 360 = 27{,}000$ Roman miles = 24,852 English miles, as against the actual 24,902 English miles.

5. The Portuguese estimate of the longitude of the Cape of Good Hope as "seventy-two degrees, a little more or less," meant, in all probability, seventy-two degrees east of the prime meridian of the Ptolemaic traditions, which was located between Tenerife and Gran Canaria, about six degrees west of Cadiz. The Cape of Good Hope is actually thirty-one degrees east of this prime meridian, and Alexandria is forty-two degrees east of it. It is possible, however, that the Portuguese reckoned from the Cape Verde Islands, from which the Cape of Good Hope is forty-four degrees east, and Alexandria fifty-five degrees east. Even so, the Portuguese error showed the crying need of Vespucci's method of determining longitude by lunar distances.

6. He begins the sentence with "But," thus dissociating it from the sentences immediately preceding. The most notable thing which occurred to him, more notable than anything which ever occurred to him, more notable than anything which ever occurred to any other navigator, transcended in importance his study of the southern stars. The end of the sentence shows that he was fully appreciative of the magnitude of his discovery.

7. He had been interested in matters affecting health ever since malaria had begun to undermine his constitution.

8. A medicinal plant; the pods yield a laxative pulp.

Chapter Nine

1. The term "Western Hemisphere" first came into use in the seventeenth century, though the idea which it expresses was clearly in the minds of the best sixteenth-century map-makers beginning with

the year 1502 when Vespucci brought to Europe the fact of the existence of the New World. I have therefore employed the term "Western Hemisphere" in my biography of Vespucci.

2. In 1397, "mondo novo" was used by an Orkney fisherman in describing North America. In the days of Columbus, Peter Martyr used the term. He was in touch with the great navigators in the service of Spain. A year after the beginning of the second voyage of Columbus, Peter Martyr thought of the possibility that Columbus had found islands previously unrecorded by the geographers, not a part of Asia. He used the words "new world" in a letter to Borromeo on October 20, 1494, thus giving expression to the skepticism which had arisen among the Spaniards in Española because Columbus had failed to lead them to the treasure cities of India as he had promised. When Columbus brought home popinjays from his fourth voyage, in November, 1504, Peter Martyr wrote that he was convinced by their brilliant plumage that Columbus had found Asia, though he previously had doubted it. Popinjays had so rarely been brought to Europe that they seemed to argue a land of riches. This idea of a new world which had been in and out of Peter Martyr's mind for ten years, was an individual opinion that did not and could not recommend itself to the minds of others or, indeed, permanently to his own mind. Later on he accepted the fact that there was a new world because of the evidence which Vespucci had presented, as we know from his own statement quoted in the text of Chapter Ten. Credit for priority properly goes to the man who succeeded in communicating to all of Europe the concept of the New World in the sense of a hitherto unknown Western Hemisphere.

3. H. R. Ratto, in *Acotaciones nauticas*, Buenos Aires, 1931, says: "The discovery of the New World is an accomplishment not consummated in the expeditions of Columbus. . . . The glory of Vespucci is, indubitably, to have formulated the concept of the American continent."

4. The sketch map ascribed to Bartholomew Columbus is from marginal drawings in a copy of a letter by Christopher Columbus from Jamaica, July 7, 1503, discovered by Franz R. von Wieser. See Franz von Wieser's *Die Karte des Bartolomeo Colombo über die vierte Reise des Admirals*, or see page 15 in *A Book of Old Maps* by Fite and Freeman.

5. How far Columbus was from realizing that there was a New World is to be seen from his words: "I think if the river mentioned [the fresh water current in the Gulf of Paria] does not proceed from the Terrestrial Paradise, it comes from an immense tract of land situated in the south, of which no knowledge has been hitherto obtained. But the more I reason on this subject, the more satisfied I become that the Terrestrial Paradise is situated in the spot I have

described." He believed, of course, that the Terrestrial Paradise was at the eastern end of Asia.

6. The Portuguese portolano of 1502, now called the Richard King Portolano, is in the Huntington Library.

7. Quoted by Rambaldi.

Chapter Ten

1. The title of the German text of *Mundus Novus* was *Von der neüw gefunden Region,* 1505.

2. Another publication erroneously ascribed to Vespucci was *Paesi nuovamente retrovati,* Vicenza, 1507, called in its French translation, *S'ensuyt le Nouveau Monde*, Paris, 1515. This was an account of a voyage supposedly made by Vespucci from Lisbon to Calicut in 1505–1507, but is a "sheer imposture," as Harrisse said, for Vespucci was in the service of Spain from 1505 until his death.

3. The "first" of the *Four Voyages.*

4. Ferdinand Columbus made an invaluable collection of manuscripts and early printed works, which after his death was neglected; it then passed into the possession of monks who "purged" it. In recent years, when the Spanish government awoke to its value, two-thirds of it had disappeared.

5: *Hispanic American Historical Review,* February, 1938.

6. *Letter to Piero Soderini, Gonfaloniere, the Year 1504,* tr. . . . by George Tyler Northup.

7. The original letter was unearthed by Navarrete and is in the collection of the Duke of Veragua, an indirect descendant of Columbus.

Chapter Eleven

1. Dictionaries do not substantiate the view expressed in the *Edinburgh Review* for July, 1892, that "Amalrich" means "steadfast." Loredan Larchey, in *Dictionnaire de noms,* said that "*Emeric*" means "riche par le travail," or "rich through work."

2. A house in Saint-Dié bears a plaque placed in 1921 by the American Legion: "This house was the baptismal fount where workmen of the Vosgian School composed the 'Cosmographical Introduction' and where the name of America was given to the new western continent."

3. Johannes de Stobnicza, the editor of *Introductio cosmographia,* Cracow, 1512, said he was "indebted not only to Ptolemy, but to

Amerigo Vespucci." The truth of this statement was proved after the discovery of the unique copy of Waldseemüller's map, in 1901, for it was then seen that Stobnicza had copied from Waldseemüller the small inset maps of the Eastern Hemisphere and the Western Hemisphere. Thus, without knowing it, J. B. Thacher, in 1896, was speaking of Waldseemüller's work of 1507, which was based upon Vespucci's discovery of a New World, when he said of this Johannes de Stobnicza edition: "Not only does it plainly connect the two continents of the Western Hemisphere, but it gives their general contour with an accuracy which is marvelous," and it is "distinguished over all others in the early sixteenth century for advanced knowledge and correct geographical surmises."

4. After his first voyage Columbus said that "guanines" or "goanines" had been handed to him by the natives of Española, who told him "that there had come to this island from the direction of the south and the southeast black people, and that they had the points of their spears made of a metal which they call 'guanin.' " "Guanines" was a native African name. African guanines were alloys of gold containing copper for the sake of its odor, for it seems the negroes liked to smell their wealth. The guanines brought home by Columbus were assayed in Spain and were found to contain the same ratio of alloy as those in African Guinea, for "of 32 parts, 18 were gold and 6 silver and 8 copper." On his third voyage Columbus learned that in the Cape Verde Islands there "had been found canoes which set out from the coast of Guinea and steered to the west with merchandise," and on his return he reported the presence of negroes in lands he had visited. In the proper season it was quite feasible to cross the Atlantic near the equator from Africa to South America in small open boats.

5. The editorial on Lieutenant Charles Wilkes appeared in the New York *Times* for August 9, 1940.

6. The world map of La Popelliniere, Paris, 1582, is called "The Three Worlds"; that is, the Old World, the New World (meaning South America), and the Third World (North America).

7. The map maker Ortelius, about 1570, proposed "Columbana" as a name for North America, leaving "America" for South America.

8. As for the priority of Columbus or Vespucci, neither of them was the first European known to have touched a western continent. The honors must go to Leif Ericson, who crossed the Atlantic at the beginning of the eleventh century. The question of priority is a relative matter that must be limited in time. We must give credit to Columbus, and also to Vespucci, for being the first during the Great Age of Discovery (late fifteenth and early sixteenth centuries) to do certain things.

9. An interesting problem is whether that other Italian, John Cabot, reached the shore of the northern continent before Columbus reached the southern. Cabot sailed from Bristol in May, 1498, reached the east coast of Greenland early in June, turned south on June 11 from 67° 30′ N. on that east coast, rounded the southern cape of Greenland, and went up the west coast an unstated distance, crossed Davis Strait to 66° N. on the east coast of Baffin Land, and then turned south, first touching the coast of the continent in northern Labrador; thence he followed the coast to about thirty-six degrees north, "to the latitude of Gibraltar," as his son Sebastian is reported to have said, and eventually reached England late in the autumn. At approximately what date did Cabot touch Labrador and thus the continent? Was it before or after the August date of the sighting by Columbus (August 2) of the mainland of South America?

10. It is not known how Waldseemüller had learned, by 1513, that the "first" voyage, dated "1497," in *Four Voyages,* had never taken place.

Chapter Twelve

1. The quotation from Werner is a translation from the Latin which may be found in "Amerigo Vespucci, erster Erfinder der Meeres-Länge durch Monds-Abstände," by Von Zach, in *Monatliche Correspondenz zur Beförderung der Erd- und Himmels-Kunde,* XXII (Gotha, 1810), 530–541.

2. A letter of Amerigo Vespucci to the cardinal archbishop of Toledo (Ximénes de Cisneros) giving his opinion about the goods that ought to be carried to the Antilles. English translation in the Proceedings of the Massachusetts Historical Society, with emendations by the author.

"Very Reverend and Magnificent Sir:

"I feel obliged to show my gratitude for the confidence which your most reverend lordship has shown me, and I will not fail to declare my opinion, without allowing any interest to influence me, although I could have no desire to speak of that; and now I am to answer in regard to what is to be carried to the islands, whether it is better that it should pass through one person's hands, and that your Highness should derive a profit, as the King of Portugal does from the trade with the Mina del Oro, or, as I think I have heard is your Highness's opinion, whether everyone should have liberty to go and carry what he wishes.

"I find a great difference between the traffic of the King of Portugal and that which we are considering; inasmuch as the first consists of sending to the country of the Moors, and to one single place, a few kinds of goods appraised at a fixed price; and for these the factors whom he has there are responsible for the amount of the valuation, or for the goods themselves. The exact contrary is our case, since what has to be taken out to the islands consists of all sorts of things that persons there may be in need of, as, for instance, clothes, and many things necessary for their buildings and farms, of which no account can be kept. So that I should think it very difficult and almost impossible for your Highness to order the business to be done in that manner, especially since many things that are needed in the islands can be procured more conveniently from other countries than this. For instance, from the Canaries and the Portuguese islands from which they get livestock and provisions, and other necessary articles. And there would have to be an agent for each thing, and of many things no account could be given, for some are consumed, others damaged, and still others spoiled. For this reason, in my opinion, the business cannot be transacted in that way; and, if the attempt is made, I think time will show that I am right.

"By either of two ways it seems to me possible that your Highness may always derive a profit from the importation of goods that are carried to the islands, without trouble or expense on your part. The first is to lay a fixed tax on all that is taken to the islands, as it may seem right to your Highness, and to allow everybody to go freely and carry whatever he chooses. The other is to commit the traffic to merchants who shall share the profit with your Highness, they furnishing all that is needed without your Highness giving any care to the matter. In such a partnership, this arrangement would have to be made: that in the said islands the treasurer of your Highness and the agent of the merchants should be charged jointly with the business of receiving and selling all goods sent thither, each of them keeping his book in which, by the hands of two persons, everything that was sold would be set down.

"And there should be a statement of the cost of all goods sent in each ship, signed by the merchant and the treasurer, or some other agent for your Highness appointed to be in Seville or Cadiz, in order that, by means of this account, those in the islands can correct their accounts of all that each ship brings, and that each person may take his share of the profit, the merchant receiving back the cost of the goods with the charges and freight. And in this way there would be order and agreement, and no opportunity for fraud or deceit. In reference to the things that would be carried from other countries than our own, or from the islands above mentioned, and to their cost, the merchant and the agent of your Highness, who resides in Seville or Cadiz, could entrust this to some person who seems to them suitable.

"This is my opinion with due submission to those who know more. From Seville, the 9th day of the month of December, 1508.

"I humbly kiss the hands of your most reverend lordship.

Amerigo Vespucci
Chief Pilot."

3. In reference to Leonardo da Vinci's portrait of Amerigo Vespucci as an old man, Edward McCurdy in *The Mind of Leonardo da Vinci*, p. 19, writes: "Brookhaus has suggested that the Amerigo Vespucci referred to may have been the grandfather of the navigator who died in 1472, in which event the portrait must have been one of Leonardo's earliest works. . . . With the rapid growth of the idea (that America should be the name of the new world) grew also the fame of the navigator, and it seems therefore more natural to assume that Vasari's statement is intended to refer to him."

4. The heads of Toscanelli and Vespucci are carved on the façade of Santa Maria del Fiore, along with those of Galileo, Ficino, and Columbus. In April, 1898, Toscanelli, Vespucci, and eight lesser Florentine navigators were fêted, and a monument to them was erected in Santa Croce. Inscribed upon it was the line from Dante: "The way I pass ne'er yet was run." Medallions on each side give the portraits of Vespucci and Toscanelli, while below are eight shields for the others.

5. Some years after the death of Amerigo, Peter Martyr wrote of Amerigo's nephew Giovanni, "He is my particular friend, a witty young man in whose company I take great pleasure, and therefore have him often for my guest."

6. Vignaud says, in *Améric Vespuce:* "His merit is in the surety of his judgment, in his critical clarity, in his knowledge of ancient geography, which made him see and enabled him to be the first to discover that the world led to by Columbus was a new world entirely distinct from Asia. This perception sets him above all the navigators of his time."

VESPUCCIAN TEXTS

Letter from Seville, July 12, 1500 – cod. Riccardiana, 2112 bis, Biblioteca Riccardiana, Florence.

Letter from Lisbon, 1502 – cod. Strazziano, coll. dei mss. Galileiani, Cimento, parte III, Carteggio, vol. 18, carte 137r°-139r°, Biblioteca Nazionale, Florence.

Letter from Cape Verde, June 4, 1501 – mss. of Pier Voglienti, n.1910, page 48, Biblioteca Riccardiana, Florence.

Mundus Novus, published August 1504 (a mixture of genuineness and forgery).

Letter from Amerigo Vespucci to Piero Soderini, Gonfaloniere, the Year 1504, September 1504, generally called Four Voyages, in many editions and languages. The "First" Voyage, dated 1497, may be spurious.

BIBLIOGRAPHY

Anghiera, Pietro Martire d'. De orbe novo [1530], the eight Decades of Peter Martyr d'Anghera; tr. from the Latin with notes and introduction by Francis Augustus MacNutt. New York and London, 1912.

Baldelli-Boni, Giovanni Battista. Il milione di Marco Polo. Florence, 1827. Contains first publication of Vespucci's Cape Verde letter of June 4, 1501.

Bandini, Angelo Maria. Vita e lettere di Amerigo Vespucci, gentiluomo fiorentino. Florence, 1745. Contains first publication of Vespucci's letter from Seville, of July 18, 1500.

Bartolozzi, Francesco. Apologia delle ricerche istorico-critiche circa alle scoperte d'Amerigo Vespucci. Florence, 1789. Contains first publication of Vespucci's letter from Lisbon, of 1502.

Batalha-Reis, J. "The Supposed Discovery of South America before 1448, and the Critical Methods of the Historians of Geographical Discovery," *The Geographical Journal*, IX (1897), 185–210.

Bunbury, Sir Edward Herbert. A History of Ancient Geography among the Greeks and Romans. 2 vols. London, 1879.

Canovai, Stanislao. Viaggi d'Amerigo Vespucci. Florence, 1817.

Cánovas del Castillo y Vallejo, Antonio (Antonio Vascáno, pseud.). Ensayo biográfico del célebre navegante y consumado cosmógrafo Juan de la Cosa. Madrid, 1892.

Caraci, Giuseppe. "Nuova luce sull'opera e la figura di Amerigo Vespucci," *Rivista geografica italiana*, XXXII (1925), 15–36.

Celoria, Giovanni. Sulle osservazioni di comete fatta da Paolo dal Pozzo Toscanelli e sui lavori astronomici suoi in generale. Milan, 1921. Reale osservatorio di Brera, Pubblicazioni No. 55.

Clerke, Ellen Mary. "Toscanelli and Vespucci," *Dublin Review*, CXXIV (1899), 60–77.

Columbus, Christopher. The Voyages of Christopher Columbus. Translated and edited, with an introduction and notes, by Cecil Jane. London, 1930.

Cook, James. A Voyage to the Pacific Ocean. 3 vols. London, 1784. Volume III by Captain James King.

Cutright, Paul Russell. The Great Naturalists Explore South America. New York, 1940.

Eames, Wilberforce. Description of a Wood Engraving Illustrating the South American Indians (1505). New York, 1920.

Fischer, Joseph, and Franz, Ritter von Wieser. Facsimiles of the Waldseemüller Maps. London, 1903.

Fite, Emerson D., and Archibald Freeman. A Book of Old Maps. Cambridge [Mass.], 1926.

Force, Manning Ferguson. Some Observations on the Letters of Amerigo Vespucci. Cincinnati, 1885. Read before the Congrès international des américanistes, at Brussels, September, 1879.

Gallois, Lucien Louis Joseph. Améric Vespuce et les géographes de Saint-Dié. Nancy, 1900. Reprinted from Société de géographie de l'est, Bulletin, année 21, 1er trim., pp. 66–87, 88–94; 2e trim., pp. 221–229.

—— "Toscanelli et Christophe Colomb," *Annales de géographie* (Paris), XI (1902), 97–110.

Gay, Sydney Howard. "Amerigo Vespucci," in Justin Winsor, ed., Narrative and Critical History of America, Boston and New York, 1884–1889, II, 129–179.

Gomez Imaz, José. "Monografia de una carta hidrografia del Mallorquin Gabriel de Valseca," *Revista general de marina*, XXXI, Madrid (1892), 430–524, and folded map.

Greenlee, William Brooks. The Voyage of Pedro Alvares Cabral to Brazil and India. London, 1938. Works issued by Hakluyt Society, 2d series, LXXXI.

Harrisse, Henry. Americus Vespuccius. London, 1895. "A critical and documentary review of two recent English books concerning that navigator."

—— The Discovery of North America. London, 1892.

—— Les Corte-Real. Paris, 1883.

Herrera y Tordesillas, Antonio de. Historia general de los hechos de los castellanos en las islas i tierra firme del mar oceano. Madrid, 1601–1615. 8 parts.

Hugues, Luigi. Di alcuni recenti giudizi intorno ad Amerigo Vespucci; osservazioni critiche. Turin, 1891.

—— "Sopra un quinto viaggio di Amerigo Vespucci," in International Geographical Congress, 3d, Venice, 1881, II (Rome, 1884), 291–300.

Jayne, Kingsley Garland. Vasco da Gama and His Successors, 1460–1580. London [1910].

Jervis, Walter Willson. The World in Maps; a study in map evolution. New York, 1938.

Kimble, George Herbert Tinley. Geography in the Middle Ages. London, 1938.

Kline, Burton. "America Discovered Many Times before Columbus Came," *World's Work*, L (May, 1925), 35–42.

Kretschmer, Konrad. Die Entdeckung Amerika's in ihrer Bedeutung für die Geschichte des Weltbildes. Mit einem Atlas von 40 Tafeln in Farbendruck. Berlin, 1892. Contains facsimiles of 93 maps.

Las Casas, Fray Bartolomé de. Las Obras. Seville, 1552.

Lester, Charles Edwards, and Andrew Foster. The Life and Voyages of Americus Vespucius. New York, 1846.

Letter to Piero Soderini, Gonfaloniere, the Year 1504. Translated, with introduction and notes, by George Tyler Northup. Princeton, N.J., 1916. Purports to be an account of four voyages by Vespucci.

Logoluso, Pietro. Su le origini del nome "America." Trani, 1903.

McAuliffe, E. "Amerigo Vespucci and the Italian Navigators," *Catholic World*, LXVII (Aug., 1898), 603.

McClymont, James Roxburgh. Pedraluarez Cabral. London, 1914.

Magnaghi, Alberto. Amerigo Vespucci; studio critico, Rome [1926]. Pubblicazioni dell' Istituto Cristoforo Colombo, No. 30.

—— "Amerigo Vespucci," in International Congress of Americanists, *Atti*, I (1928), 73–96.

—— "Amici . . . portoghesi di Vespucci," *Rivista geografica italiana*, XLIII (May–August, 1936), 73–119.

—— Precursori di Colombo?—Il tentativo di viaggio transoceanico dei genovesi fratelli Vivaldi nel 1291, Rome, 1935. Memorie della Reale società geografica italiana, Vol. XVIII.

—— "Una supposta lettera inedita di Amerigo Vespucci," *Bollettino della Reale società geografica italiana*, Series 7, II (1937), 589–632.

Major, Richard Henry. The Life of Prince Henry of Portugal, Surnamed the Navigator. London, 1868. Contains account of Vivaldi brothers, p. 99.

—— The Voyages of the Venetian brothers, Nicolò and Antonio Zeno, to the northern seas, in the XIVth century. London, 1873. Works issued by the Hakluyt Society, No. L.

Manfroni, Camillo. "Amerigo Vespucci secondo le nuove ricerche," *Rivista marittima*, LVIII (1925), 653–663.

Markham, Sir Clements Robert. Amerigo Vespucci; Letters and Other Documents Illustrative of His Career. London, 1894. Works issued by the Hakluyt Society, No. XC. Contains evidence of Alonso de Hojeda respecting his voyage of 1499, and an account of the voyage of Hojeda (1499–1500) by Navarrete.

Masetti-Bencini, Ida, and Mary Howard Smith. "La vita di Amerigo Vespucci a Firenze," *Rivista delle biblioteche e degli archivi*, XIII (1902), 170–189; XIV (1903), 45–61. Contains seventy-one letters in Italian written to Vespucci.

Masini, Enrico. "La data della nascita di Amerigo Vespucci," *Rivista geografica italiana*, V (1898), 86–88; also in *Atti* dell' VIII Congresso geografica italiano, II (March–April, 1921), 278–280.

Menkman, W. R. "Vespucci en Ojeda in de deschiedenis van Curaçao," *West-Indische Gids*, XVIII (1937), 257–273.

Morison, Samuel Eliot. Portuguese Voyages to America in the Fifteenth Century. Cambridge [Mass.], 1940.

Müller, Johannes (Regiomontanus). Ephemerides. Venice, 1484. Editions also published in 1488 and 1492.

Mundus Novus; Letter to Lorenzo Pietro di Medici, Vienna, August, 1504; tr. by George Tyler Northup. Princeton, N.J., 1916. Purports to be a letter to Lorenzo di Pier Francesco de' Medici containing an account of Vespucci's voyage to fifty degrees south.

Navarrete, Martín Fernández de. Colección de los viages y descubrimientos . . . Madrid, 1825. Contains documents pertaining to Vespucci.

Nordenskiöld, Nils Adolf Erik. Facsimile-Atlas to the Early History of Cartography. Stockholm, 1889.

—— Periplus; an essay on early history of charts and sailing-directions. Stockholm, 1897.

Nunn, George Emra. The Geographical Conceptions of Columbus. New York, 1924.

Ober, Frederick Albion. Amerigo Vespucci. New York and London, 1907.

Oberti, Eugenio. Amerigo Vespucci alla scoperta del continente Sud-Americano. Turin, 1932.

Oldham, H. Yule. "A Pre-Columbian Discovery of America," *The Geographical Journal*, V (March, 1895), 221–233.

Olschki, Leo S. Storia letteraria delle scoperte geografiche. Florence, 1937.

Olsen, Örjan. La Conquete de la terre; tr. by E. Guerre. Paris, 1933.

Pigafetta, Antonio. Magellan's Voyage around the World; with English trans. by James Alexander Robertson. 2 vols. Cleveland, 1906.

Pons, Roberto Giorgi de. "Amerigo Vespucci nella critica storica," *Nuova antologia* of *Rivista di lettere, scienze ed arti*, CCLXVII (September, 1929), 81–92.

Priestley, Herbert Ingram. *The Coming of the White Man*, New York, 1929. History of American Life.

Ptolemaeus, Claudius. Almagestũ . . .

—— Cosmographia. Editions of 1475, 1477, 1478.

—— Tetrabiblos, or Quadripartite.

Rambaldi, Pier Liberale. Amerigo Vespucci. Florence, 1898.

Ravenstein, Ernest George, ed. A Journal of the First Voyage of Vasco da Gama, 1497–1499. Translated and edited, with notes, an introduction and appendices. London, 1898. Works issued by the Hakluyt Society, No. XCIX.

Santarem, Manuel Francisco de Barros. Researches respecting Americus Vespucius and His Voyages. Boston, 1850. Translated from the French ed., Paris, 1842, by E. V. Childe.

Stevens, Henry. Historical and Geographical Notes on the Earliest Discoveries in America, 1453–1530. New Haven, 1869.

Stevenson, Edward Luther. Early Spanish Cartography of the New World. Worcester, Mass., 1909.

—— Maps Illustrating Early Discovery and Exploration in America, 1502–1530. New Brunswick, 1903.

—— Terrestrial and Celestial Globes. New Haven, 1921.

Sumien, N. La Correspondance du savant florentin Paolo dal Pozzo Toscanelli avec Christophe Colomb. Paris, 1927.

Thacher, John Boyd. The Continent of America; Its Discovery and Its Baptism. New York, 1896.

United States. Hydrographic Office. Pilot Charts.

Uzielli, Gustavo. La vita e i tempi di Paolo dal Pozzo Toscanelli. Rome, 1894. Pubblicati dalla Reale commissione colombiana pel quarto centenario dalla scoperta dell' America, Raccolta di documenti e studi, Parte 5, Vol. I.

—— "Toscanelli, Colombo e Vespucci," *Atti* del IV Congresso geografico italiano, April, 1901, pp. 559–591. Milan, 1902.

—— Illustrations and annotations by Gustavo Uzielli, in *Vita di Amerigo Vespucci*, by Bandini, Florence, 1898.

Valentini, Philipp Johann Joseph. "Pinzón-Solís," in Zeitschrift der Gesellschaft für Erdkunde zu Berlin, XXXIII (1898), 254–282.

Varnhagen, Francisco Adolpho de. Amerígo Vespucci; son caractère, ses écrits (même les moins authentiques), sa vie et ses navigations. Lima, 1865.

—— Le Premier Voyage de Amerígo Vespucci definitivement expliqué dans ses détails. Vienna, 1869.

—— Nouvelles recherches sur les derniers voyages du navigateur-florentin, et le reste des documents et éclaircissements sur lui. Avec les textes dans les mêmes langues qu'ils ont été écrits. Vienna, 1870.

Vespucci, Amerigo. Three letters to Lorenzo di Pier Francesco de' Medici: (1) from Seville, July 18, 1500 (see Bandini); (2) from Cape Verde, June 4, 1501 (see Baldelli-Boni); (3) from Lisbon, 1502 (see Bartolozzi). The reader is also referred to the spurious Mundus Novus and Letter to Piero Soderini.

Vignaud, Henry. Americ Vespuce, 1451–1512; sa biographie, sa vie, ses voyages, ses découvertes, l'attribution de son nom á l'Amérique, ses relations authentiques et contestées. Paris, 1917.

—— Americ Vespuce; l'attribution de son nom au nouveau monde. [Paris], 1912.

Waldseemüller, Martin . . . The Cosmographiae introductio of Martin Waldseemüller in facsimile, followed by the Four Voyages of Amerigo Vespucci, with their translation into English; to which are added Waldseemüller's two world maps of 1507, with an introduction by Prof. Joseph Fischer . . . and Prof. Franz von Wieser; ed. by Prof. Charles George Herbermann. New York, 1907.

Wieser, Franz, Ritter von. Die Karte des Bartolomeo Colombo über die vierte Reise des Admirals. Innsbruck, 1893.

Wright, John Kirtland. The Geographical Lore of the Time of the Crusades. New York, 1925.

Yonge, Charlotte Mary. History of Christian Names. 2 vols. London, 1863.

INDEX